HomeBasics

A READER'S DIGEST BOOK

Published by The Reader's Digest Association Limited
11 Westferry Circus
Canary Wharf
London E14 4HE

We are committed to both the quality of our products and the service we provide
to our customers. We value your comments, so please feel free to contact us on
08705 113366, or by e-mail at cust_service@readersdigest.co.uk
If you have any comments about the content of our books, you can contact us at
gbeditorial@readersdigest.co.uk

Copyright © MQ Publications Ltd. 2001
Text copyright © Gill Chilton

ISBN: 0 276 42615 0

A CIP data record for this book is available from the British Library

This book was designed by Axis Design Editions Ltd., and edited and produced by
MQ Publications, 12 The Ivories, 6–8 Northampton Street, London N1 2HY

Printed and Bound in Great Britain by Butler & Tanner Ltd, Frome and London

® Reader's Digest, The Digest and the Pegasus logo are registered trademarks of
The Reader's Digest Association, Inc., of Pleasantville, New York, USA

HomeBasics

THE COMPLETE GUIDE TO RUNNING TODAY'S HOME

Gill Chilton

PUBLISHED BY THE READER'S DIGEST ASSOCIATION LIMITED
LONDON • NEW YORK • MONTREAL • SYDNEY

Contents...

chapter **1**

homecare

Basic repairs inside your home

■ ■ ■**Always tackle repairs as soon as you notice a problem. They soon become a bigger and more expensive job if you do not deal with them right away** ■ ■ ■

before you start ■ ■ ■

■ Consider what is required and make sure that you have enough time to complete a job.

■ Read the *How to fix the problem* sections and be sure you understand what to do.

■ Consider anything that might affect how you complete the task at hand; you may need a particular tool.

■ Check that you have all the materials you need – the right sized screws, nails, and fittings.

■ If you are uncertain how to complete a job, consult a comprehensive DIY manual or check out the Internet.

common problems ■ ■ ■

Squeaky floorboard

This happens when floorboards work loose from the joists which support the floors or grit is caught between two close-fitting boards. When the boards are walked on, they flex and make a squeaking noise as they rub against each other.

How to fix the problem

To stop wood planks from rubbing, sprinkle talcum powder between the boards. For a more permanent solution, you will need to fix any loose boards back to their joists. Unless you can easily lift the floorboard to check for pipes or electrical wiring, locate the holes where the boards were previously fixed in place and hammer in floor brads. These should be hammered flush with the floor level. If you think that you may need to remove the floorboard at a later date, use screws. Drill a screw hole with a narrow drill piece and screw in a larger-sized screw until it is flush.

Gaps between floorboards

Over time, and particularly where there is central heating and air conditioning, floorboards shrink away from each other, leaving gaps.

How to fix the problem

Where boards are hidden under floor coverings, fill the narrow gaps between fixed and tongue-and-groove boards, with a flexible filler. A tube of wood-coloured filler with a nozzle attachment is the most practical method. Simply squeeze the filler into the gap and wipe off any excess with a damp cloth.

For gaps that are wider than 5mm (¼in), and in polished wood floors, buy a narrow strip of softwood and insert between each gap. Coat each side with PVA glue (see page 22, *All about glue*) and gently hammer into place. Once the glue has dried, plane or sand the wood strip until it is level. Wipe over the joins with white spirit to remove any dust and then re-apply the finish.

Repairing cracks

How to fix the problem

Small hole: Small holes and cracks in wood can be filled with ready-mixed filler. Clean out any loose dust and debris from the hole, dampen the area to avoid shrinkage, and put the filler into the crack or hole using a wide filling knife. Smooth it over and allow to dry for one to two hours. When the filler is dry, rub it smooth with fine-grade sandpaper.

Larger hole: For a larger hole in a solid wall that is more than 2.5cm (1in) deep or wide, it is better to apply a base layer of filler. Let it dry, then apply a second layer, finishing as described.

Plasterboard

To fill a hole in a plasterboard wall, that measures less than 5cm (2in) wide, start by applying meshed jointing tape over the hole. Spread filler over the tape (some will squeeze through the mesh), then use a wide filling knife or a caulking tool to smooth it level. When dry, rub smooth with sandpaper.

For larger holes up to 20cm (8in) wide, see below.

Knocks and dents in woodwork

How to fix the problem

Painted woodwork: Rub over the dent with fine-grade sandpaper. Fill it with wood filler and leave to harden. Rub over the filled area with fine sandpaper and paint it to match the existing paint finish.

Varnished woodwork: Prepare and treat as for painted woodwork (above) but finish with varnish to match. If the dent has not exposed the natural wood, a quick repair can be made with clear nail polish.

Natural woodwork: Tape a small piece of wet cotton wool or a wet cotton bud over the dent. Leave to swell the fibres overnight. If the dent is still too deep, apply colour-matched filler and rub smooth when dry.

repairing a hole in plasterboard

1 Measure the hole and cut a piece of plasterboard lath, slightly larger than the hole. Attach a length of string to the lath by drilling a small hole, threading the string through, and securing it at the back. Dampen the edges of the hole and the lath and apply dabs of filler around and behind the hole and on the corners of the lath.

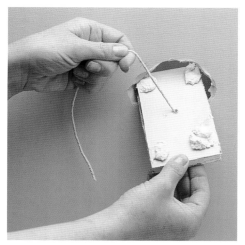

2 Carefully place the lath into the hole, and, using the string to pull the lath into place, position it to cover the hole with the dabs of filler against the back of the plasterboard. Hold the lath in place by the string tie, for a few minutes, while the filler sets enough to hold firm until it dries completely.

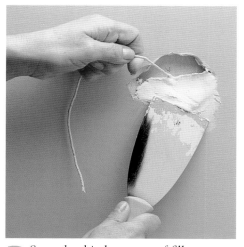

3 Spread a thin base coat of filler over the lath, making sure it is not as deep as the hole. Roughen the surface with the edge of the filling knife and leave to set. When the base is dry, remove the string with clippers and apply a finishing layer, skimming carefully to make it flush with the wall. Lightly sand before painting.

Repair a dripping tap

Always turn off the water at the mains before beginning repairs. There are four main types of sink tap: a compression tap, usually with two separate handles that control the hot and cold valves, the rotating ball type of tap, which is controlled by the circular movement of a single handle, and disc and cartridge taps, which are generally controlled by a single handle that moves forward and back, and side-to-side. The first two are the most common.

Ball type tap

Lift the tap handle so that you can insert a screwdriver into the screw inside the hole. Unscrew and remove the handle. Using tapered pliers, unscrew the cap directly beneath the handle, then unscrew the retaining nut that holds the ceramic disc cartridge in place. Replace the disc (check that you have got the right type).

Light bulbs

Keep a selection of spare light bulbs to fit all the lamps in your home. When a bulb burns out, disconnect the electricity and turn off the lamp.

Bulbs come in a variety of shapes and sizes. Find out which type you use the most and keep a good supply.

Wait five minutes for the bulb to cool down or protect your hands with oven gloves. Dispose of the old bulb safely. Check that you have the correct size and wattage for the fitting. Fit the new bulb.

Knobs on cupboards and drawers

With constant use, the knobs on kitchen cupboards and drawers become loose and sometimes break off. These are usually fastened from inside the cupboard door or drawer, and are simple to repair or replace.

How to fix the problem

Remove the screw, and knob if it is still attached. Choose a screw and matching washer. Make sure the

repair a dripping compression tap

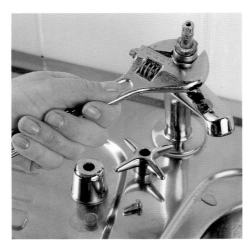

1 Prise off the index cap on the top of the handle and undo the screw underneath to remove the handle. With a 20cm (8in) adjustable wrench, loosen the hexagonal retaining nut and remove the stem assembly.

2 Remove the washer screw at the bottom of the stem assembly and carefully examine the washer. If it shows signs of wear, replace it (check your local DIY shop for the right product).

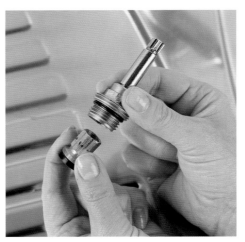

3 Near the centre of the stem assembly is the O-ring, frequently the cause of leaks. Unscrew the threaded spindle in the centre of the stem assembly. Take off the O-ring and replace it if it looks worn.

replacement screw is slightly longer and thicker than the current screw. Insert this into the screw hole from behind and re-thread the knob while holding the screw steady with a screwdriver.

If the knob has broken away with the screw tip inside, it is usually simpler to replace both the knob and the screw. Most cupboard knobs are available from hardware shops, DIY stores or kitchen furniture shops.

Mending a broken drawer

After use and time, drawers often come apart. The base panel or a runner separates because the wood shrinks, or the glue disintegrates so that the joints no longer connect with each other and the front panel comes away from the rest of the drawer.

How to fix the problem

Dowel joints: Clean the surfaces of both joints and sand them. Use wood glue around the protruding dowels and ease them back into place.

Dovetail joints: Clean the joint surfaces and sand them lightly. Apply glue to the edges and ease the joints back, tapping gently with a lightweight hammer if necessary.

Loose base panel: It is often possible to simply tap the panel back into place with a lightweight hammer, but if it has come apart, place a thin line of glue along the inside of the groove and tap the base firmly back into place with a light hammer. Wipe away excess glue with a damp cloth.

Detached runner: Clean and sand both surfaces and glue the runner back into its previous position. For added strength, secure the runner with panel pins or small screws. See pages 22 and 23 for tips on using glue and screws.

Tip

■ To stop a softwood drawer from sticking, run a wax candle along the top and bottom edges of each side of the drawer.

■ Preserve and maintain drawers and cupboard doors with an occasional application of oil to all moving parts.

■ When glueing joints, clamps are the ideal holding tools, but the joints can also be held in place with strong adhesive tape while the glue dries. Gently remove the tape when the glue has dried.

Blocked waste disposer

Waste disposers are a wonderful invention, but, if not used properly, will become blocked and stop working. Common causes of blockage are foreign objects, usually cutlery, fibrous foodstuffs, grease, or not running sufficient cold water to flush away the waste. Always check your manual for the specific instructions for your model.

How to fix the problem

Food blockage: Run small bones through the disposer with plenty of cold water. This will help to break up the blockage and move it along the pipe.

Grease blockage: Run hot, soapy water through the disposer. Remember to never put uncooked waste fat or cooking oil in the disposer.

A foreign body: Disconnect the power to the disposer. Use the release tool to expose the underside of the unit. Open the inspection chamber and remove the obstruction. Re-seal the inspection chamber and press the reset button.

If you're buying a waste disposer, try to buy one with a release button on the base, as shown above. This will make the task of clearing blockages much easier.

Replace a broken tile

How to fix the problem

Wear safety goggles and protect the area below the tile with a dust sheet. Follow the steps below. When the new tile is in place, you will need to re-grout the tiled area. Work the grout into the spaces and wipe off any excess with a damp cloth, working it around the tile to give a smooth finish. Before it sets, wipe off any grouting on the tile itself, as it is difficult to clean it off once it hardens.

Tip

■ Grout saws are an inexpensive purchase for your toolbox. Buy one from a tile shop. Glass cutters make this job much easier and can be hired.

Top tips around the house

■ Regularly oil hinges, locks, and door handles.
■ To loosen a stiff lock, oil the key and turn it in the lock in both directions.
■ Regularly check for loose screws on furniture and fittings.
■ In case of emergencies: keep replacement fuses, light bulbs, and a torch in a safe and convenient place.
■ Regularly move drawers around – the top one probably gets far more wear than the bottom.
■ Maintain some ventilation to reduce condensation, especially in the kitchen and bathroom.

■ When dismantling anything, make notes and a diagram of exactly which part goes where so that you can put them back together accurately.
■ Reduce problems with electrical appliances by keeping vents and grills dust and fluff free. Replace or clean filters as recommended by the manufacturers and have your appliances regularly serviced.
■ Before calling an engineer to repair your electrical appliances, check the power socket and plug. If this is not the problem, call the manufacturer's customer service number. You may only need a replacement part, such as a rotating bar on a vacuum cleaner.

---

replace a broken tile

1 With a grout saw or blunt chisel, remove the grout around the tile. Cut a large X shape right through the tile with a glass-cutter, or drill holes to mark the shape.

2 Tap the centre point with a hammer and chisel to break up the tile. Scrape away the old adhesive and re-apply fresh tile adhesive using the applicator supplied.

3 Insert the new tile into the space and use plastic tile spacers, or adhesive tape, to hold the tile in position. Allow 24 hours for the adhesive to dry.

Basic repairs outside your home

■ ■ ■ **The exterior of your home needs regular maintenance to protect it against the effects of the elements. Major jobs are best left to experts. However, there are many ways to repair and improve your home that need only basic DIY skills. If you don't own your home, check your lease or rental agreement to see who is responsible for carrying out any work; external repairs may be part of a maintenance contract** ■ ■ ■

EQUIPMENT CHECKLIST

- Protective gloves and safety goggles
- Extension ladder
- Polythene sheeting: to cover plants and pathways while you work
- Wire brush: for removing dirt
- Hot-air gun: to strip large quantities of paint
- Sandpaper: for smoothing
- Exterior fillers: wood and/or cement to fill cracks
- Filling knife: to apply and smooth filling materials

- Fungicide: to treat any mould patches
- Paintbrush: 15cm (6in) bristle brush
- Paint roller: 23cm (9in) wide with an extension pole, for painting above your head
- Paint kettle: a handled pot that lets you carry both paint pot and brush with one hand
- Masonry (exterior) paint
- Wood and metal primers
- Exterior gloss paint or wood stain

---

protecting your home ■ ■ ■

Protecting the outside of your home is vitally important if you want to minimize expensive repairs and keep your house looking good for longer. Damage can come from:

- Rain beating on external walls. This will be absorbed by brick and stone, and will cause timber wall cladding to rot.
- Holes and large cracks in rendered and timber-clad walls, or excessive water on unprotected stone and brick walls, will cause penetrating damp to the inside of the house. This can be very costly to repair.
- Broken or blocked downpipes, overflow pipes, and guttering can cause rain water to splash onto the walls. Over time this will saturate the area of wall surrounding the water pipe problem.
- Water leaking through cracks in the roof.

- Water soaking through door and window frames (maintaining paintwork will help to avoid this).

If you suspect that you might have damp in your external walls, check them in daylight. Particularly where cracks in the wall and under window frames allow water access. If water has penetrated you should be able to see darker patches in the wall.

Seal the walls of your house every three to five years, and re-seal any repairs that you make. At the DIY shop, check out:

- Micro-porous sealants, including paint – allows surfaces such as render, brick, timber and tile-clad walls to breathe, yet offers water protection.
- Bituminous paint – gives extra protection against water for plastic gutters.

common problems ■ ■ ■

Sticking external door

There are a number of possible factors that could result in a sticking door: a problem with the hinges; the door might be warped; or paint has built up around the closing edge.

How to fix the problem

Start by examining all around the door and frame and note where it is sticking. This will often reveal the reasons why.

Loose hinge screws: Try tightening these with a screwdriver. If the problem is an enlarged hole, replace the screw with one slightly wider.

Protruding hinges: To fix this, undo the screws and remove the hinges from the door frame. Use a chisel and mallet to shave away more wood and deepen the fixing point under the hinge. Sand this smooth and replace the hinge.

Paint build-up: If too many layers of paint have made the door too big for its frame, strip off the paint. Sanding back the door with sandpaper will often be enough if the problem is very slight. If the paint has built up to a thickened layer, a hot-air paint stripping gun will take off the paint as far as the original wood. Confine the heat to the edge of the door to avoid affecting the rest of the paintwork. Seal and repaint the wood to match.

Warping: If the door sticks only at certain times of the year, humidity changes are to blame. Wood expands with moisture and contracts in dry weather. Sanding or shaving may be enough to ease the door into place but if it is necessary to plane it, be very cautious about how much you remove. When the wood contracts you may have too big a gap between door and frame.

Blocked drains

When debris, such as hair, grease, and food wastes are not flushed away properly they can become compacted after leaving the sink or washbasin and become stuck at a bend in the drainpipe. This can accumulate until the drain becomes blocked.

How to fix the problem

Chemical drain cleaner: Buy this from the DIY or hardware shop. This will tackle the problem from the inside. Pour the chemical cleaner down the sink drain and it will usually clear small blockages. Follow the manufacturer's instructions and always wear gloves because the chemical is usually caustic.

Blockage in the main drain: Stubborn blockages in the drainage system can be cleared with drain rods. Wear old clothes and protective gloves. Remove the lid from the drain inspection chamber – this is usually in the garden and near to the house. Connect several lengths of drain rod (these can be hired) and attach a plunger to the end. Feed this into the drain until it reaches the blockage. Work the rods to and fro to break up the blockage and push the particles through until the drain clears. Flush the pipe with plenty of water to remove any remaining debris and replace the cover. Hose down the drain rods before returning them or putting them away.

Tip
■ Although not a difficult job, it can be unpleasant, and there are many drain-clearing companies that will do the job quickly and efficiently for you.

Blocked gutters

Particularly during autumn; leaves and debris can collect and create blockages in gutters. Rainwater then pours up and over the edge of gutters which will cause a penetrating dampness in the walls.

How to fix the problem

Securely position a ladder just below the affected gutter. Take a small bucket with a handle and a garden trowel or scoop, climb until you're at shoulder level with the gutter, then use the trowel or scoop to remove the leaves and debris into the bucket.

Roof leaks

Water can penetrate cracked or loose tiles, and cause damage to the roof lining underneath. It is always better to deal with roof leaks before any water penetration causes secondary problems.

How to fix the problem

Find the source of the leak. If this is not apparent from the ground, use binoculars to spot broken tiles. At this point, decide whether the problem needs to be repaired by a professional roofing contractor. If the problem area is difficult to reach, this may be the safer alternative. (See *All about ladders* on page 21.)

Plain tiles: To replace a damaged tile, lift up the one above it and prise out the roofing nail. Slide the matching replacement tile into place and secure it with a nail. To avoid damaging the tiles when hammering, place the crowbar over the nail head and hammer that instead.

Slate tiles: These often slip out of place and can easily be nailed back into position. If the slate has split, lift off the surrounding slates and remove the part that is still attached, taking care not to damage the roofing material underneath. Slide the replacement slate into place, making sure it is lined up with the adjacent slates, and secure it with tile nails. Replace the surrounding slates.

Flat felt roof: This type of roof is prone to blistering and splitting. Cut across the blister with a retractable knife and carefully ease open the edges. Spread bitumen inside the hole. Cut a patch of roofing felt that is 5cm (2in) bigger than the hole and slide it inside, pressing down the edges to seal it against the bitumen. Seal the split with bitumen and allow it to dry.

Roof flashing: Re-attach any loose nails and cover them with bitumen to seal the holes. Corrosion holes up to 2cm (¾in) wide can be patched with matching roof flashing. Cut a piece larger than the hole, roughen up the area and fix the patch with bitumen. Then seal over the patch with bitumen. Badly corroded flashing will need to be replaced.

Tip

■ Don't work on any kind of roof unless you are very confident about your skills and have the right equipment. It is very easy to cause further damage to the roof or to yourself.

Plant growth on walls

Climbing plants such as ivy or other types of vines attach themselves directly to walls. In addition to obstructing light, these plants also draw moisture from walls, which damages mortar joints.

How to fix the problem

Cut vine trunks at the base of the wall as low as possible. Their tendrils will loosen after two to three weeks, as the severed plant dries out. To remove the vegetation, wear safety glasses and pull the branches away, peeling upward from the bottom. If you need to reach higher branches with a ladder (see page 21), it is essential that the ladder be anchored and that you pay close attention to your balance while pulling off the branches. This is a task that is completed more safely with a helper. Finally, dig up the roots or apply a herbicide (a plant centre will advise you).

White deposits on new brickwork

When houses are newly built from bricks or blocks, it is quite common for water-soluble salts to be drawn to the surface as they weather. This is more likely to occur in damp conditions and is an unavoidable, but only temporary problem.

How to fix the problem

Remove the white (salt) deposits with a dry wire brush. Resist the temptation to scrub them away with water and a cloth or brush – you will only add more moisture and make the problem worse.

Broken or cracked window

Most broken windows are caused accidentally, but cracked glass can be the result of shifting pressure caused by a warped frame. If the window is accessible, replacing the glass is not a difficult job.

How to fix the problem

Metal and plastic window sashes usually hold the glass in place with spring clips, a rubber seal, and moulded glazing bars.

CAUTION
Always wear safety goggles and protective gloves when working with glass.

Measure the replacement glass and have it cut or made to order if it requires double glazing. Remove the glazing bars and insert the glass, securing it with the spring clips, and replace the glazing bars.

Wooden window frames: Place strips of strong adhesive tape across the broken glass to prevent further breakage. Holding a cloth between yourself and the pane, tap out the glass with a hammer. Dispose of the broken glass safely. Clear away the old putty and any retaining pins with a chisel and pliers. Measure the inside of the frame accurately, allowing 2mm (⅛in) less on all sides, for clearance, and have the glass cut to size. Apply a line of putty or glazing compound around the frame, gently press the replacement glass into place, and secure it with retaining pins tapped into the frame every 15mm–20mm (6–8in). Apply more putty in a thin line, using the putty knife to seal a neat edge. Let it dry before painting to match.

Maintaining wall surfaces

Regular maintenance on the outside of your home is always highly rewarding. Many tasks do, however, take a lot of time, such as painting wall rendering, and for this you may choose to hire a contractor.

Cement render (high maintenance): This is a very versatile wall surface that can be painted the colour of your choice. With regular maintenance the surface will last a long time but, once neglected, cement render will deteriorate rapidly.
Repairing render: To repair worn patches, mix up new render following packet instructions (or use ready-mix). Brush off all loose chips with a wire brush. Prime the area with a PVA sealant, then use a steel float to smooth the render on to the wall, until it sits just below the surrounding surface. Let this dry, then apply a second coat of render and blend it into the surrounding surface with a damp sponge.
Painting render (high maintenance):
Choose a day that's dry, but not overly hot, because the paint can bubble in these conditions. Avoid painting in direct sun – ideally, work on a part of the house that the sun has just left, because it is easier to see what you are doing in shadow. Clean up the existing paintwork with a hard brush. Fill any cracks

or worn patches. It is safer to work from a moveable scaffold tower, but if you use a ladder, make sure it is always securely placed (see page 21). Paint with a roller, or an extension pole, or use a paint spray system that you can hire.

Brick (low maintenance): If the bricks on your house take a long time to dry after a rain shower, the brickwork is most likely porous and may benefit if you paint on special brick protection.

To remove mould growth from bricks, scour them with a hard wire brush.

Stone (low maintenance): Natural stone looks good, but can become dirty and dull over time.

Remove mould growth with a hard wire brush. Next, scrub with a softer brush, using water. If you still can't remove it, try applying a solution of one part bleach to four parts water.

Cement paint can hide cracks on stonework around doors and windows, and can make dull stone look more attractive.

Timber (high maintenance): Unpainted wood needs regular sealing to keep out moisture. Always use products made especially for this, and re-seal your wood regularly. Always check the instructions for the product you use.

Painted timber offers some protection from damp weather but can blister easily, particularly if exposed to extreme conditions. Remove flaking bits with a hot-air gun before repainting.

Stone cladding, stone brick, or stone block is easily maintained and will last a long time.

Handy hints

Make use of your neighbours! Their home may be made of similar materials – and will certainly face the same weather conditions.

■ **Swap tips on maintenance.**

■ **Save money by getting jobs done by the same contractor.**

■ **Check out exterior decoration ideas.**

The best – and worst – examples of what works are on view for all to see.

Timber houses are beautiful but the upkeep can be costly because of the necessary high level of maintenance.

Good bricks are durable and can be easily and inexpensively maintained.

The tool box

■ ■ ■ The range of available tools is vast. A good starting point is to put together the basic tools needed for home DIY projects. Start with twelve core items and then add as your enthusiasm – and skill – at home maintenance grows ■ ■ ■

twelve essential hand tools ■ ■ ■

Screwdrivers (a)

There are two types of screwdriver which both come in various sizes, to fit large and small screws. A screwdriver set, with one handle and a selection of heads, means you can find a match for every screw. Alternatively, start off with a medium-sized screwdriver and a much smaller one – these should cope with most jobs.

Standard screwdriver (also known as a flat-head screwdriver)

This type of screwdriver is used with screws that have one straight slot. These screwdrivers can be used for tightening wall sockets, constructing some types of furniture, replacing door hinges, and for most jobs around the house.

Write down the type of tool that you need before you go to the hardware shop or DIY store. Ask about hiring the tools that you need for specialist jobs.

Phillips Screwdriver (cross-head)
This kind of screwdriver is used as a standard, but with screws that have a cross shape in their heads.

Hammer (b)
This can be made entirely of steel, or have a steel tip on a wood handle. Swing the hammer in the shop to check its weight; it should not be too heavy, and should have the correct width for a good grip. A double-headed hammer has a claw end that can be used for removing nails.

Pliers (c)
Pliers are used to cut, bend, or stretch wire. They are also good for holding nuts in place when tightening bolts with a wrench.

Retractable knife (Stanley knife) (d)
A retractable knife is a safe way to cut tough materials with accuracy. The blades are replaceable and can be withdrawn into the case for safety.

Tape measure (e)
A retractable measuring tape can be used for general measuring, and is essential for measuring large areas (such as room widths). Some have a spirit level fitted.

Adjustable wrench (f)
This type of wrench has a roller ball that adjusts the head to fit around most nuts. It is essential for tightening loose joints and connectors in plumbing, though you still might need a small wrench for delicate jobs.

Sandpaper (glass paper) (g)
Sandpaper is sold in varying weights – fine, medium and coarse – but is cheap enough to buy in a mixed packet. Use it to smooth surface irregularities and scratches in wood and plaster. It also roughens smooth surfaces to prepare them to grip fresh paint.

Cross-cut saw (h)
This long, graduated saw will cut through planks of wood and composite boards, from floorboards to beading strips.

Hacksaw (i)
This thin blade cuts through metal and plastics easily and safely.

Spirit level (j)
A level provides a true horizontal and vertical line, thus ensuring perfect results for all DIY projects that rely on a level surface. This tool is essential for marking straight shelves and wallpaper borders.

Bradawl (k)
This pointed hand tool makes small starter holes in walls and woodwork. These holes serve as a guide for nails and screws, making the job more accurate. They also make the job safer – an electric drill is less likely to slip when the fixing point is already started.

Oil (l)
Oil lubricates moving parts, and oiling cures squeaks, and ensures the smooth movement of metal parts.

safety first ▪ ▪ ▪

Use protective aids and keep your tools properly stored and cared for.

▪ Wear plastic safety goggles while cutting, using chemicals or power-tools, and working with glass. If you wear spectacles, you can buy goggles to fit on top.
▪ Face masks are needed for very dusty work or when using strong-smelling chemicals.
▪ Wear secure, non-slip shoes or boots.

▪ A properly planned workbench provides a safer workplace and keeps the mess in one place.
▪ Use a strong canvas bag or a toolbox to carry large tools around the house.
▪ The safest storage place for sharp tools is on a wall rack. Keep them out of the reach of children.
▪ Worn tools can be dangerous and some tools wear out fast. Even with moderate use a cheaper saw will need replacing every two years.

power tools ▪▪▪

A DIY enthusiast should have a powerful and easy-to-use jig-saw. But for smaller projects, a hand-saw is sufficient.

Cut down on the elbow grease and hire an electric sander from your local hardware shop.

Increasingly inexpensive, an electric drill is becoming an indispensable piece of equipment for the home.

Electric power tools help you get jobs done faster and with less effort. They aren't essential – you can do practically all basic household jobs with manual hand tools – but they are invaluable.

Electric drill: This is generally used to make holes but can often be fitted with attachments that perform other functions, such as sanding or tightening screws.

Jig-saw: This saw cuts through tough materials, including wood, plastic laminate, and steel. It can be used for cutting precision shapes.

Sander: An electric sander smoothes large, rough areas effortlessly. It is ideal for renovating doors and floorboards.

Power screwdriver: This is a lightweight alternative to using a drill attachment.

Circular saw: This saw cuts thick, straight pieces of wood up to 5cm (2in) deep.

Power tool tips

▪ It is worth buying cordless tools. They give complete flexibility and solve the problems of trailing cables and locating power sources.
▪ Hire expensive tools that are used only occasionally.
▪ Always wear safety goggles and never leave power tools unattended in homes with children.

ADHESIVE TAPES

Masking (low-adhesive tape): Use this tape around window frames and anywhere that needs protective boundaries. This tape is invaluable for maintaining borders when painting.

Double sided (adhesive on both sides): This tape is perfect for any job where two surfaces need to be joined, but you prefer not to use glue, (either for convenience, or for situations where the rigidity of tape is needed). Double-sided tape is good for mending book spines, holding photos in mounted frames, and repairing dried-out wallpaper edges.

Insulating (wraps around electrical cords): Insulating tape is good for temporarily repairing worn electrical cords, but should not be used on severed cords where wires are exposed – these should always be replaced.

Clear adhesive (transparent adhesive tape on a roll): This tape has no major uses, but 101 minor ones, from mending rips in paper to securing packages.

Carpet tape (very strong, double-sided tape): Carpet tape fixes carpet and vinyl to the floor. It is available with permanent or temporary adhesion.

all about ladders ▪ ▪ ▪

Extension ladders

Hiring or borrowing extension ladders from a neighbour can make sense, especially if your storage space is limited. Be sure to check that each rung is sturdy before you start. Working with care will help you to avoid mishaps.

■ Prop the ladder away from the wall. A safe angle is around 70°, or one quarter of the height of the ladder. For an 8m (26ft) ladder, that is approximately 2m (6ft 6in) from the wall.

■ Secure the base with a strong, level board (on soft ground), or with stabilisers (on hard ground). A sandbag, or other deadweight, placed in front of the ladder provides extra support.

■ Face the wall as you climb the ladder. Don't lean or look down. If you lose confidence, come down immediately.

■ Never stand above the third-highest rung of the ladder, as it is easy to overbalance from this position.

■ Try to keep one hand on the ladder at all times and never over-reach.

Stepladders

A folding stepladder with four to seven rungs is ideal for indoor use. Stepladders are usually versatile and can often be unfolded to reach the highest ceilings. Two stepladders with wooden planking between them make a sturdy platform from which to work.

■ Stepladders must be locked into position before you start.

■ Place your stepladder parallel with where you want to work.

■ Never twist or stretch as you work. When you can no longer reach comfortably, move the stepladder.

■ When the job is done, don't store your ladder by hanging it upright from a peg; this may cause the rung to buckle.

Ladder safety tips

■ Always follow the 70° positioning angle. This is a good safety rule for all ladders.

■ Check for nearby or overhead hazards where you are working, such as open windows or overhanging branches.

■ When working above first floor level, it is wise to have a work partner.

A circular saw makes cutting wood easy. Follow the manufacturer's instructions carefully, and avoid the danger of slippage by having a workbench or solid base to work on.

A power screwdriver has changeable heads to match different types of screw and takes the hard work out of inserting screws.

all about glue ▪▪▪

There are many forms of glue available, which provide fast, permanent bonds. Glue is ideal for repairs. It needs little skill to apply, and can also be used in conjunction with screws to make a strong reinforced joint.

PVA (polyvinyl)

This white, multi-purpose acetate glue is soluble. It is useful for large areas such as laying floor tiles or laminate. PVA bonds composite wood together, mends wood furniture, and can be diluted with water to make a sealant.

Cellulose clear

This strong transparent glue is sold in small tubes. It makes invisible joins, and is good for mending china. Useful when working with handicrafts, leather, glass, and rigid plastics.

Epoxy resin

Epoxy resin is a clear, very strong glue and hardener. It forms a strong waterproof bond on most surfaces, including wood, fabric, paper, and vinyl. Epoxy resin takes several hours to reach full strength.

Super glue

This clear, permanent adhesive bonds in seconds. It is invisible and extremely strong, and can bind the surfaces of different materials together.

Glue gun

This tool delivers a steady stream of molten glue, which is ideal for DIY crafts and upholstery. It also works well for large areas of wood or fabric.

Tips on glueing

■ Let the glue sit for at least twenty-four hours before testing joined materials. Some glues take several days to reach full strength.
■ Buy only what you need: glue deteriorates after its container is opened.
■ Plan carefully. Once you have joined two surfaces together, you may not be able to rectify a mistake.
■ Follow instructions carefully. The same glue may need to be applied differently, depending on the materials used. For instance, absorbent surfaces like wood and paper may need to be glued on only one side, while non-absorbent surfaces like china and metal may need glue on both surfaces.

CAUTION
■ Think through the job at hand to avoid the glue touching any surface that should not be bonded – including your skin. This is especially important when using permanent, instant adhesives such as super glue.
■ Keep strong and/or toxic glues out of the reach of children.

all about nails ▪▪▪

Nails are a quick, cheap way of joining two objects. Standard nails, made of steel, are usually sold by weight (not number), in a number of widths and lengths, from 2.3cm (1in) to 15cm (6in).

Masonry nails

These are extra-strong nails with regular points. They are typically used for nailing directly into walls.

Galvanized nails

Galvanized nails are usually coated with zinc to resist rust. This makes them suitable for use in outdoor projects, such as fencing and roofing.

Carpet tacks

These are steel pins with angled points and flat heads. Use carpet tacks to nail carpets to a wooden floor.

Heavy-duty staples

These U-shaped nails, which come in different sizes, may be used, among other options, to fix indoor cables or to mend outside fencing.

Nailing tips

■ When nailing something thin to a thicker surface, such as a batten onto a wall, choose a nail length that is two and a half times the thickness of the batten.

■ For joining two surfaces of the same thickness, the nail should be long enough to penetrate just over half of the bottom surface.

■ To hammer a nail into wood, hold the hammer with one hand, the nail with the other, and carefully hit the nail with rapid, light blows. You can also use gum or putty to hold the nail in place while you hammer it in.

■ Before nailing into walls, locate power sources and switches, and establish where the pipes and cables run. A cable locator will find electric wires with accuracy.

■ Keep nails accessible as you work. Use a nail pouch or improvise with a loose pocket.

all about screws ■ ■ ■

Screws are sold by length and diameter, and ensure a stronger connection than nails. They can also be easily removed. This makes them ideal for projects that you may need to take apart later. Most self-assembly furniture uses screws.

Countersunk head

These screws feature a straight slot with a head that sinks into a surface. They are often used in furniture to leave a neat finish and for fixing door and cupboard hinges that should be flush with the wall.

Cross-head screws

These screws, used with a cross-head (Phillips) screwdriver, allow for a more secure driving action. They can be used for all projects.

Plugs

Plugs are made of plastic or wood and come in many different sizes. They are used to provide a strong anchor for screws drilled into walls, wooden shelves, or wooden furniture.

Screw tips

■ Always match the correct screw size with the correct plug.

■ Rubbing screws with dry soap will make them screw in more easily.

■ Never use steel screws in oak, because the wood may discolour. Use brass or stainless steel ones.

■ A small butter knife can tighten a flat-topped screw.

Inserting a screw

■ Make an entry hole with a bradawl.

■ Using a hand or electric drill, make a hole to receive the selected size and type of plug.

■ Place a wooden or plastic wall plug into the hole.

■ Push the screw into the plug and, using a screwdriver, drive the screw home.

(a) **screwdriver**
(b) **hammer**
(c) **plugs**
(d) **staples**
(e) **plastic box for keeping nails and screws.**

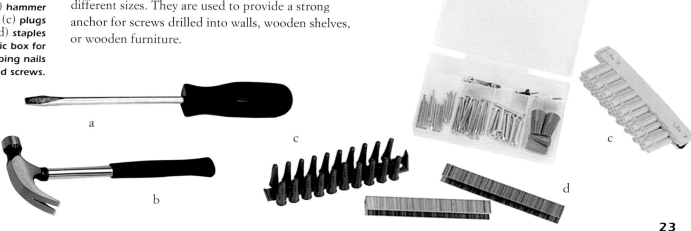

23

Household cleaning

■ ■ ■ **Household cleaning can often become unwelcome and intrusive; but a regular routine really does reduce the effort involved and prevents all those necessary jobs from taking up too much valuable time** ■ ■ ■

TOP TO BOTTOM IN TWO HOURS

The Top-to-Bottom guide outlines an adaptable once or twice weekly routine. This keeps regular jobs under control and it's all done in two hours maximum!

15 minutes — **Bedrooms and bathrooms**
- If weather permits, open windows to let fresh air inside.
- Fold back bedding, and air the beds.
- Gather and sort laundry, load it in the washing machine, and start the wash cycle.
- Put away clothes and other items.
- Dust surfaces and make the beds.

5 minutes
- Vacuum bedrooms.

15 minutes
- Clean toilets, bath, and bathroom basins. Use a non-rinsing shower cleaner.
- Close the windows.

5 minutes
- Vacuum stairs (if you have them), as well as the halls and corridors.

25 minutes — **Living room**
- Put things away in their places.
- Throw out rubbish or used materials, such as old magazines.
- Shake and arrange cushions and throws. Dust, working from higher shelves down, over all hard surfaces, including tables, chairs, and entertainment equipment.
- Vacuum the floors.

45 minutes — **Kitchen**
- Check the refrigerator for any food that has gone bad. Load the dish washer, or hand-wash any dishes.
- Put the dishes away. Clear the worktops.
- Clean the cooker top and all surfaces.
- Wipe the doors and handles of cupboards and appliances.
- Clean the backsplash, sink, and taps.
- Empty the dishwasher and transfer dishes to cupboards.
- Clean the floor.

10 minutes
- For those occasional jobs like cleaning windows or airing a wardrobe.

which cleaner? ■ ■ ■

Always check the labels on your cleaning products and treat them with respect. Modern cleaning agents are powerful and effective – a little goes a long way.

Liquid bleach

■ This powerful cleaner destroys germs and breaks down grease. Use this product with some caution as splashes will mark clothes.

■ Dilution: 600ml bleach to 10 litres water (1 pint bleach to 2 gallons water).

■ Never use this undiluted, except in toilets or drains.

■ Bleach can be useful for general cleaning of floors and walls. Don't use it on enamel, wood, plastics, stainless steel, laminates, paint, or aluminium.

■ Always rinse well after use.

Powder bleach

■ An abrasive cleaner for hard, scratch-resistant surfaces such as oven interiors or use to scour pans.

■ Always rinse well after use.

Liquid disinfectant

■ This is a cleaner that also destroys germs. Use diluted to clean walls, tiles, and hard surfaces.

Multi-surface cleaners

■ A combination of detergent and water softener (and sometimes a little bleach), these cleaning agents don't need rinsing off and can be used on most hard surfaces around the home.

■ Specialized kitchen and bathroom products contain only the amount of bleach that's safe for the recommended use.

■ Don't use them on wood, aluminium, or on painted or lacquered surfaces.

Cream cleaners

■ These fluid and mildly abrasive cleaners are for hard finishes (such as cookers, kitchen appliances, stainless steel, enamel, chrome, and laminates). Do not use on aluminium. Always rinse off well.

Soda crystals

■ This is a traditional, all-purpose cleaner. It is not very convenient to use, and has now been replaced by many single- and multi-purpose cleaners.

Anti-bacterial cleaner

■ This kind of product cleans and disinfects surfaces while destroying the bacteria that can cause food poisoning. It is a good choice for both the kitchen and nursery.

Washing-up liquid

■ This mild detergent has many uses. Diluted in warm water, it can be used on most washable surfaces around the home, including aluminium. Washing-up liquid must always be rinsed and dried off surfaces to avoid streaking.

If you don't like to have too many chemicals in the house, there are many cleaning solutions that can be made from everyday ingredients.

> **CAUTION**
>
> Many household cleaners contain bleach and strong detergents, particularly those used in the kitchen and bathroom. Protect your hands and clothes by wearing rubber gloves and an apron, and wash off any splashes immediately.
> Never mix chemical cleaners. They may react with each other and give off noxious gases.

Natural remedies

Many ingredients found in the grocery shop make effective cleaning agents.

Lemon

■ Rub lemon juice onto copper or brass. Wash off. Two drops in the final rinse restores the shine to glassware.
■ Lemon juice removes soap scum from bathroom taps.

Salt

Pour a strong solution of salt water down drains to prevent blockages and to eradicate smells.

Bicarbonate of soda

Use bicarbonate of soda to soak off burnt-on food from pans. Mix a paste with water to clean stainless steel sinks and glass oven doors without scratching.

Vinegar

■ A cloth soaked in white vinegar shines plastic and coated kitchen tables and chairs.
■ Vinegar stops mould forming inside bread bins.
■ It can also remove water stains left by dripping taps and can remove limescale.

Chemical-free cleaners

Increasing concern about the effects of chemicals means that there are more chemical-free (or low-chemical) products available in our shops, through specialist mail order catalogues, and on the internet.

hints and tips on household care and cleaning ...

Entrance

Doormats

■ Shake the mat outside and away from where people walk to prevent the dust from being brought back inside. To be truly effective, your doormat needs to be long enough so that people can walk across it and brush off their shoes as they enter – a metre (yard) long mat is large enough to save the rest of your floor from soiling.

Living rooms

Sofa and armchairs

■ Regular vacuuming will keep the fabric looking clean and fresh.

■ Shake and turn seat cushions frequently to keep their filling evenly distributed and to prevent uneven wear to the fabric.

■ Be careful with upholstered furniture placed in direct sunlight. Ultra-violet light will fade the colours and weaken the fibres. Use blinds if you have them. Close curtains during the brightest part of the day or protect your furniture with a throw – it will look good and protect the upholstery.

Rugs

■ Shake rugs outdoors and, preferably, hang them outside to air. Vacuum to remove any remaining surface dust and fibres. If the rugs are colourfast (see page 46 for test), shampoo them as you would a carpet, (see page 46, *Fabric care guide*).

Walls

■ Wash painted walls and washable wallpaper with a mild solution of detergent and warm water. Make sure that your cloth is completely clean before you start, and wring it out well. Clean non-washable paper by dusting or vacuuming. Spot-treat marks with a pencil eraser, a ball of fresh white breadcrumbs or a damp cloth.

Vacuuming carpets

■ Use the nozzle attachment along skirting boards and hard-to-reach corners. It is quicker and more efficient to vacuum in straight lines – this also prevents you from missing any areas. Spot-treat small stains with dry-foam stain remover for carpets. If you are shampooing your carpet, see pages 46–7, *Fabric care guide.*

Floors

■ Hard floors – cork, wood, laminate, ceramic, stone, slate, and marble – should be swept or vacuumed regularly. Go over them with a damp mop to keep them fresh. Special cleaners are available for different types of hard floor which will enhance their appearance. Polish sparingly and be careful – a highly polished floor will be slippery!

Lighting and lampshades

■ Use the crevice tool on the vacuum cleaner, if you have one, for fabric and paper lampshades. Glass fittings are best cleaned by hand with a feather duster or soft cloth, and occasionally wash them in mild washing-up liquid to keep the glass sparkling. Dust light bulbs, too.

Curtains

■ Use the upholstery tool of the vacuum cleaner to clean curtains. Pay close attention to the outer folds, as these move less and retain more dust (see page 47, *Fabric care guide*).

Venetian blinds and wood slat shades

■ Venetian blinds are awkward to clean but regular vacuuming with the upholstery tool will keep them dust-free. A useful tip when cleaning venetian blinds is to wear washable cloth gloves, dip your fingers into soapy water, then run a finger along each slat of the blind. Rinse your gloved hands in clean water and repeat the process to remove any soap. Wooden slat blinds can be cleaned in the same way, but keep your gloves dry.

Entertainment systems

■ Televisions and music systems create static, which attracts a lot of dust. This can then be drawn into the internal workings of the machines. Dust or vacuum regularly and use anti-static wipes, especially on the television screen.

Fireplace area

■ Vacuum regularly to remove ash and dust. Painted and natural wood, tiled, and brick areas can be brushed clean with a soft brush dipped in mild detergent.

■ Marble areas need more care, as marble is porous and stains easily. Avoid using general household cleaners and wipe over with a damp, soft cloth instead. Gently clean with a soft brush if especially dirty.

Ornaments

■ This job is easier if you remove everything from the shelves and place them on a tray, then dust each piece individually and replace it. (See page 40, *Taking care of special things.*)

Many household cleaning agents contain strong chemicals. Always use protective gloves when you are working with them.

Dining rooms

Table and chairs

■ If your furniture is polished wood, maintain its finish with natural wax polish. This feeds the wood and smells really good too.

■ Spilt candle wax can be removed from table linen, chair upholstery, and carpets by placing two or three layers of paper towel over the wax and applying a hot iron. Don't let the iron come into contact with the carpet or upholstery surface in case it scorches. Spot clean the area to remove any residual grease.

Home office

■ Turn off the power to your computer. Dust its keys with an unused paintbrush – as particles can fall between the keys. If stains are present, use a cloth or a cotton bud dipped in methylated spirits or lighter fluid and rub gently until the stains are gone.

■ Use anti-static wipes on the screen to reduce dust.

■ Apply the same methods to printers, scanners, fax machines, and any other equipment.

Telephones

■ Use a cotton bud dipped in methylated spirits to clean around the dial pads. Disinfect the handset with a cloth dampened with an anti-bacterial cleaner.

Kitchen

■ Germs found in some uncooked foods, such as chicken, thrive in warm, moist surfaces – think 'hygiene' and keep food preparation areas scrupulously clean. Cleaners labelled 'anti-bacterial' give added peace of mind; bleach and liquid disinfectant also kill germs.

■ Non-rinse cleaners save time and wipes pre-moistened with detergent speed the cleaning of switches, door handles, and knobs.

Extractor fans and cooker hoods

■ Avoid a build-up of grease by cleaning with a damp cloth wrung out in a solution of hot, weak, detergent. Change filters as recommended and, if possible, clean them every week.

Refrigerators

■ Check the manufacturer's details if you have them but, in general, refrigerators should be cleaned out every two months or so to keep them hygienic and smelling fresh.

■ Empty the shelves before you clean them and use the opportunity to check and clean water and ice dispensers.

■ Use a specialist refrigerator cleaner, or, alternatively, use a solution of bicarbonate of soda in warm water (this absorbs odours) or mild detergent. Wipe jars and containers as you put them back.

■ Use a fresh, dry, cleaning cloth to remove crumbs from the rubber seal around the door. Condenser coils should be vacuumed several times a year to prevent dust build-up.

■ Clean the outside with a damp cloth and soapy water, or a non-abrasive cream cleaner. To buff large appliances generally, use specialized polish.

Freezers

■ Sort through the contents of your freezer at least twice a year and discard anything that has passed its expiry date. Check storage times on page 136. Check plastic packaging for leaks, as this causes 'freezer burn' on food and can dehydrate and spoil it as well.

■ Even if your freezer defrosts automatically, an annual cleaning and defrost will keep it in good condition.

■ Choose a time when your stores are low, as you will need to temporarily remove the contents to insulated bags and boxes. Picnic coolers are ideal. For an upright freezer, switch off the power, empty the contents, and place a deep tray on the bottom shelf to catch melting ice. (A towel will also help to mop up water.) Chest freezers usually have a drainage system. If not, the water will have to be baled out. Wipe out the inside and the racks with a proprietary cleaner or bicarbonate of soda dissolved in warm water. Switch on the power and return the food when freezer is cold. To clean outside, see *Refrigerators* (above).

Dishwasher

■ Cleaning the dishwasher's filter after each wash is recommended, but at least once or twice a week is essential; otherwise, particles will simply stick to the next load of dishes. From time to time, clean inside the dishwasher by setting it to run through a complete cycle while empty of dishes.

Microwave

■ Wipe out the inside regularly. If your microwave shows a build-up of food matter, especially at the top, place a bowl of steaming water in it for ten minutes to soften the food deposits, then wipe the top clean with a damp cloth. A solution of bicarbonate of soda in warm water or a slice of lemon will remove odours.

Cookers

■ Cleaning the cooker is usually everyone's least favourite job in the kitchen. Wiping up any spills and splashes as they happen will help you avoid having to do a major clean too often.

For regular maintenance:

Gas cookers: Remove the metal burners regularly and wash in hot diluted washing-up liquid. Use a cream cleaner on the cooker top (and the burners if necessary) to remove burned-on food.
Electric cookers: Check the manufacturer's instructions first.

■ Switch off power before cleaning electric cookers.

■ Brush solid electric hot plates with a wire brush.

■ Remove drip pans under the rings and soak in soapy water before scouring them with a steel pad. Pat these dry with kitchen roll and replace.

■ Wipe ceramic and metal cooker tops with a damp cloth and a proprietary cleaner.

Ovens: Remove racks and wash in soapy water.

■ Always follow the manufacturer's instructions for self-cleaning ovens, and remember that ordinary oven-cleaning products may damage your oven lining. Most just need an occasional brushing out with a stiff brush. For normal ovens, use a branded cleaner and carefully follow the instructions. Wear gloves, protect the floor with newspaper, and ventilate the room. Treat these products with caution; they usually contain sodium hydroxide, which can burn skin and mark floors and paintwork.

■ For a quick clean, preheat the oven to 110°C (225°F, gas mark ¼), spray the inside with oven cleaner, leave for ten minutes, then turn power off and wipe the cleaner away with a damp cloth, taking care, as oven will be hot. Rinse frequently (make sure that you have plenty of ventilation).

Cast iron cooker (Aga): These are self-cleaning. Use a stiff wire brush on hot-plates (but be careful, these will always be hot). To clean the vitreous enamel top and sides, use a damp soapy cloth, then wipe dry.

Sinks and drainage areas

■ Synthetic resin can be wiped with a damp cloth dipped in bicarbonate of soda or a cream cleaner.
■ Porcelain can be cleaned with a cream or specialized cleaner.
■ Stainless steel can be wiped clean with diluted dishwashing liquid. Remove water stains and smears with a proprietary cleaner and polish with a kitchen towel. Do not use chemical cleaners on stainless steel, because they can spoil the finish. See *Bathrooms* for guidance on cleaning taps.

Tables

■ Wipe laminates and varnished wooden tables with anti-bacterial spray and kitchen roll.
■ Scrub unsealed wooden tables with soapy water and a scouring cloth or small brush.

When cleaning stainless steel sinks and worktops, try to use the mildest possible effective method and rinse thoroughly afterwards as dried deposits of cleansers and detergents will affect the finish.

Bathroom

Toilets

■ Every day, clean the inside of the toilet bowl with a toilet brush. This will reduce build-up of limescale.
■ Give wooden seats an occasional wax polish and plastic seats some silicon polish (check the manufacturer's instructions).
■ Thick liquid toilet cleaner left overnight, or a rim block, will keep the toilet clean and hygienic and help to prevent lime build-up. Bleach can be used to remove stains inside the bowl, but it doesn't remove lime scale and can damage porcelain after a few hours.

Baths

■ An acrylic bath should be rinsed each time it is used to stop build-up of dirt and limescale. Clean the bath with a mild detergent, non-abrasive cream cleaner or bathroom mousse, and rinse thoroughly. Occasionally use a limescale remover if needed, but check the label for suitability.
■ Do not bleach an acrylic bath because it can damage the surface. Steel baths need to be cleaned with soapy water, then rinsed thoroughly. Avoid bleach and only use a bathroom cleaner or mousse that states it is safe for enamelled baths.

Showers

■ For showers, see also *Baths* above.
Non-rinse shower spray cleaners will prevent a build-up of water stains. Spray the shower floor and sides immediately after showering.

Basins

■ Vitreous china basins are similar to porcelain – see porcelain sinks in *Kitchen*. Hard objects can cause china to chip and crack, so avoid storing glass jars above sinks.
■ For acrylic basins, see *Baths* above.

Taps

■ Rub inside the spout with a toothbrush dipped in limescale remover. For chrome taps, use a specialized cleaner or warm water and very dilute dishwashing detergent. Rinse, then polish them dry with a soft cloth to prevent smears.
■ Clean gold-plated taps as you would chrome, but use extreme care and be mindful not to let limescale

remover splash onto them. Gold can wear away very quickly and scratching will be highly visible.

■ Brass taps can be cleaned in the same way as chrome, and maintained with metal polish.

■ Avoid bleach or scouring products, including cream cleaners. Splashes of perfume and strong disinfectant can cause damage, too.

Mirrors

■ Spray glass cleaner onto a paper towel (not directly onto the mirror) then use this to polish. Use anti-mist spray to stop the mirror from steaming up.

Grout

■ To clean and restore tile grout, fill an empty washing-up liquid bottle with diluted bleach, 75ml bleach to 600ml water (2½ fl oz to 1 pint) and squeeze the bottle to direct the cleaning solution along the lines. Rinse well. If the grouting is very grey or stained, use a small brush over it and then rinse well.

Showerheads

■ Descaling will shift limescale build-up that can block water holes. Unscrew the showerhead and place it in a plastic bowl of diluted descaling solution. Follow the product instructions, then rinse thoroughly.

Shower curtains

■ Remove mildew with a paste made from bicarbonate of soda and lemon juice. Leave to soak, then rinse in warm water. Check their care labels as many shower curtains are machine washable (although you will still need to discourage mildew). Wash them with fabric conditioner to remove soap build-up, particularly on the curtain edges.

Shower enclosure

Tiles: Most tiles are glazed, so use bathroom mousse or non-rinse cleaner that states it is suitable for ceramic tiles. Alternatively, use a solution of mild detergent and wash it off. Buff it to a shine with a dry cloth. Wash matt tiles with soapy water.

Condensation marks

■ These small brown stains usually form on the ceilings of insufficiently ventilated rooms when steam from hot showers and baths hits a colder wall and ceiling. You can reduce condensation by opening the window, or installing an extractor fan. Clean off stains with bathroom cleaner; use one that contains a little bleach. To prevent stains recurring, re-paint with anti-condensation paint.

Bath mats

■ Most can be laundered in the washing machine. If not, see Rugs in *Living Room* on page 27.

Bedroom
Bedding

■ Wash on a high temperature to remove dust mites and perspiration. (Our bodies loose as much water at night as they do in the daytime.) Turn back the covers completely every morning to air-dry and keep the bed fresh.

Cotton sheets should be machine washed with like colours using warm water. Fabric softeners are not necessary because cotton grows softer naturally with repeated washing.

Headboards

■ On fabric headboards, use dry-cleaning foam, following application instructions. On metal, just wipe with a wrung-out cloth, then polish dry. Wood should be wiped with warm water and dilute detergent, then dried. A little wax polish will keep the wood in good condition.

Mattresses

■ Use the vacuum upholstery tool. Turn over and rotate sprung mattresses to stop sagging in one area of the mattress. Use dry-cleaning foam to spot-treat stains. See *Buying furniture basics* on page 67 for more information on mattresses.

Stairs

■ Vacuum from the bottom, so you don't tread dirt into the carpet. For hard floors, (see pages 100–1) mop from the top but be sure to wait until the stairs are dry before using them again. If you need to keep using the stairs, mop alternate steps, leave them to dry, then mop the remainder.

Pets

■ Lay pet beds on a washable floor surface. Wash plastic beds with very dilute bleach, 300ml bleach to 2.5 litres water (½ pint to ½ gallon). If you choose a foam pet bed, buy one that is machine washable. Cats like boxes. A cardboard box lined with old woollens is hygienic and saves on cleaning.

Handy hints

■ **Try using a cotton bud or cocktail stick to dislodge particles of dirt trapped in corners and small spaces such as control switches and dials. Be sure to cover the sharp point of the cocktail stick with a tissue to protect surfaces.**

■ **Use adhesive tape, sticky side out, wrapped around your hand, or a brush, to remove threads and pet hairs from cloth.**

■ **To rescue small items trapped in inaccessible places, use the crevice tool on your vacuum cleaner, after covering the end securely with the foot of an old stocking or even a thin sock.**

CLEANING CHORES CHART

DAILY
■ Clean bathroom washbasin
■ Clean lavatory bowl
■ Spray shower enclosure
■ Wipe kitchen worktops
■ Disinfect kitchen sink
■ Air the beds
■ Empty and clean kitchen waste bin

WEEKLY
■ Air and vacuum throughout
■ Dust/clean bedrooms and living rooms
■ Clean bathrooms
■ Wash kitchen floor, plus surfaces
■ Clean cooker top
■ Check through refrigerator
■ Polish wood furniture
■ Dust computing and entertainment equipment

PERIODICALLY (6–8 WEEKS)
■ Clean out storage cupboards
■ Clean the oven
■ Clean and polish delicate and special items
■ Spend a cleaning session spring-cleaning one room
■ Clean windows
■ De-scale the kettle and shower head
■ Clean shower tile grouting and shower curtains

OCCASIONALLY
■ Move beds and sofa and vacuum underneath
■ Take down and clean light fittings
■ Shampoo carpets; polish hard floors
■ Take down and clean curtains and nets
■ Thoroughly clean appliances, including dispensers and filters
■ Empty and clean bathroom cupboards
■ Wash all paintwork, including skirting boards

help in the home ▪ ▪ ▪

Domestic help is a real advantage for busy people but should be thought through carefully first. These pointers are a useful guide to follow:

▪ Decide exactly what you want your help to do and how much you are willing to pay for the work. Be aware of minimum wage laws. Use the 'Top to Bottom in Two Hours' chart to measure how much they should be able to complete in a given time.
▪ Personal recommendations are always a good way of finding help. Ask amongst your friends.
An agency is the next best way, but decide whether you want to employ an individual for continuity or a cleaning company where you might have a different person each time. Ask for references and always follow them up.
▪ If your budget is limited, reduce costs by limiting the number of rooms cleaned. The kitchen, bathroom, and living room are regular essentials, while other rooms could be rotated week to week. To achieve the most satisfactory results, spend a little time explaining to your helper, what you want done, how you like things to be done, and anything that requires special care.

cleaning windows ▪ ▪ ▪

Cleaning the windows can be just one job too many. To clean the outside of windows, make use of a window cleaner. Most areas have several companies that clean on a regular basis. This is essential if you live above the first floor, unless your windows open to allow easy cleaning (and you may still not be keen to wash them yourself if you live in a flat in a high-rise block).

For cleaning the inside of the windows, try to make sure that when they are drying, the room is not too humid. When cleaning windows follow this guide for perfect results.

▪ If you want to do a thorough wash then start by removing loose dirt with a soft brush. Concentrate on the window frame which can become very grimy – particularly on the outside.
1. Use a specialist soluble window cleaner in a bucket of warm water.
2. Using a squeegee, (a hard-edged rubber blade on a rod) go from top to bottom along the window in even, downward strokes. Clean the squeegee between each stroke.
3. Spray window-cleaning liquid sparingly onto the glass, and then rub to a shine with kitchen roll.
▪ For more frequent, less thorough wash days, just use a spray window-cleaning product.
▪ Never clean windows in direct sunlight because the glass will become streaky.

Household pests

■ ■ ■ From ants marching across the kitchen to wasps' nests in the eaves, prompt action is needed if your home is besieged by pests or vermin. Many infestations can be stopped as they occur, but for some longer term or potentially hazardous problems, an expert will bring greater peace of mind ■ ■ ■

common pests ■ ■ ■

Ants

Spray ants – especially lines of ants – with ant-killer. Follow the trail back to their nest, and pour boiling water on it. Follow this up by leaving ant traps by their nest, or use a slow-acting spray. Ants covered with spray will introduce the poison to other ants in the colony.

Prevention: keep floors and worktops clean and mop up sweet spills immediately, especially in hot weather.

Cockroaches

Cockroach infestation has mostly been confined to commercial kitchens and premises but in recent years has also been found in domestic houses. These are among the most difficult household pests to eradicate, and it is essential to deal with them very thoroughly. As well as having an unpleasant smell, cockroaches carry bacteria that may cause food poisoning. They need food, water, warmth, and dark places to hide in – behind and under sinks, in the motor compartment of refrigerators, and under tabletops. Spray them with specialized pesticides. Remove dead insects, clean the area, and then repeat the treatment as an extra deterrent to stop them coming back.

If you are irritated by household insecticides, consider alternatives such as boric acid to control ants and citronella oil to repel mosquitos.

Dust mites

Unpleasant though it is to imagine a bed full of microscopic mites feeding on particles of dead skin, these tiny creatures aren't a problem unless you are asthmatic or develop an allergic reaction. You can't eliminate them from a home, but you can cut their numbers drastically.

■ Use an anti-allergen cover for your mattress and an anti-allergen pillow, or protective covers for pillows and duvet.
■ Avoid synthetic bedding. Recent research shows that feather bedding harbours fewer mites than synthetic bedding.
■ Thoroughly vacuum beds and furniture regularly.
■ Wash sheets and duvet covers at a high temperature.
■ Consider switching from carpets to hard floors.
■ Children's soft toys – which also harbour mites – can be put in plastic bags, then popped into the freezer to kill the mites, and then machine-washed.

Fleas

If you own a cat or dog, there's a big risk that the animal will carry fleas – which then jump off the animal to bite you. There are many methods and products available to keep your pet and your home free from fleas, and your vet can advise you on the best way to deal with it. Common treatments include a liquid applied to the animal's skin, and a powder that is added to food. Both of these render the fleas sterile. More traditional methods include powder pesticides to treat animals and bedding, and the use of flea collars. Your pet shop will have a range of suitable products.

Flies

Reduce the presence of flies in your house by keeping your rubbish bin lid tightly closed and by putting away food. If you have convenient corners, hang old-fashioned slow-release fly-killer strips. These are very effective. Regularly check and remove insects. If there is a particular problem in the kitchen, try a plug-in fluorescent trap that draws flies to the light, then zaps them.

Mice

Unless you have a cat, which will bring you direct evidence, you may not know you have mice for some time. Look for signs of nibbled food or chewed wiring, usually in the kitchen, basement, or attic. To tackle the problem, you may want to contact your local pest control services. They will use poisoned bait placed in small boxes away from children and pets. Alternatively, you could employ a private pest control contractor or buy traps and poison from a DIY shop to use yourself.

Moths

The plain, brown clothes moth lays eggs that hatch into white grubs. These grubs then eat holes in anything containing wool – carpets, furnishings, and clothes – and usually focus on a favourite sweater. To eradicate them, use a specialized moth killer. See page 57 for tips on clothes and moths.

Mosquitoes

Mosquitoes and gnats can be a big problem when the climate is hot and humid. Kill them with a specialized insecticide. If your home is near water you can reduce their entry by placing mosquito screens on windows and doors or keeping windows shut. Mosquitoes breed in standing water, so cover any reservoirs used to collect rainwater, and put petroleum jelly in gutters to prevent water from collecting in pools and stagnating.

Rats

Rats carry serious disease and organisms like Salmonella bacteria, parasites, viruses, and worms. They continually gnaw on solid objects and damage to buildings can prove costly. It is therefore important to address the problem quickly. It is best handled by your local authority's pest control office, who will also be able to advise you on how to prevent re-entry. Steps you can take to eliminate rodents include:

- Keep garbage cans covered.
- Remove rubbish and tall weeds from property.
- Place large traps around the home.
- Always wear gloves when removing dead rats.
- If you have a vegetable garden, be sure to check vegetables for teeth marks.

Silver fish

These are small crawling insects that eat starch and glue. They like to hide in dark places, especially if it is damp, and are often an indication of lack of ventilation or low-grade damp. They may damage wallpaper and paper in picture frames and book covers. Destroy with insecticide.

Wasps

A few wasps can be dealt with using a specialized spray. Large numbers indicate that you may have a nest under the eaves, or around the base of your house. Employ a contractor who will remove the nest.

Woodworm

Woodworm attack furniture and cause holes the size of pinheads. In older furniture, some damage may have been done years ago. To see if woodworm is currently active, look for very fine sawdust that falls from the holes when you touch them. It is important to act promptly, because woodworm can move easily from one piece of furniture to an adjacent piece. You can treat an isolated infestation in furniture with woodworm eradication kits, but if you think any part of the house may have an infestation, it is better to contact a contractor.

> **SAFETY TIP**
> Always remember that insecticides are toxic, and may harm pets (including fish). It is unsafe for people to touch or breathe their fumes. So keep children far away from them.

Waste disposal and recycling

■ ■ ■ Putting rubbish out for collection is easily done without a thought but much of what we throw away can be recycled if we think about how we collect our household waste ■ ■ ■

disposing of your waste ■ ■ ■

Dust bins

Dust bins are available in plastic or metal. Plastic is lightweight, easy to clean, and won't rust. Metal bins are arguably better looking, and because of the extra weight, are more stable when empty. Always have a dust bin with a secure lid. Without this, wind and animals can disperse your rubbish throughout the neighbourhood.

Dust bin checkpoints

■ Site the bin near your front door. Ideally, screen it from view.

■ Write your house number on both bin and lid.

■ Regularly wash the bin with disinfectant.

Indoors

Placing a small wastebasket in every room makes it more likely that paper and packaging will be thrown away promptly.

■ Simple wicker baskets are fine for dry waste. A plastic liner is hygienic and makes emptying quicker.

■ Where you may have wet waste – in the bathroom or children's rooms – choose a metal or plastic wastebasket that can be washed out.

■ Wastebaskets that have anything other than paper in them should be emptied every day.

■ Lidded bins are essential when what's put inside them may develop a smell. A rubbish bin with a

swing lid in the kitchen saves time and means less hand contact with the bin.

■ For easy recycling, a kitchen bin that's divided into two or more compartments lets you put glass or cans only in one side, and non-recyclable waste in the other.
■ A flip-top rubbish bin that sits under the sink is convenient in smaller households, but is not big enough for families.

Kitchen waste hygiene

Germs love rubbish bins, so emptying the kitchen bin needs to be done daily, whether it's full or not.

■ Have a set time when you do this job – preferably at a time that won't be changed.
■ Wipe the lid daily with an anti-bacterial wipe. Clean inside and out weekly with a bleach solution or disinfectant.
■ Make sure the bin is completely dry before putting in a fresh bin liner.

Waste disposers

Many kitchens include a waste disposer alongside, or integral to, the main sink. This provides a convenient and hygienic way to dispose of most kitchen food waste.

■ Always read the instructions to get the most out of your disposer and how to avoid problems.
■ Don't cram a lot of waste in at once.
■ Always run plenty of cold water when the disposer is in use.
■ To clear a blockage, see page 8, *Basic repairs inside your home.*

Disposal checkpoints

Never leave items that are flammable, toxic, or labelled as 'household hazardous waste' out with general rubbish. Also do not put things into the rubbish that might injure the workers who empty your bins.

Broken glass

Wrap breakages securely in thick newspaper, secure with tape and label clearly. Put beside the bin. Large glass pieces, such as whole windows, should be taken away by the contractor who fits replacements.

Medicines

Take unfinished or expired medicines to any pharmacy or doctor's dispensary to be disposed of safely.

Hazardous household waste includes:

■ Paint
■ Anti-freeze
■ Petrol
■ Solvents
■ Car batteries
■ Needles/syringes

General waste

Cooking oil

Pour unwanted liquid grease or oil into a rigid container; an empty jar or bottle is ideal. When the fat has cooled, put the container into the rubbish.

Raw food and cooked scraps

Use the waste disposer if you have one, except for bones (wrap these thoroughly before placing them in the rubbish). Use this same method to get rid of all meat and fish trimmings if you do not have a disposer. Don't put these items directly into the bin where they will smell and encourage animals and insects. Use waste jars or food packaging in which to seal these items before adding them to the rubbish.

General food waste

Strain food liquids down the sink and put food scraps in containers. Always drain milk and juice cartons, wine bottles, and other similar items before placing their containers in the rubbish.

Vegetable peelings

Even if you only have flower pots, get composting. If you have a garden, a compost-maker will soon turn kitchen scraps into compost. If you live in a flat, a wormery will do the same job, and your flower pots will be wonderful.

Clothing, glasses, used postage stamps, furniture, PCs, domestic appliances

These items can be donated to organizations that provide them to the needy. Look in the Yellow Pages under charities, and look out for campaigns in the local press.

Recyclable items

Aluminium cans, tin cans, paper (including newspaper) and glass bottles can all be recycled at your local recycling centre. A few councils recycle certain plastic containers as well – look on the bottom of containers to see if they are recyclable. Take washed items to your local recylcing centre and place them in the appropriate container.

Some councils will collect some or all of these items from your doorstep at no charge and will even provide you with your own recycling bin. Contact your council to find out more details.

SPACE-SAVING TIPS	
Cereal boxes	Undo base flap, then flatten.
Cans	Open both ends, then flatten. Crush aluminium cans.
Cans/tubes	Fill with other waste first, to use the space inside.
Paper waste/tissue	Fold, don't scrunch.

home recycling ■ ■ ■

■ Attend a car boot sale, or take items directly to shops selling secondhand books, clothes, or furniture.
■ Buy products with less packaging, such as refills or bigger sizes (they use proportionately less packaging).
■ Take your own shopping bags/baskets for your supermarket groceries.

Taking glass and cans to your local recycling centre is great – but it's better to find a way to re-use things in your own home. Doing so saves energy that would be spent on re-processing materials and transporting them back and forth in their new form. You also save money and make more room in the rubbish bin.

Item	New uses
Old clothes and fabric	■ Rags for cleaning. ■ Cut sleeves from jumpers to make pet blankets or woollen cushion covers. ■ Net curtains make garden cloches to protect vegetables from frost. ■ Duvet covers make curtain liners for extra warmth in winter. ■ Sheets and old clothes are great for children to play dressing-up.
Newspaper	■ Line cat-litter trays with it and use in rabbit hutches, in place of straw. ■ Make papier mâché with your children. ■ Use as an economy liner under foam-backed carpets, but not in bathrooms. ■ Use as plant mulch, instead of bark, to prevent weeds. Cover with topsoil. ■ Make seed pots for easy planting outdoors. Use existing plug pots for shaping, then, when ready, set both plant and newspaper pot straight into the ground. As the plant grows, the newspaper disintegrates. ■ Individually wrap garden fruit for storage.
Plastic food containers	■ Large, clear, upturned bottles with the bottoms cut off make individual 'greenhouses' for delicate seedlings. ■ Use plastic containers to store food in your refrigerator. ■ Empty milk containers – thoroughly cleaned – can store soup in your freezer. Don't overfill them, as food expands when frozen. ■ Ice cream tubs make good sandwich boxes.
Cans and jars	■ Catering-size tins of instant coffee have airtight lids; cover them with sticky-back paper and use them as storage containers. ■ Use screw top bottles for salad dressing. Pour in ingredients, shake, and serve! ■ Make a summer lantern – place tealights in empty jars, tie string around their rims and hang them on trees. ■ Small, coloured glass bottles make single-stem vases, or café style candle holders. ■ Re-use metal boxes and jars for biscuits, tea, coffee, spices, holding nails, etc.
Toothbrushes	■ Toothbrushes are good for scrubbing small, fragile items and for cleaning delicate areas about the home. See the *Household cleaning* section, page 24.
Paper products	■ Paper printed on only one side is fine to use again in the printer, but check for staples first. ■ Cut a stack of used paper in half to make a telephone message pad.

Taking care of special things

■ ■ ■ **Some valuables you may store carefully for safety – but others will be exposed to the rigours of being on shelves or walls or even being used, albeit on special occasions. This guide is designed to help you keep the items you value in pristine condition. Some things you will be able to do yourself, but, from time to time, you may need to seek out specialist cleaning or repairs. If in any doubt, seek advice from professionals** ■ ■ ■

care and maintenance ■ ■ ■

Antique lace
Never wash nineteenth-century fine lace, as it may contain horsehair and will fall apart. Take it to an antique textile specialist or a museum for cleaning advice. Twentieth-century lace can be hand washed. Squeeze it, don't wring it, and pull it into shape while it is hanging to dry. Moths aren't interested in cotton lace; the main danger here is from yellowing. So keep pieces rolled around white acid-free tissue paper (from a stationer's) and store in a closed box.

Bamboo
Vacuum bamboo regularly with the brush attachment. Wash each summer with warm soapy water. To re-stiffen your furniture add salt to the final rinse. Air-dry it outside.

Books
The drying effect of central heating can be a problem for books – over time, the glue used to bind the spine of the book can dry out. A humidifier helps, and even a bowl of water will offer some benefit. Books benefit from careful treatment.

■ Always grasp a book firmly on both sides – don't pull it out by its spine.

■ Give it enough room on the shelf – squashing a book damages the binding.

■ Each year, take out each book and dust it, starting from the top shelf and working your way down.

■ Damp conditions can quickly cause mildew on books, so don't store boxes of books in the attic or basement. These two places have the highest humidity in the house. If you do find mildew, fresh deposits can often be wiped off with a soft cloth. You can also try dusting it with cornflour, but old or widespread mildew may not come off.

■ Leather bindings can be polished annually with a smear of petroleum jelly, but let them dry for several days before returning them to the bookcase.

■ Grease spots may come out of book pages if you place blotting paper on either side of the spot and press the page with a warm iron.

■ Placing sheets of tissue paper between affected pages can repair damp or flood-damaged books. Weigh the book down and leave in the airing cupboard to dry out, or use a hairdryer, on low setting.

Brass

■ The air quickly tarnishes non-lacquered brass – which is a manmade mix of copper and zinc. Brassware, such as candlesticks, doorstops, and ornaments, needs regular cleaning and polishing with a soft cloth and a specialist cleaning solution.

■ For a first-time clean, scrub with an ammonia solution to remove ingrained dirt and any green patches (verdigris).

■ Lacquered brass simply needs dusting, but it may look less authentic. It should last at least ten years, but if it gets damaged it will need to be professionally re-finished.

Bronze

■ Dust lacquered bronze. Never wash un-coated bronze if you think it is valuable, because the metal could corrode.

■ Seek specialist advice – try antiques dealers or museum staff. If your piece isn't valuable, but is dirty, wash it with mild detergent and water. Rinse and wipe it very dry.

Cane

Dust cane lightly with a feather duster. A spray cleaner is safe for unvarnished cane. If the piece is varnished, just use soapy water.

Chrome

This was a popular material used in Art Deco artifacts from the 1930s. Restore shine by washing it with warm water and detergent. To treat stains, use a specialized chrome cleaner.

Christening gowns

Hand wash after use, but don't starch or iron these. Store them in acid-free tissue paper, placing pads of tissue inside the sleeves and body. Every year, take the gown out and give it a shake to change the folds and then replace it in the acid-free tissue paper.

Clocks and watches

Always leave these for an expert. Never attempt to clean the working parts of clocks and watches. Take old clocks to a clock repairer. Return new watches or clocks to a department store or jewellers, or contact the manufacturer directly for servicing.

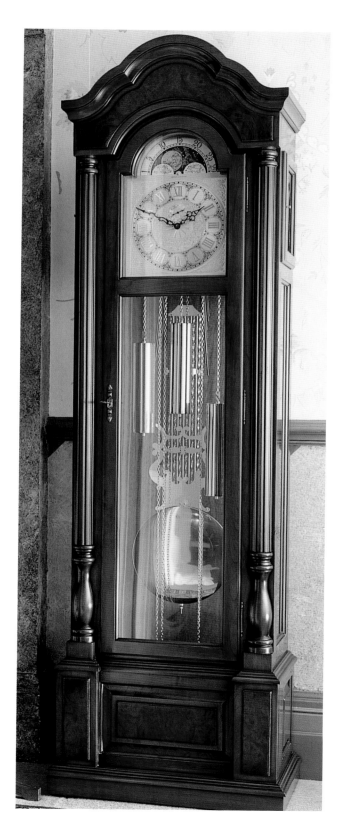

Coins

For an immaculate collection, don't polish these; scrub them with hot water, using a toothbrush.

Copper

Copper is easily cleaned with any metal polish that specifically says 'suitable for copper'. It is fine to wash it between cleanings with water and detergent, then a clear rinse. Be sure to dry it well.

Diamonds and precious stones

As you'd expect of one of the world's hardest substances, diamonds can cope with rigorous cleaning solutions. Some experts have even recommended shining them with denture cleaner!

■ A weak liquid detergent is a more traditional way to clean these. Clean them in a cup, never the basin.
■ Check the settings of rings, ear-rings, and necklaces regularly. If a ring starts to 'catch' on clothes, it's probably due to a claw that has worked loose and you will need a jeweller to correct this.
■ Take care with other precious stones; opals and emeralds need professional cleaning.

Glass

It is the hot temperature of the water, plus thorough air-drying, which gives glasses washed in dishwashers that great shine. Try to mimic these conditions when you hand wash glass.

Glasses

Use warm, soapy water to clean and then rinse them in clean, hot water. Hold glasses by the stem and drain them dry on a soft cloth. Resist the temptation to do the drying yourself; even a glass cloth can leave pieces of lint on the glass.

Decanters

Remove tidemarks by filling to just above the mark with water and vinegar, then adding a handful of un-cooked rice. Shake firmly. The mark should disappear.

Gold jewellery

Your grandmother may have declared that dropping her rings into alcohol restored their shine, but a weak solution of washing-up liquid will cut the grease and grime, too. Afterward, polish them with a soft cloth.

■ Gold is most likely to get scratched in your jewel case, when it rubs against other metals and hard stones. So use separate compartments!
■ Wrap chains in tissue paper.
■ Keep jewellery you don't wear often in its original padded box, inside a safe if you use one. This way, the items left in your jewellery box will have sufficient space. Every month or so, swap things around.

Home videos

Quality video and camcorder tapes are designed to permanently store sounds and images.

You don't have to keep ornaments safe by displaying them in cabinets or storing them where they can't be enjoyed. Just ensure that your ornaments are out of reach of pets and children, and keep them away from busy thoroughfares where they are likely to be knocked over.

- Keep tapes away from dampness and light.
- Keep tapes away from sources of magnetism such as stereo speakers.
- Keep tapes safe. Protect valuable tapes by removing the safety tabs so they can't be recorded over.
- Make a back-up copy of irreplaceable wedding tapes, and box, label, and store them separately.

Ornaments

When you clean or move and display fine china or glass ornaments, use the utmost care.

- Use both hands to pick something up and support its weight underneath.
- Washing can be simpler than trying to accurately dust very intricate figures. Be careful and gentle; use a plastic bowl or improvise with an empty food container and wash each piece separately. Air-dry, by standing the ornament on a cloth.
- Displaying a collection behind glass cuts down on cleaning. If you have cats, it can also make good sense to protect items from being knocked over.

cleaning silver

1 A quick and easy way to clean silver is to use specialist silver polish. Clean a small area at a time, applying the polish and rubbing the silver with a cloth.

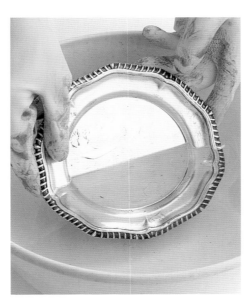

2 A more old-fashioned method is to apply a paste of bicarbonate of soda and water to silver. To remove tarnish, place it directly on a cloth, then rinse in water.

3 No matter what method you choose to clean your silver, it's always best to finish off by rubbing it with a dry lint-free cloth to make it shine.

Photographs

■ Protect photographs on display with a firm backing behind, to prevent wrinkles, and a glass frame in front, to protect from dust and dirt.

■ Never place photographs in direct sunlight.

■ Negatives need to be clean and stored dust-free in acid-free paper, not plastic sleeves. Store in a metal file box, for complete darkness.

■ Store photographs not on display in the dark (inside an album is fine) at 24°C (75°F) or lower.

■ Because fumes from wood preservatives, paints, and varnishes can harm photographs, it's better to keep your albums on open bookshelves than in closed drawers.

Silver

Silver is a soft metal that needs to be protected from scratches. Be careful when washing it, use hot water with washing up liquid – never use scouring powder – or polish it with specialized silver polish.

Silver cups, shields, and trophies

Clean the dirt from engraved names and mottos with a soft toothbrush that has been immersed in silver dip. Brush away any dirt with sweeping left-to-right strokes. Remember that cleaning silver is an abrasive process and you are removing the surface layer of silver from the item that you are cleaning. You must take particular care when cleaning silver plate, because you could eventually remove the silver layer entirely. Regular cleaning with a soft cloth will avoid this.

Handy hints – use a safe

A simple way to make more secure the items that you cherish is by choosing to keep them in a strong, steel container. You will be protecting them against damage by flood or fire, too. Fitting a basic safe is a simple home improvement project. The safe comes complete – all you need do is find a discreet place, perhaps under a wooden floor (with a trapdoor cut for access), inside a cupboard, or in an unused space, like a blocked-up fireplace. (See pages 62–4 for information on securing your home.)

Silverware

■ Your dishwasher will state whether it can safely clean silver. However, the patina, caused by fingering, is best removed by washing and drying by hand.

■ Never put stainless steel items in the same wash or your silver will become damaged.

Silver jewellery

■ Jewellery that is regularly worn does not usually tarnish. If you have to store your jewellery, clean it first and store in a dry plastic bag or container with anti-tarnish paper.

■ Frequently clean silver in mild washing-up liquid and remove tarnish using a commercial silver dip or specialist polish.

■ If a clasp begins to irritate your skin, it may have lost some of its silver coating, and your skin could be reacting to the base metals underneath. Paint clear nail polish on it to stop direct skin contact.

Wood furniture

Polish restores the shine to most woods – but the deepest shine comes from elbow grease. Antique furniture will stay in good condition with regular dusting and a twice-yearly polishing with a traditional furniture cream. If you want to darken the wood, use a polish with a deeper dye. For modern woods, like pine and beech, choose a polish that matches the colour of the wood.

■ Disguise scratches by filling them in with a waxy substance that is a close colour match – for example, an eyebrow pencil can be used for mahogany, and tan shoe polish or a wax crayon for oak and pine.

■ Go for prevention, not cure, and use placemats on untreated wooden tables.

■ Whole books have been written on treating stains on wood. If you try one method that doesn't work move on to the next. Water marks and heat stains may come out if you rub *very* gently with fine steel wool, then re-build the grain and finish with linseed oil.

■ Learn to view your wooden furniture as a living item whose condition and appearance will age and even look 'lived in' over time. If this bothers you, have the wood varnished or professionally waxed.

Fabric care

■ ■ ■ **Regular cleaning of soft furnishings to remove dust, dirt, and any staining will preserve the colours and freshness of fabric and greatly increase the life of your furnishings** ■ ■ ■

sunlight ■ ■ ■

The greatest damage is often done by sunlight. As well as causing fading, prolonged exposure to direct sunlight may weaken the structure of material, particularly silk. Synthetic carpets are also highly susceptible to it.

■ If you can, close curtains in unoccupied back rooms during the day. Those visible to the street are best left open, so that your home looks occupied.
■ Install blinds for rooms that you use by day.
■ Move upholstery out of direct sunlight.
■ Rotate throws and rugs to reduce the sun's effect.
■ Curtains made of velvet are easily faded by the sun, so tie them back, away from direct sunlight.

special surfaces ■ ■ ■

Furnishing fabrics and bedding should have a care label, just as clothes do. However, that may not be the case for items you have made-to-order, created yourself, or inherited when you move into a house. If you have no instructions, you must decide whether your item is typical of its fabric type and suited to the treatment outlined on page 49. If in doubt, seek professional advice. Most dry cleaners will advise you on how to care for washable fabrics, or you may want to take a sample to a fabric shop for advice.

how to test for colour-fastness ▪ ▪ ▪

Before you attempt to clean furnishings or carpets, you will need to know if the colour will wash out in water. If it does, you must decide if the level of fading is acceptable or if you wish to use a non-water – that is to say a dry-clean – method.

▪ Dampen a patch of fabric in a discreet place – inside a seam is ideal, or a corner of carpet behind a door. Place a piece of white fabric, such as an old handkerchief, on the material and iron over it. If colour transfers to the white, your item is not colourfast.

▪ Non-colourfast items must be either washed separately or with same-colour items. Alternatively, the item will have to be dry-cleaned.

cleaning ▪ ▪ ▪

Blankets

▪ Many wool, wool blend, and all synthetic blankets can be machine or hand washed. Size may dictate that you need to use a commercial machine or take it to the cleaners. Never use a self-operated dry-cleaning machine because toxic fumes tend to linger in the material.

▪ *Electric blankets*: These must be serviced every two to three years. Hand wash them, if care instructions allow, but dry very thoroughly. If non-washable, contact the manufacturer who may offer cleaning and servicing as a combined package.

Carpets

▪ If colourfast, shampoo carpets with a deep cleaner. If not, use a dry-foam cleaner (this is best done professionally, however).

▪ To remove stains, use a dry-foam stain remover and follow instructions.

▪ Cut out cigarette burns and other impossible-to-shift stains on cut-pile carpets. Use nail scissors and snip the fibres below the mark. This is not a perfect solution, but it makes the mark less noticeable.

▪ To minimize stain damage, have carpets treated with stain protector. This covers carpet fibres with a fine layer of a liquid-repelling coating, so that stains sit on the surface, ready to be cleaned off.

Curtains

- Decide whether the material is washable (see chart on page 49).
- Unlined washable curtains are a straightforward laundering job. Take out the hooks and mark their place with a laundry marker pen. Wash as instructed. For lined curtains, follow care instructions for the gentlest fabric (for instance, on damask curtains with polyester lining, follow the care instructions for the lining).
- Consider having lined curtains that are cotton or linen-based professionally cleaned, as these materials are prone to shrinking. If a lining shrinks more than its top fabric, you'll need to separate the two pieces of fabric, then re-attach them, or the curtain won't hang smoothly. Take non-washable curtains to be dry-cleaned, or use coin-operated dry-cleaning machines. To dispel toxic fumes, air them thoroughly in a ventilated room (not in a bedroom).

Net Curtains

- Use warm soapy water and a large bowl for these. Don't squeeze or wring them – simply move the fabric around in the bowl.
- Use net curtain whitener in the final rinse to restore their brightness. Tumble-dry them if you have a low heat setting; otherwise, line-dry them. Re-hang them over the window while they are still damp to avoid creases.

Duvets

These are machine washable, but most are too heavy for domestic machines. Unless the label specifically says you can wash these at home, use a commercial washing machine at a launderette or have them professionally cleaned.

Pillows

Fibre-filled pillows generally must be machine or hand washed. Do not use fabric softener and rinse them very thoroughly. Feather pillows must be washed by hand, then put into a very short spin cycle. Once saturated, a feather pillow may become too heavy to safely go into a tumble dryer. Instead, secure it lengthwise on a clothes line, shaking and hanging it from opposite ends regularly. Air it thoroughly before using.

Rugs

Oriental rugs: The backing and front fibres may be made of different materials and may not react well to washing. Always seek professional advice.
Wool rugs: If colourfast, clean with carpet shampoo suitable for wool carpets. Use warm water only – if it is too hot it will shrink the fibres.
Polyester/Acrylic rugs: Check to see whether the rug is colourfast. If so, clean it with carpet shampoo; if not, use dry shampoo.

Sisal flooring

Clean only when you must and use a dry foam carpet shampoo. Secure the edges of the mat to a solid surface like a clean, outdoor patio – to help reduce shrinking. Take care not to over-wet the matting. Dry it naturally.

Cotton-based upholstery

Wash loose upholstery covers according to the maker's instructions. Traditional stretch-covers are light enough for a home machine wash. A heavy linen cover may need to go in a larger launderette machine or be washed in a bath (but not in an acrylic bath). Even if only one seat cover is stained, you must wash all covers together to keep the colours even. Replace covers just before they dry completely – they go on more easily. For fixed covers, use a foam carpet shampoo for washable fabric, and a dry-clean (that is, non-water) preparation for fabrics that aren't washable. Alternatively, professional upholstery cleaners may come to your home to do the job. Look in your Yellow Pages for possibilities.

Synthetic velvet and dralon upholstery

■ This is most often made of acrylic velvet on a cotton blend backing and needs careful handling. Loose covers should be dry-cleaned.
■ Vacuum fixed covers first, then test shampoo in an unnoticeable corner and let it dry completely before cleaning the whole item. Avoid over-wetting, as this may make the fabric shrink. Use shampoo lather, applied with a cloth. Work in shampoo following the direction of the pile. Allow it to dry, brush thoroughly, and then vacuum it again.

cleaning fabrics

Remove stains on carpets regularly to reduce the expense of using professional carpet cleaners or hiring carpet-cleaning machinery. Most supermarkets now stock specialist cleaners, such as the one above, that comes with a soft brush for agitating difficult stains, and does require rinsing off afterwards.

If you just have a stain on your curtain, and don't need to, or can't wash it, you can use a specialist stain remover that can be bought in a supermarket and used on the brightest of colours. But make sure that you've bought the right cleaner for the colours and type of fabric used in your curtain.

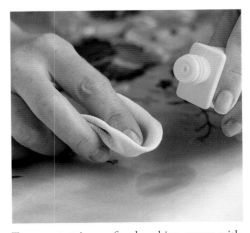

Treat spot stains on fixed cushion covers with a specialist or general upholstery cleaner. Agitate difficult stains with a soft cloth, dabbing gently. Do not scrub because you can ruin the fibres, and ultimately, the appearance of the fabric. Try to find a cleaner that does not need rinsing off afterwards.

Leather upholstery

■ Dust or vacuum, then clean with saddle soap when needed. Polish with a soft cloth. Twice a year, clean with shoe cream or (for pale leather) petroleum jelly. Be very thorough about rubbing off excess product.
■ Have any repairs done by an expert.

Quilts

Follow care instructions, but generally wash quilts as you would duvets. Have patchworks professionally cleaned, unless all the patches are from the same fabric.

Towels

Machine wash, separately for deep-dyed towels. Over time, fabric softener makes towels less absorbent, so leave this out if you use a dryer. If you line dry, towels will be too hard without a softener.

WASHING POPULAR FURNISHING MATERIALS

Fabric type	Washing instruction	Ironing instruction
Boucle	■ Gentle machine wash	■ Cool iron, press on wrong side with damp cloth
Chiffon	■ Gentle machine wash/dry-clean	■ Cool iron, no steam
Chintz	■ dry-clean to retain glaze	■ Cool iron, press on wrong side
Corduroy	■ Hand or gentle machine wash	■ Press on top of a towel. Use steam to revive pile
Cotton	■ Hot wash	■ Hot iron
Damask	■ Hand wash or dry clean	■ Medium iron, under a cloth
Dralon	■ Warm wash, cold rinse	■ Cool iron once dry
Fur fabric	■ Gentle machine wash/dry-clean	■ Clean press on wrong side, on top of a towel
Gingham	■ Wash at up to 59°C (140°F)	■ Hot iron
Linen	■ Warm wash or dry-clean	■ Hot iron
Muslin and voile	■ Gentle wash	■ Cool iron
Silk and satin	■ Gentle wash/dry-clean	■ Medium iron, no-steam medium iron, no-steam with a cloth
Velvet	■ Dry-clean	■ Medium iron on wrong side

For information on using fabric in the home, see Soft furnishings *section on page 94*

The home laundry

■ ■ ■ **Washday is no longer just on Monday! If you lead a life that's already full to bursting, you may prefer to do your laundry in the evening or a quiet corner of the weekend. With the right equipment and a little planning, that's no problem ■ ■ ■**

washing ■ ■ ■

A washing machine is a priority purchase for anyone setting up a home. As well as saving both time and labour, each wash costs a fraction of what you will pay at a launderette. Modern detergents have further eased the burden; cleaning enzymes designed to give impressive results at low temperatures mean that practically everything can now go into the machine.

WASHING MACHINES
■ Consider how much noise the machine will make and how much space it will take up.
■ Look for extras that you want such as a fabric softener dispenser, and an individual spin cycle.
■ Don't be tempted by fancy features. Most laundry needs one of three options: low temperature with a short spin; colourfast/medium wash and short spin, and cottons/maximum hot wash with a long spin.
■ A front loading machine is more compact, lets you store things above, and is more energy efficient than a traditional top loader. However, its washing times are longer and it is more expensive to buy.

WASHING TIPS
■ Read the operational instructions for your machine, plus care labels on clothes.
■ Prepare clothes for the wash by emptying pockets, pulling off loose buttons, fastening bras, and closing zips. Separate clothes by colour and/or fabric type. One load might be colour t-shirts and underwear, another cotton bedding, and a third white shirts. This is important, because the dye in a dark or bright colour could run into a lighter item.
■ An overloaded machine will not wash well and may even damage the machine.
■ Choose the right detergent. Some detergents contain soap and synthetic cleaners as well as natural enzymes, which break down dirt at lower temperatures. Other detergents contain no enzymes or bleach. These are often chosen by families that want a more skin-friendly detergent.
■ Colour-safe detergents are bleach-free. They won't make bright or dark clothes fade.
■ Fabric softeners work by coating fabric fibres with a layer of silicone to make clothes feel softer and prevent matting. However, people with allergies may want to avoid adding synthetic residue to their clothes.
■ Care symbols show maximum washing temperatures. If the item just needs freshening up, you may want a quicker, low-temperature programme.

stain removal ■ ■ ■

Most stains will come out – if you act fast. First assess whether a particular fabric will cope with the stain re-mover. Take care with delicate fabrics – you may remove the stain, but be left with a bleached-out patch, ruining the item. You may often be instructed to work from the inside of the garment so that the stain is lifted out of the right side onto a cloth. Here are some basic rules that may need to change according to the stain:

- Scrape off excess deposits.
- Rinse under warm or cold running water.
- Spot-treat with soapy water.
- Machine wash with a biological powder.
- If this fails, try stain remover.
- Never use hot water as it may 'set' the stain.

STAIN REMOVAL

Tea and coffee	Washing in biological washing powder will usually work. If not, try a stain remover.
Beer	When you're away from home, dilute with cold clear water. At home: dab with a solution of wine vinegar and warm water. Rinse and machine wash.
Beetroot	Rinse in cold running water then machine wash fast.
Blood	Soak in cold, salty water, then rinse and wash in a detergent with enzymes.
Chewing gum	Remove what excess you can, then put the item into a plastic bag and place it in the freezer for an hour. The frozen gum then breaks off quite easily.
Grass	Spot-clean with methylated spirits, then machine or hand wash.
Paint	Wash emulsion paint before it dries, and it will come out easily. For gloss paint, apply white spirit from the inside of the fabric. Hold a clean cloth against the paint, to absorb it. Caution: once completely dry, it will be almost impossible to shift both types of paint.
Ink	Rinse fabric with cold water, then rub in liquid detergent and rinse it again. You can also buy specialist ink removers.
Jam	The traditional way to get rid of this type of stain is with a solution of borax from the pharmacist. You can also use a specialisd fruit and wine stain remover.
Ketchup	Scrape off excess. Rinse under cold water. Loosen the stain with a solution of warm water and glycerine before washing.
Cosmetics	Soak in weak ammonia solution. 10ml to 1 litre of water (2tsp to 2pts). Rinse then wash. Dab lipstick with vegetable oil and leave for 15 minutes. Mop up with a dry cloth.
Oil	Dab stains on washable materials with a solvent. If the stain is on leather, sprinkle it with talcum powder to absorb the grease, then polish.

drying ...

Automatic washing machines spin out excess water but the job still has to be finished by tumble-drying or air-drying on a clothesline outside, in the laundry room, or on a rack over a bath.

Hanging outside
- Wipe off the clothes line with a damp cloth before pegging out clothes.
- Turn coloured clothing inside out to prevent sun-fade.
- Don't let clothes become over-dry before ironing.

Hanging inside
- Hand-washed delicates can drip over the bath, and be switched to racks once all the dripping has ceased.
- To prevent condensation, keep the window open while clothes are damp.

Dryer checkpoints
Tumble dryers are great time-savers – they mean less ironing, as well as the certainty that you can wash and dry an outfit in about two hours. Always buy a dryer with two heat settings: delicates and wools will shrink in hot temperatures.

- *Vented tumble dryers*: These dryers need a hose to release the damp air outside, which means they must be positioned near an outside wall or a window.

- *Condenser tumble dryers*: These collect damp air in a reservoir and cool it. The reservoir is emptied as necessary. Although more expensive, these dryers are usually better and can be placed anywhere near a power point.

ironing ...

Environmentally friendly washing
- Always wash at the lowest temperature possible.
- Pre-wash very dirty clothes.
- Fabric care guides show maximum temperatures, but you can always go lower.
- Wait until you have a full laundry load.
- Choose 'green' washing products that use soap and natural vegetable detergents but avoid bleaching agents, enzymes, brighteners, and perfume.

Between driers and fabric softeners, ironing is not the chore that it once was. Many items just need a shake and placing on a hanger to air. An adjustable ironing board and a good iron are both essential for a quick and efficient finish to your laundry.

Irons
- Steam irons and steam/spray irons are available with a cord, or cordless, for easier manoeuverability. A reservoir of distilled water inside the iron turns to steam when it reaches the hot plate of the iron. This creates a damp surface and makes a smoother finish on fabric.
- Distilled water is sold in hardware shops and supermarkets. If you run out, use boiled water.
- Steam/spray irons have the added function of delivering a shot of steam. This means you can work out a particularly stubborn crease.
- Synthetics, delicate fabrics, and items without deep creasing won't need steam. Dry ironing is sufficient.
- Always choose a steam iron over the traditional dry iron.
- Spray starch gives a firm finish to shirts and bed linen. Spray one side of item just before ironing.

Ironing boards
- Check for good height adjustment and useful extras, such as a storage rack underneath.
- If you iron in a kitchen, consider a space-saving pull-out ironing board that fits into a utensil drawer.
- Wash and change the cover regularly.

Laundry checkpoints
- Follow care instructions for the most delicate part of an item. A cotton pillow with silk trim needs to be washed as if it is silk.
- To hand wash wool: use fingers and thumbs to gently rub the fibres. Rinse, then rinse again, and add fabric softener.
- Drip-dry skirts with pleats. Use clothes pegs to hold pleats in place.
- Perspiration weakens silk, so hand wash or dry-clean promptly after each wear.
- Wash corduroy inside-out. Try to avoid ironing corduroy, but if you must, iron inside-out.
- Iron jumpers, satin, and linen suits, and anything with a special finish, inside-out to prevent shine.

FABRIC CARE SYMBOLS

WASHING

 Cotton wash (no bar)
A wash tub without a bar indicates that normal (maximum) washing conditions may be used at the appropriate temperature.

 Synthetics wash (single bar)
A single bar beneath the wash tub indicates reduced (medium) washing conditions at the appropriate temperature.

 Wool wash (broken bar)
A broken bar beneath the wash tub indicates much reduced (minimum) washing conditions, and is designed specifically for machine washable wool products.

 Hand wash only
Wash by hand

The number in the wash tub shows the most effective washing temperature.

BLEACHING

 Chlorine bleach may be used.

Do not use chlorine bleach.

IRONING

 Hot iron

 Warm iron

 Cool iron

Steaming may be beneficial to remove unwanted creasing.

DRY-CLEANING

 Must be professionally dry-cleaned. The letters contained within the circle and/or a bar beneath the circle will indicate the solvent and the process to be used by the dry-cleaner.

 Do not dry-clean.

TUMBLE DRYING

 May be tumble dried:

 with high heat setting,

 with low heat setting,

 Do not tumble dry.

A cross through any symbol means "DO NOT".

Caring for clothes

■ ■ ■ **For most of us, at least part of our wardrobe is something of an investment, even if only in time and effort. It makes sense to look after that investment and get the best value from each garment** ■ ■ ■

organizing your wardrobe ■ ■ ■

Clothes should be hung on hangers in a dark, well-ventilated wardrobe or folded correctly and stored flat. Although space may be at a premium, it's important that each item has sufficient room. Natural fabrics need to breathe and too many clothes hanging together leads to crushes and creases in all types of fabric.

■ *Hang*: shirts, jackets, trousers, coats, dresses, skirts.
■ *Lay flat on shelves*: underwear, t-shirts, jumpers, cardigans, swimwear, joggers and other sports kit.
■ *Keep on racks*: ties and belts, hats and scarves.

Trousers
■ Fold along the crease and drape over the bar of a trousers hanger, or use a grip hanger.
■ If you wear formal trousers to work, an electric trouser press ensures they stay immaculate. The press, which can be fixed onto a wall, removes knee-creasing and can also store trousers overnight.

Skirts
■ Hang these by the waistband loops. Don't use pressure hangers that expand to fit the garment on skirts with elastic waists. They can make them stretch.

Shirts
■ Fasten the buttons and give each shirt a hanger!

Dresses
■ Hang inside-out if rarely worn to protect them from dust. If a dress is too long for the cupboard, sew loops inside the waist seams and hang it from these.

Jumpers

Fold the arms behind the back, and then fold in half width-ways (see page 57). Otherwise hang them.

T-shirts and sweatshirts

Hang these if space permits; otherwise, store them flat. Fold across, never lengthways.

Jackets

Hang on quality padded or wooden hangers.

Coats

Ideally, hang these in a cloakroom. If you prefer to use a wall peg near the door, use a hanger to hold the coat.

Wardrobe checkpoints

■ Clothes that are worn frequently need to be accessible. This is particularly true of work clothes when dressing time may be limited.

■ If you have a half dozen work shirts of the same style, devise a simple rotation system to ensure even wear. For example, place newly washed shirts on the left and take shirts to wear from the right.

■ Group clothes together by type and colour – for instance, black skirts, then navy skirts.

■ Avoid using metal coat hangers as they distort shoulder shapes. Use wood or plastic instead.

Making more room

■ Re-organize built-in furniture. Remove drawers inside wardrobes to create shelf space for shoes. If you remove several shelves, you'll have room to fix a hanging rail for shirts or skirts.

■ To make twice as much hanging space for separates, install a second rail halfway up the height of the main wardrobe.

■ Make space by taking out of the wardrobe anything that doesn't currently fit you or you haven't worn since the previous season.

■ To make more shelf space in your wardrobe, buy some shelving made from heavy cotton that can hang from your wardrobe pole.

Making the most of the space in your wardrobe will help to ensure that your clothes last longer, require less attention through the years, stay fresher, and are quick and easy to find when you're late for the office!

take good care of footwear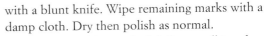

■ Store shoes in original boxes, if you have room, so that they don't get scuffed. Label the box with a felt-tip pen, so you can quickly see what's inside. As an extra time-saver, add tights or socks to match.

■ Keep trainers in the laundry room or back hallway on slatted racks, to aid air circulation.

■ Avoid wearing the same shoes two days in a row. This allows moisture to evaporate from the shoes.

■ Stuff wet shoes with newspaper to maintain their shape as they dry.

■ Regularly machine-wash trainers, if care instructions say you can. Wrap them inside socks to deaden the noise in the machine.

■ Your shoes will last longer and look better if you work at improving your posture. People who slouch end up with shoes that 'lean' as they do.

■ Cover scratches on heels by marking over them with the same colour felt pen. Seal them by painting over with clear nail polish.

■ Have shoes re-heeled promptly. Once the heel pad has worn on one side, you'll walk less evenly.

■ To remove mud: let it dry out, then scrape off with a blunt knife. Wipe remaining marks with a damp cloth. Dry then polish as normal.

■ To remove white marks left from walking through puddles or a snow bank, rub them off with saddle soap while still damp.

Polishing shoes

Leather

Fast cleaning: use shoe-cream with a built-in applicator. Rub evenly into the shoe, then buff to a shine by rubbing vigorously. Ideally, use a small velvet pad. Otherwise a soft brush or duster is fine.
Traditional cleaning: use a wax shoe polish and a set of shoe brushes. Take off surface dirt with a stiff brush, then use a medium brush to apply polish to the shoe. Rub it in gently then buff with a soft brush.

Patent leather

Clean this with a soft, damp cloth and diluted detergent. Add shine with petroleum jelly. Buff well to remove excess grease.

Suede

Treat this with suede protector and clean with a specialized cleaner. Use a small suede brush to remove dirt and a new eraser to rub out marks.

Synthetic and vinyls

Wipe these with a soapy cloth. Man-made uppers can't absorb polish, but you can add surface shine with a silicone-impregnated sponge. This is sold as an instant shoe shine product and is suitable for all colours.

Canvas

Treat this with a fabric protector. Wash off dirt by sponging it with carpet shampoo.

Satin

Do not polish or wet this. Brush it over lightly with a soft cloth. Satin can be re-coloured with fabric dye and this may be your best option for stained, pale satin.

If you find that keeping all your shoes in boxes is not practical, use a shoe rack like this one to store your shoes in the short term.

longer-term storage ▪▪▪

Clothes you won't wear until the next season need to be packed away with care.

▪ Wash or dry-clean your clothes before you put them away. This is essential, as stains may develop over time, and moths are attracted to food stains on clothes.
▪ Fasten buttons and zips.
▪ Fold a jumper with its arms behind its back, and then bring the back of the neck to the hem.
▪ Make sure that where you store your clothes is dry and dust-free. Avoid excessive heat or damp, as fabrics may yellow, or develop mildew.
▪ Use vacuum storage containers to store your clothes. Once the air is removed, your out-of-season clothes will take up only a fraction of the space they otherwise would.
▪ To guard against moths, hang clothes on cedar hangers. Moths hate cedar as well as lavender and citrus peel, so scatter some gauze herb bags. Man-made fibres are already moth-proof.
▪ Don't keep anything in your wardrobe that you haven't worn in over a year. Donate it to a local charity now (see *home recycling* on page 39).

▪ Two cotton sheets sewn together will protect a wedding dress from yellowing. But for long-term storage, seek professional advice. A premium dry-cleaning service may include permanent packing in acid-free tissue paper, to prevent discolouration.

Tips and tricks
▪ **To ease a sticking zip, rub pencil lead over it.**
▪ **If you regularly use the jacket hook in your car, turn items inside out or store them in a garment bag to eliminate sun damage.**
▪ **Always empty pockets before you put clothes away – to help the pockets lie flat.**
▪ **Keep a shallow dish next to the wardrobe for loose coins and odds and ends.**
▪ **Double-sided tape is great for lifting off pet hairs.**
▪ **Wash shirts sold in packets before a first wear. It will be quicker and easier than ironing out the folds.**
▪ **If you're at a hotel and need to wear a garment again the next day, hang it up in the bathroom overnight. Bathroom steam will remove light creasing.**

folding clothes

1 Always button up before folding jumpers and fold in any rollneck collars. Place the jumper face down. Pull the right arm across to the left and, with a fold at the shoulder of the right arm, fold the arm back on itself.

2 Repeat with the left arm so that both arms are almost parallel with the sides of the jumper. Carefully fold in half, at the back. Storing clothes this way will keep them tidy, save room, and preserve appearance.

Sewing repairs

▪ ▪ ▪ Basic stitching is simple and doesn't take a minute if you have a sewing kit to hand ▪ ▪ ▪

Here's what you need in a basic sewing kit:
- Package of needles in assorted sizes
- Small, sharp scissors
- Steel pins with coloured heads
- Pin cushion
- Safety pins
- Tape measure
- Selection of threads
- Spare buttons
- Iron-on hemming tape (or fabric)
- Elastic
- Chalk for marking fabric if necessary

Before you start stitching

You need to secure the thread. Choose from:
1 Rolling a knot: wrap thread-end twice around a forefinger. Roll the threads between finger and thumb, then slide the loop from the finger. Continue twisting these threads as you pull on the other end to make a knot.
2 End stitching: sew three small, straight stitches exactly on top of each other where you want to begin sewing.
To finish, sew three small stitches on top of each other, then snip the thread.

basic types of stitch ▪ ▪ ▪

These are either temporary, and used to hold the fabric in position while sewing, or permanent, and stay in place as part of the finished work. The main stitches in repairs are:

Tacking stitch

Large, straight stitches made by going in and out of the fabric with the needle.

- A temporary stitch used when joining a seam before machine stitching, or to hold a hem in place.
- It's best done in a colour-contrast thread, because easily-seen stitches will be more quickly removed later.

Running stitch

A smaller, neater version of basting that is used to join seams permanently. Ideally, stitches are around 3mm (⅛in) long.

- Working from right to left, take the point of the needle in and out of the fabric about four times. Pull the needle and thread through completely. Repeat.
- Can also be used to gather fabric. Take the stitching to the end then pull up on the thread until you have as many gathers as you want.

Hem stitch

Securely and evenly holds fabric that's been turned up, without showing stitching on the front. The quickest type of hem stitch is the slanting hem stitch.

- Working on the inside of the fabric, secure thread at a side seam just above where you want to hem.
- Bring the needle up through the hem edge then, moving slightly to the left, pick up one thread of the underneath fabric. Be careful not to go through. If you do, simply re-stitch.
- Go back up through the hem edge again to complete the stitch.
- Make the stitches loose to allow for any stretch in the material as it is worn.

Back stitch

A very strong stitch used for heavy-duty seams, especially on thick fabric like denim.

- This stitch is made by starting a small 3mm (⅛in) stitch, and then drawing the needle backward to where the last stitch ended. Continue in this way.
- On the right side, you see a row of even stitching without gaps; on the reverse, there's doubled thread.

measure and stitch a hem ▪▪▪

▪ Ideally, have someone help you. Wear the garment and ask him or her to measure up from the ground. Mark the hemline with horizontal pins.

▪ Alternatively, lay the garment flat on a table and use a tape to measure from the top to keep the hemline even. Then pin.

▪ Turn up the fabric, using the pins as your guide. Secure with more pins by pushing through both layers of material near the top of the hem.

▪ Baste stitch it in a contrasting thread.

▪ Try on the garment to check the length.

▪ Adjust the hemline if necessary, then stitch it by using thread of matching colour.

Speedy method

Use iron-on web from fabric shops and supermarkets.

▪ Measure and pin new hem, as above.

▪ Iron it in place.

▪ Open the hemfold and place the tape inside.

▪ Place a dampened cloth on top and press slowly with the hottest iron your garment can safely take.

▪ Let cool – and the job's done.

Making false hems

Trousers and skirts can be lengthened right to the end of the fabric if you make a false hem with ready-made hem or bias binding.

▪ Unpick existing hem and press it open.

▪ Put binding on the edge of the material, with both right sides together.

Iron-on webbing makes hemming easy for even the most inexperienced seamstress. Just follow the instructions on the packet, or on this page, for an instant quick-fix hem.

▪ Sew a line of running stitches, keeping 5mm (¼in) from the edge.

▪ Turn the binding over and press along new seam.

▪ Hem stitch the binding to the fabric.

Shortening trousers and skirts

Standard lengths on trousers and skirts are often too long and need raising. Some shops will do this for you, but it is a simple task if you do it yourself.

▪ Unpick the existing hem, and note its length.

▪ Measure required length, and pin.

▪ Cut off excess (allowing enough fabric for turning).

▪ Press the hem fold and stitch it into place.

basic types of stitches

Running stitch

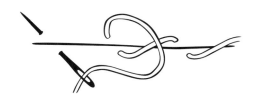

Hem stitch

Back stitch

sewing repairs around the house ■ ■ ■

Replacing buttons

Loose buttons will always come off at the wrong moment but you can avoid this by checking and securing buttons when garments are washed or dry-cleaned. To securely replace buttons, follow these pointers.

■ Knot your thread and start on the wrong side. Push the needle up through the material and into one of the holes in the button.
■ When there are two holes, simply come back down through the adjacent hole and repeat several times.
■ With four holes, make two parallel lines of stitching on the button.
■ Halfway through the job, make a thread stem for the button by coming up through the material, but not through the button, and twisting the thread several times around the button stem.
■ Sew a 'guard' button on the underside on delicate fabrics, using a smaller, flat button.

Hemming curtains

This can be a time-consuming task, but, when done well, it will finish your curtains to perfection. It is an especially useful skill to have if your windows are of an unusual size and you need to make curtains fit.

■ As fabric may drop when hung, it is wise to hang the curtains for several days before altering or making hems.
■ Pin and tack hem to the correct length, as explained on page 59.
■ For floor length curtains, the fabric should actually be 1cm (½ in) above the floor, so that it hangs easily.
■ To avoid a great deal of hand stitching, use iron-on bonding web provided that the fabric can withstand a medium iron (see page 59 for bonding web).
■ Lightweight materials will hang better if you add a hem weight (sold at fabric shops) inside the bottom corner of each curtain. Old coins can be used also.

Darning a hole

Traditionally, hand-knitted socks were darned when holes appeared, but nowadays we simply buy new ones and darning is forgotten. But it is a useful skill and will repair a snagged or worn hole in that favourite jumper.

■ Slip a piece of cardboard, or a darning mushroom, if you have one, underneath the area that has the hole.
■ Use a darning needle, with thread that matches the garment in both colour and texture (darning wool or, if you have it, spare wool from the original).
■ Work small running stitches around the hole to strengthen its edge.
■ Next, imagine you're making the base of a weaving loom and sew close parallel rows of stitches across the hole. Be careful not to pull the hole together.
■ Fill in your loom by weaving in and out of the parallel base stitches. Catch each side of the hole as you go.
■ To darn the heels of sock, use a tennis ball inside, instead of cardboard, so that your darn will be rounded.

Holes in pockets

Holes in pockets can be a real nuisance and should be repaired quickly before something important is lost.

■ Pocket base: cut out any fraying material and stitch a new pocket seam higher up. Use backstitch for strength.
■ To replace with a new pocket – unpick the old pocket to use as a pattern. Join seams with backstitch or machine sew and stitch back into original position. It's also possible to buy ready-made replacement pockets that can be stitched into place.

Patching up tears

If a tear is just above a hemline, it's easier to take up the hem than mend the tear.

Small tears

Iron-on webbing is the easiest method.

■ Cut out a piece of iron-on webbing just larger than the tear and place this on the inside.
■ Working from the outside, gently pull together the torn edges, so that they meet.
■ Cover with a damp cloth and iron them with high heat to bond the patch to the material.

Larger tears

Make a patch from matching fabric or, if the garment is very casual, use an iron-on patch.

■ Try to use the same material to make the patch – take a piece from the hem or a side-seam.
■ Cut a fabric patch and double-sided webbing that is 8mm (⅜in) larger than the hole.
■ Cut out the patch shape from the webbing, leaving a thin ring of webbing around 8mm (⅜in) wide.
■ Position webbing and patch on the fabric then press with a hot iron to bond the patch in place.
■ Neaten raw edges with small, slanting stitches.

Mending a split seam

This is the simplest of repairs.

■ Trim any loose threads visible on the exterior of the garment, and turn it inside out.
■ Make small running stitches (or machine sew) over the length of the split, plus an additional 5mm (2in) on either side to provide extra support.

Replacing zips

This is a more difficult sewing repair. A dress zip can fit more snugly when hand stitched, but trousers zips are best done with a sewing machine.

■ Unpick the old zip; pin a new one in the same position and tack in place.
■ Backstitch in matching thread along the old machine stitch line.

Zip checkpoints

■ Get more life out of a zip that's broken at the base by over-sewing it. The zip will be a little shorter but it will function.
■ Replacing zips on jeans and trousers calls for a sewing machine, as the seams have to be strong. But it's fine to stitch cushion-cover zips by hand.
■ Replace broken zips on jackets and children's clothes with poppers, if you want to avoid any sewing. Some poppers are sold in packs with a gun that staples them directly into fabric.
■ Most dry cleaners take on basic sewing repairs. Some include new buttons, hem repairs, and other services in the price of a premium cleaning.

Repairing a cushion

If a feather filling starts to push out, install a new fixed lining.

■ Sew together two pieces of material that are marginally bigger than the existing cushion.
■ Sew three seams, and then turn right-side out.
■ Insert the cushion inside.
■ Fold and press in the edges of the final seam and stitch it with a running stitch.
■ If a zip- or button-up cushion splits, remove the cushion from the cover and stitch the fabric back together, as shown in *Mending a split seam*, opposite.
■ If a fixed cushion cover splits, unpick a complete seam, remove the cushion, and use the opportunity to make it into a removable cover. Either insert a zip, poppers, or use iron-on grip tape.

Repairing upholstery

Minor repairs can be made to loose upholstery covers, but fixed upholstery needs a professional.

■ If a seam comes undone, remove the cover then pin the seam into place and re-stitch it by machine, or backstitch it by hand.
■ A tear in the fabric can be patched with matching fabric. See *Patching up tears*, opposite.

Safety first

■ ■ ■ **Maintaining a safe home should always be your first priority. As well as ensuring that your property and fixtures, and your furnishings aren't hazardous, you need to take precautions against break-ins** ■ ■ ■

The biggest threats to your safety and that of your possessions are:

■ Personal accidents and injury
■ Fire
■ Electrocution
■ Extreme weather
■ Burglary

Not taking enough care when you make improvements to your home, can markedly increase your risk of experiencing the first three items on the list. Make your home as safe as possible.

■ Choose products and materials that meet or exceed current safety requirements. This is particularly true of items that are potentially flammable, such as upholstery and anything that involves electricity or gas. You don't need to know current safety laws as reputable products will label their compliance very clearly.

■ Know your own limits. DIY accidents have risen sharply in recent years. Never rush a task, and always use professionals for any home maintenance projects you don't feel comfortable with.

■ Keeping your home safe is an on-going project. It might be more fun to have a weekend away, but fitting new window locks has to come first.

■ For full advice on how to prevent accidents in the home, especially if there are children or older people who live with you, see page 162.

■ Install smoke alarms and carbon monoxide detectors in your home. See page 170, *Being prepared*, to find out where to place them.

■ Respect any climatic conditions that could affect your home and take suitable precautions.

■ Be prepared for emergencies in advance.

Make sure that a dead bolt lock, like this one, fits deeply into the wooden frame; otherwise, it might easily be forced away from the frame by an intruder.

home security ▪▪▪

Most break-ins happen by chance. A thief who notices a home that appears to be empty will very quickly try to break in. Research has shown that the average thief spends just sixty seconds trying to gain access to a house. If he is unsuccessful, he moves on to the next place.

External action

▪ Install a good security system if you don't have one, such as burglar alarms and external lighting. Make it second nature to turn them on, even for short trips away from home.

▪ Compare your property with others in your street. If you have easy and unobserved access to your home, or an obvious lack of security, consider how you might change things.

▪ Imagine you have no key, but need to get in. Go around your home to identify its weak spots.

▪ Prune back shrubs so that they don't obscure doors, or anyone who might be standing at them.

▪ Security paint makes drainpipes slippery.

▪ Grow prickly plants around the borders of your property and, if you like them, on the house walls.

Windows and doors

▪ Fit window-locks on first-floor and second-floor windows with easy access from single-story roofs.

▪ Thermal-glazed windows are more secure as they don't break easily. Sash windows offer the least burglar resistance and slide up for very easy access; locks here are essential.

▪ Glue slatted windows onto their supports, so they can't be lifted out.

▪ Pay special attention to doors that can't be seen from the street. The thief will have longer to work on getting these open.

▪ With sliding glass doors, a broomstick wedged in the inside track of a full-length double door will jam the track from the inside.

▪ Install new locks when you move, or after a break-in.

Precautions

▪ Securely lock away any tools or equipment that burglars could use to gain better access to your home. Use heavy duty padlocks.

▪ It's a cruel fact, but the most vulnerable time for a break-in is after a break-in. Thieves may return to steal the items you've replaced. Make sure that the entrance they used is now impossible to break through and security is improved overall.

▪ Ask the local crime prevention officer for a home security survey.

▪ Getting a dog can be an effective deterrent.

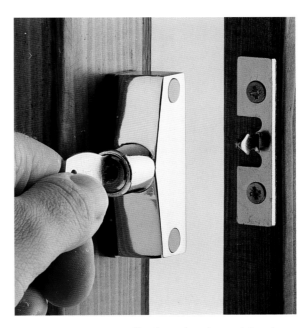

Key locks are the most effective; a burglar can't break a window and open the latch without a key. However, be careful that these locks are not used in any room that may be considered an emergency exit.

Checkpoints for flat dwellers

▪ Key-in-the-knob locks are not sufficient; change external door locks to dead bolt locks.

▪ Install hinge bolts, so the door can't be lifted from its hinges.

▪ Door chains break easily and won't keep out intruders. Install a peephole or wide-angle viewer instead.

▪ Join a neighbourhood watch group, or set up one with your neighbours.

▪ Always report burned out light bulbs in public or communal areas. Don't wait for someone else to take the initiative.

Extra precautions before you go on holiday

■ Use time switches for radios and lights to give the appearance of occupation.

■ As well as obvious musts, like cancelling deliveries, give the lawn an extra-short cut before you go on holiday, so the long grass won't give away your absence.

■ For longer absences, arrange for the post office to divert or hold onto your post.

■ Leave an answering message that says "I can't get to the phone right now," not the date of your return. Regularly call in to your answerphone and collect any messages.

If the worst happens

If you return home and see signs of a break-in:

■ Stay outside.

■ Call the police on your mobile phone (or use a neighbour's phone).

■ If you're already inside, don't call out or approach the thief. Make your priority getting back outside.

■ At night, if you think you can hear someone breaking in, but you can't get out, lock yourself in a room with a telephone and call the police.

■ If an intruder is in your room, pretend you are asleep until you hear him in another part of the house, then call the police if you have a telephone beside you. Otherwise, it is safer to wait until he is out of the house.

Security checkpoints

■ Safeguard your possessions.

■ Mark valuables with your post code using a security marker that becomes visible under ultra violet light.

■ Photograph valuable jewellery and other items, to help police retrieve them. This will also simplify insurance claims.

■ Make use of a safety deposit box at the bank.

INSTALLING A SAFE

A practical way to secure items you cherish is to install a safe in your home – the items inside don't have to be of high value. A domestic safe is a strong, steel container, which protects against flood and fire damage too. This can be a simple DIY project.

You can buy a basic safe from a hardware shop. It comes complete – all you need to do is find a discreet spot. You could choose a place under a wooden floor (you will need to cut a trapdoor for access) inside a cupboard or in an unused space, such as a blocked up fireplace.

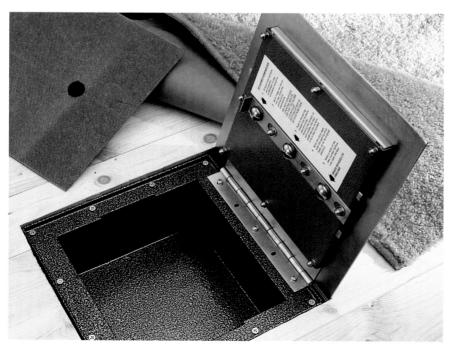

chapter

2.

décor

Buying furniture

■ ■ ■Furniture that you choose for living, sleeping, and eating areas has to fulfil practical functions, as well as look good. Beds, tables and seating may have to last some time – so it is important to get them right ■ ■ ■

> **Make sure it fits!**
> When you have made your choice, make sure you can get it into your home. Internal doors can be more of a problem than the front door, so measure both. Delivery companies will take doors off hinges, and even remove windows in order to deliver – but at a cost. If you're unsure, ask the suppliers if they will survey your home for potential delivery problems before you buy.

beds ■ ■ ■

A bed consists of two separate parts – frame and mattress. You need to think about what you want from both of these before you buy.

Divan sets
An upholstered bed base with either a padded top layer or a spring mattress mounted inside. The latter is the more comfortable, and more expensive option.

Storage divan
This is the same as a divan bed, but with pull-out drawers set into the base.

Bedstead, or slatted bed
A bed with a flat base that stands on four legs. With slats, usually pine or metal, that are fixed to the bed frame. Traditional four posters are bedsteads.

Adjustable beds
The top and bottom sections of this bed can be raised electronically by a switch. Often sold as two single beds on one base for greater flexibility.

Futon
This simple cotton filled mattress can fold into a sofa. Futons come in varying thicknesses, but all give a harder sleeping surface than a traditional mattress.

Sofa bed
A sofa with a lift or fold-out bed mechanism that conceals a foam or spring mattress. Budget sofa beds may be sold for 'occasional use' which indicates the mattress is not sufficiently supportive enough to be slept on every night.

Bunk beds
Two single bedsteads, stacked vertically to save space. This is ideal in children's rooms.

Water bed
Designed for comfort, the water is contained in a protective plastic pocket. Water's moulding ability makes it suitable for some people with back problems. However, because the water 'moves' as you do, it is noisy and can take some getting used to.

The average person sleeps seven and a half hours per night. Make sure that your bed is comfortable.

Air beds

Like water beds, these are designed for comfort. The air pockets in the mattress are controlled electronically to give very specific comfort levels. These are good for couples with greatly differing weights, and particularly good for those with back problems.

Mattresses

■ To give a comfortable night's sleep, the mattress must be firm enough to support your spine; it might feel great to sink into a soft mattress, but you will probably wake up with backache.

■ Always test a bed before buying it. Lie down alongside your partner for at least ten minutes; if the bed is sufficiently supportive, you shouldn't roll toward each other, nor should you roll if one of you moves off the bed.

■ Inexpensive mattresses often contain only foam, which is not supportive enough for every night, but acceptable for occasional use as guest beds.

■ Spring mattresses can be:

Pocket sprung: These are the most expensive, and

---

contain individual springs in separate fabric pockets, so that each is free to respond to the weight above.

Continuous sprung: The spring unit in this model is made from a single length of wire.

Open coil sprung: Hourglass-shaped springs linked top and bottom by wire and clipped to a retaining rod.

dining tables ■ ■ ■

While TV dinners and worktop breakfasts are acceptable some of the time, most of us want to be able to eat at a table too.

Before you buy, think about

Size: How many people will sit at the table? Circular tables mean more chairs can fit around, but there is less tabletop room for food dishes.

Shape: Will the shape suit your room?

Durability: Unless you always use a tablecloth, the table needs to be washable. Wood that has not been treated will soon suffer food stains. The easy-care options are varnished wood or plastic-coated surfaces.

Space-saving options

Extendable tables: These are useful when space is limited and there is occasional need for a larger table.

Drop-leaf tables: A real space saver: their sides fold down when not needed, leaving no more then the width of a narrow central section. Drop-leaf tables can also be wall-mounted when just one side will drop down.

sofas and upholstered chairs ▪▪▪

More than just somewhere to sit, the seating you choose for your living room sets the mood of the room. Mid-price upholstery should give between five to ten years of wear. After this, if the frame and springs are sound but the cover is worn, faded, or simply outdated, you can simply re-cover.

■ The strongest sofas have hardwood frames, usually made of beech or birch that are screwed and glued together (never stapled). Softwood, like pine, is less strong. Sofas are often constructed using a mix of hardwood and particleboard. The hardwood provides the frame, and the particleboard the shape.

■ The seats and cushions may be:
Foam – inexpensive and unlikely to retain shape.
Polyester fibre-filled – most practical and best for allergy sufferers.
Natural down feathers – more expensive, but excellent for comfort.

- In the shop, check that your back is well supported and your feet can touch the floor. If you like to relax sitting sideways or with your feet up, go for high, solid sides.
- If you entertain often, two sofas will seat more than a living room set of a sofa and two chairs.
- Avoid pale colours if you worry about everyday stains, or have messy pets or children. Avoid dark sofas if you have pets with white, silver, or tan fur.
- Think about how you'll cope with stains. Fitted upholstery can be treated with a stain resistor like Scotch guard. Loose covers are not suitable for treating, as the coating will wash away. They can be washed, some in a domestic washing machine, and you'll also be able to spot-treat small stains.
- Choose the right size sofa and chairs to suit your room. Remember that furniture always looks smaller in a showroom. See *Designing a room*, page 76, for how to pre-empt any problems using a graph paper plan.

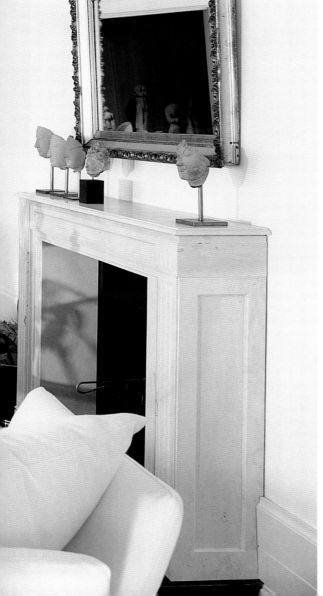

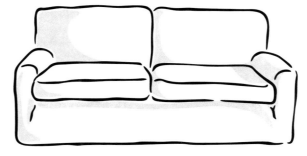

The versatile two-seater sofa: use as a sofa in small rooms, as substitute chairs in larger rooms, or have two facing each other.

The three-seater sofa is best suited to large rooms – great if you have a family.

Modular sofas are informal and stylish and allow you to change the seating combination.

The home office

■ ■ ■ **Whether you need desk space from time to time, or use your home as a permanent work place, you'll need to plan your workroom carefully** ■ ■ ■

If home working is not a main issue for you, then this room may be an office-cum-study with more emphasis on furnishing the room in a similar style and standard to the rest of your house.

However, if you are setting up a home office on a limited budget, you may prefer to concentrate on communication tools and improvise on the furniture or buy at low cost. Used office equipment is often sold off cheaply at auction sales.

communications ■ ■ ■

A powerful home PC and reliable telephone system are at the heart of today's home office.

■ Consider installing a separate office line and number. It's more professional and also helps to segregate work from home.
■ Ideally, you'll need at least two business lines, for a combination of internet/fax/voice facilities.

BASIC EQUIPMENT

Most home offices will need to accommodate the following equipment:

■ PC with internet access
■ Scanner/fax
■ Telephone/answering machine/voice mail
■ Desk
■ Chair
■ Storage system
■ Stationery
■ Calendar and diary
■ Notice board
■ Wastepaper basket
■ Paper recycling bin

power and light ■ ■ ■

You may also need to upgrade electrical wiring to provide enough sockets for all the technology. Lighting needs to be bright and clear.

■ Use directional light on the desk.
■ If your desk or work station is against a wall, avoid having the source of light behind you. Instead, increase brightness with wall lights.
■ Make sure that you can screen off sunlight when needed. Shades make a small room feel less 'hemmed in' than closing curtains during daytime.
■ Don't overload electrical sockets and secure cables so that you don't trip on them.

office maintenance ▪▪▪

▪ Choose office machinery that comes with good service support. If possible, get a PC package that includes repairs at your home, not one that insists you return the machine to the vendor.

▪ Make use of an office supply company that provides next day stationery. The printer always needs a new cartridge when you're too busy to get to the office supplies shop. Always keep a spare cartridge and replace it when you install it.

health and safety ▪▪▪

Beat backache and reduce the risk of repetitive strain injury (RSI) by positioning your desk and chair so that they are ergonomically correct and don't cause strain.

▪ Desktop height can be 64 x 76cm (25 to 30 in).

▪ Put the computer screen at eye level and place the keyboard so that your forearms are parallel with the floor and your elbows are at your side (i.e., don't reach up or down to type). Buy a wrist rest.

▪ Invest in a chair with good back support. Chairs designed specifically as PC operators' chairs are better than general office ones.

▪ Feet should be flat on the ground with knees bent about 90 degrees.

how much space will I need ▪▪▪

You can install a computer workstation under a stairway recess. If you live alone it may be a feasible working area, but for privacy and concentration, it's far from ideal. If you can't give up a complete room for work, choose a space in a room that's away from the hub of the house and interruptions. As well as desk space, think about storage. You may want space to put up shelves, in addition to a filing cabinet. A metal rack and shelving brackets system is the most versatile arrangement and gives floor-to-ceiling storage. If you work in the evenings, or need to stretch out to think creatively, you may also need room for an easy chair.

Storage

■ ■ ■ **Many homes are lacking in good storage facilities and correcting this can greatly improve the efficiency of your home. It can also provide attractive display space for treasured items** ■ ■ ■

shelves ■ ■ ■

Shelving can be made of any flat material, ranging from glass to hard woods.

Freestanding shelving units
These can go anywhere in a room and are available in designs and styles to suit every purpose and interior. Units with adjustable shelves are the most practical.

Flexible shelving
Wall mounted shelving systems are usually modular systems that you can add to as your needs grow. Some designs will take heavy weight items.

Individual shelf
Inexpensive and simple to fix. This is useful for awkward areas or for space over radiators or doors.

Cupboards and closets
Essentially these are shelves behind doors.

Freestanding shelves
Useful for storing items out of view and protecting possessions from dust, it does still need to be periodically cleaned, but can be moved around the home to suit other furniture.

Fitted shelves
This mainstay of modern kitchens and bedrooms is an ideal way to make full use of unusual or awkwardly shaped rooms. Clever devices, like turntables allow access to corners and may be made to measure, or come with standard dimensions from a prefabricated kitchen or bedroom retailer.

■ Try to get the most out of your shelving units. Adjustable shelves can be altered to accommodate larger or smaller items. Take time to store items of the same size together to save room.

■ To avoid shelving looking densely packed, try breaking up lines of books or files with a single ornament or plant.

■ Freestanding shelves may have doors that will hide storage, keeping the room looking clutter-free.

drawers ■ ■ ■

Drawers can be regarded as storage boxes and serve a dual pupose, as they not only store, but offer a surface for displaying.

Freestanding chest of drawers

This is an ideal way of keeping groups of similar things in one place and small items protected from dust and light.

Fitted drawers

Usually built into kitchens and bathrooms they provide pull-out storage for easy access. Deep drawers may be chosen instead of cupboards for larger items.

Freestanding drawer units

Unlike chests of drawers, these are simply a stack of pull-out storage units. They can be made of a variety of materials, shapes, and sizes and sometimes have wheels for greater flexibility. These can be used in just about any part of the house – from bedroom to kitchen to hallway – so long as their size is suitable for your needs.

Smaller storage

There are now many storage extras , for example, drawer dividers that create individual pockets for socks, and baskets that can slide onto shelves in the kitchen or the bedroom to hold smaller items.

making space ■ ■ ■

- Don't waste space with things you no longer need or enjoy; throw them out or recycle them.
- Put least-used items at the back.
- Group similar things you use only occasionally and store them above wall cupboards.
- Squeeze extra storage from larger cupboards by fitting racks onto the backs of doors. Hang up keys, small tools, ties, etc.
- Pack bookshelves effectively. Adjust the height brackets to avoid wasting space above books. Stack too-tall books in horizontal piles.
- Leave one cupboard per room empty as a quick hideaway for clutter if guests suddenly appear.

more storage ■ ■ ■

Look around your home to find usable space:
- Above coat pegs: a shelf for hats and bags.
- Above radiators: a display shelf for ornaments.
- The kitchen ceiling: racks, lowered by a pulley for cooking pans and utensils.
- Utility room ceiling: rack for airing clothes.
- Space above doors: shelving for little used files.
- Above the toilet: a cupboard for cleaning supplies.
- Around the basin: add a vanity unit.
- The backs of doors: great for hooks.
- Under beds: store out-of-season clothes in dust-proof packing.
- Under desks: many are just tall enough to house a filing cabinet.

under the stairs ■ ■ ■

- Create a home office, for occasional use. Install a desk and computer, and a shelf or two. Add lighting and a set of metal stacking drawers under the desk.
- Make a sewing station with the same desk, chair and lighting, but use stacking storage containers under one side of the table to hold the materials you're working on.
- Insert a floor-to-ceiling bookcase. Install a vertical metal shelving rack, then cut wooden shelves different lengths to fit the space available.
- Get an estimate for converting the space into an extra bathroom. This is most likely to work in homes with a full height walk-in cupboard under the stairs.
- House a wine rack or build a shoe and boot tree.
- Create a coat room or sports locker.

Add a hook – gain a drawer
To free storage space around the home, hook these to the wall:
- **keys**
- **shopping bags**
- **long-handled gardening tools**
- **coffee cups above a kitchen worktop**
- **bathroom sponge and shower cap**
- **games equipment**
- **aprons and overalls**

garages, cellars, and attics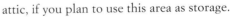

When the only way is up, down, or outside, you need to take care to protect your possessions.

■ Cellars and basements offer cool, dark conditions, just right for wine storage. But remember that they can also be damp and prone to flooding.
■ Check if there is any history of problems before using an area for storage.
■ Fit a drop-down ladder at the entrance to the attic, if you plan to use this area as storage.
■ Consider laying floorboards, to create a safe walkway in the roof space.
■ Install sufficient lighting in storage spaces so that you can see what you have there!
■ If you plan to move within the next five years, think seriously before you fill the attic with objects. What has gone up may take a very long time to get down.

CHILDRENS' ROOMS

This is a real challenge, as children tend to have the smallest rooms, yet need to store more possessions.

■ Initially, safety must be your watchword. Never use anything which could cause injury as a storage container, such as plastic bags or lidded boxes large enough for small children to climb into. Open-top rigid plastic crates, or lidded compartments made from rigid plastic with air holes, are practical and easy to stack and store.
■ A raised bed allows for storage underneath, for example, a desk. A sofa bed is useful for when friends spend the night.
■ If you rotate young children's toys, keep the changeover toys in crates with handles and store them out of sight.
■ For children over the age of five, storage needs to be simple if they are to keep the room tidy themselves. It is much easier for them to put away jumpers on shelves than in drawers.
■ Get down to your child's eye level to help him or her become organized. Look at your child's space, storage furniture, and possessions from his or her eye level. The view may surprise you!
■ Provide box files and lidded boxes for school work.
■ Keep objects off the floor with fun pegs and hooks on the wall.
■ Fit an upright edge of wood trim on the front of shelves, so that things don't fall off.
■ Keep a lidded box somewhere safe where you can save the paintings and letters that might otherwise be thrown away, which will be priceless memories tomorrow.

keeping paper safe ■ ■ ■

In the course of running a home, you'll need to store:

- Receipts and guarantees
- Care information
- Bill payment records
- Contractors' contact numbers and service helplines
- Journals and magazines

Expanding folders (a)
Concertina-style folders that open to reveal a file for each letter of the alphabet are handy. They are great if your home affairs are quite simple.

Ring binders
Hole-punch your papers, then insert them in a binder. Use dividers to identify the contents. Label and store binders vertically on shelves to take up minimum space.

Home computer
Be bold and go paperless! You'll need a scanner to record documents you receive, and it is always a good storage sense to keep all records on a 'back-up' disk.

Magazine files (b)
These boxes hold magazines or journals vertically with the spine showing for easy access and storage.

Filing cabinet
If the traditional four (or two) drawer filing cabinet takes up too much room, use a half-width set of filing drawers. It can sit discreetly in a corner.

Boxed storage (c)
Buy lidded card or plastic boxes and use dividers to separate papers. Label and store boxes on shelves. Box files, like a boxed ring binder but with only one central holding device, can be economically stored vertically on shelves.

Storage checkpoints

■ **The best time to think about storage is before you really need it. When you move into a new home, or start re-designing a room, think about how you'll add storage space as you go along.**

■ **When buying furniture, look for storage extras, such as a kitchen table with an inset drawer, a bed with drawers, or a cupboard with shelving.**

■ **Make sure that what you want to store will fit into the new storage unit. Test capacity: take along a dinner plate to the shop if you're buying crockery cupboards or measure the shoulder width of suits before buying a cupboard.**

■ **Storage is big business nowadays. Think about what you want to store and where. If you're storing items that you're unlikely to use much in the next couple of years in a garage, you might need a protective container. For example, paper files might go mouldy in a cardboard box, so use a lidded plastic box.**

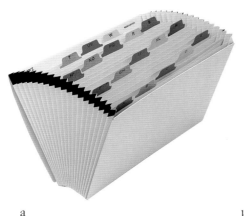

a

b

c

Designing a room scheme

Think practically as you plan because although white is a good, bright, neutral colour, it can soil easily.

starting a design project ■ ■ ■

Accurately record the dimensions and any limiting factors in your room, for example, furniture or furnishings that you will keep. While you can pay professionals to take over at any stage of the process, you'll cut your budget and achieve a room that exactly matches your vision if you keep the project to yourself.

■ Be clear about what you want the room to achieve. Include the mood you hope to project, as well as practicalities, such as 'somewhere to watch TV', or 'space for two guests to sleep'.
■ Do some practical research. This is the 'fun' part of the project: department stores, catalogues and magazines are good sources for inspiration.
■ Plan how to turn your design into reality.

assess the room ■ ■ ■

Make a modelling plan
■ Use a tape measure to find the dimensions of the room. Plot this on graph paper, making one square foot in your room at least four squares on the graph paper.
■ Add breaks for doors (include which way they open), windows, and air conditioning and heating units.
■ Measure at the base any furniture that you want to stay in the new room. Make paper cut-outs to scale, and put weak adhesive on the back of them, so you can move them around.
■ Take contrasting colour paper and cut to scale things you'd like to go in the room, such as a dining table in the kitchen.
■ For bathrooms and kitchens, you may want a

professional overview. Many companies offer free, no-obligation quotes. These can save time by identifying flaws you hadn't thought of (for example, a kitchen appliance that has to have an outside wall, or plumbing which will dictate shower types).

■ Write down design aspects that are important to you, for example, a hardwood floor, or a particular theme or style, such as Mexican style. These will form the starting point of the next stage, which is to find a focus.

finding a focus ■ ■ ■

A room needs a theme to pull everything together. You may have set ideas – a style that you like, such as New England Shaker, or an object you already have – perhaps a special vase. It's also fine to incorporate several styles into a room. But with the whole world of design out there, you will use your time more effectively if you establish preferences, even if you later change your mind.

These could be based on:
Colour: "I want a yellow room."
Mood: "It must be relaxing."
Period: "I want Art Deco."
Function: "I need to work or give dinner parties here."

> **Money-saver tip**
> Think carefully before you commit to knocking down walls between rooms or extensions. Changing colours, lighting, and furniture can make a room dramatically different – and for far less cost and disruption than employing builders.

You might narrow the search further with:
Practical: "All fabrics and furniture must be easy-care."
Environmental: "I want natural materials only."
Budget: "I have a maximum price that I'm willing to pay for each element of my design."

A trip to the local DIY store is indispensable. Pick up colour swatches to help you with ideas and check out the different kinds of paint finishes that are on sale.

sources of inspiration ▪ ▪ ▪

Professional interior designers make flat boards for their clients with fabric swatches, strips of paint, and carpet samples of everything they think might go into a room they are decorating. It's a good way to see how colours and textures work together. It is quite easy to do the same at home: just cut out and stick onto a piece of board or cardboard everything that you would like to use. On the back, or in a separate folder, be sure to write down the manufacturer and price details. While paper 'tear outs' are useful, it is always better to get a real sample. Most shops are happy to help with this.

Look for ideas in:
- Home magazines
- Department stores
- Home shopping catalogues
- Specialized design and decorating books
- Friends' houses
- Hotels, cafés, and restaurants
- Specialized shops for fabric, carpets, and lighting
- TV home make-over shows
- Home exhibitions
- Display homes in new housing developments
- Museums and galleries

key elements in a room ▪ ▪ ▪

You will need to consider the key factors listed below.

- **Walls** How you want to finish them with paint, wallpaper, or special paint effects.
- **Floor** Hard or soft materials, present or desired.
- **Ceiling** Complementing or contrasting shades, or textural effects you have or want.
- **Windows** Whether to thermal glaze them or change the style.
- **Window treatments** Whether you want formal drapes, casual curtains, shades, or nets.
- **Lighting** Whether to change fittings to suit existing fixtures or create additional light sources.
- **Features** A fireplace or other distinctive. architectural features that are present.
- **Soft furnishings** Upholstery, cushions, rugs.
- **Storage** Furniture or shelving systems you may want to add.
- **Fixed furniture** What wall-mounted cupboards, floor to ceiling fittings you have or want.
- **Free-standing furniture** Whether to keep what you have or update existing items.

Every room has its own additional priorities. To ensure that you don't miss anything, do the bulk of your planning in the room that you want to design. Look at existing fittings and think what else you might need, or what to remove.

planning the work ▪▪▪

Setting a schedule is essential. This is especially true if you plan to work in stages.

- Have any structural work done first.
- Complete anything that involves taking up floorboards, fixing or fitting. Having an extra radiator fitted or more power sockets and light fittings would both fall into this category.
- Install curtain poles and tracks.
- Build fixed shelves for cupboards, etc.
- Paint ceiling and doors.
- Paint or paper walls.
- Install carpet or lay wood flooring.
- Hang curtains.
- Bring in new furniture.

> **Planning checkpoints**
> - If the room is to be colour-coordinated, buy everything at the same time, even if it will be some time before the room is completed.
> - If the project is going to be a gradual process, paint the walls a neutral colour as a temporary measure.

Using colour

■ ■ ■**Don't just reach for the beige. There's an infinite choice of colours and shades out there. Discovering how different shades contrast and harmonize with each other is the easiest and quickest way to give every room in your home personality and style** ■ ■ ■

The hundreds of shades in a paint chart have their roots in just three primary colours: red, blue, and yellow. From these come the secondary colours – violet, green, and orange. Combinations of these make up all the colours within a colour wheel. This is a vital tool for anyone working with colour, because you can see at a glance how different shades complement and contrast with each other.

For *complementing* colour schemes, find the colour that you like, and then choose a shade from either side of it. This creates a softer effect than contrasting ones do, because complementing colours come from the same primary colours.
For *contrasting* colour schemes, find the colour you like, and then add the colour that is its opposite. This creates a colour scheme that looks stronger than complementing colours.

Red

Red Orange

Orange

Yellow Orange

Yellow

Yellow Green

colour checkpoints ■ ■ ■

■ To test a colour, paint or wallpaper a piece of board about 60cm square (2 feet sq) or use four pieces of copy paper taped together and hang this on the wall for several days.
■ Don't be tempted to paint tiny test squares. The colour sample needs to be this large to give you an accurate impression; you know already that you like the colour, but this is to see if the colour and shade work well in the room. It will show you whether the colour is too light or dark, whether it enhances the room's furnishings, and so on.
■ Remember to look at your colour sample at

different times of the day, to gauge the effect of sunlight upon it.
■ Only look at one colour test at a time. If you put a row of squares together, you won't be able to assess the new look accurately.
■ Be your boldest with paint, not paper; if you grow to hate your colour scheme, it will be simpler to re-paint a wall than re-paper one.
■ Curtains and carpets create blocks of colour; when choosing colours for these, use the colour wheel to pick shades that complement or contrast your overall scheme.

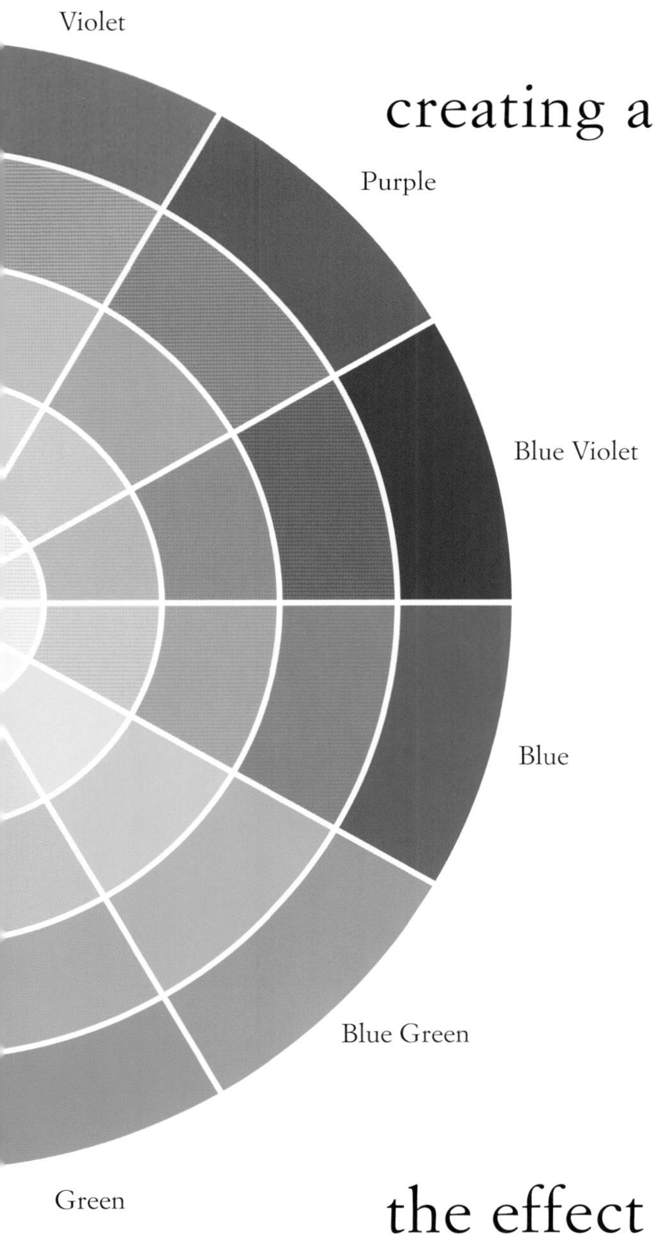

Violet

Purple

Blue Violet

Blue

Blue Green

Green

creating a mood ■■■

Lively

Reds	Make a room welcoming	Halls, north-facing rooms
Oranges	Create a cozy, intimate atmosphere	Living rooms
Yellows	Good for rooms that are primarily used when they are artificially lit	Formal dining rooms
Fuchsia pink	Adds drama	Living rooms
Blue Violet	Used sparingly, can enliven without overpowering	Children's playrooms

Calm

Hints of colour	Soft hues are very 'liveable'	Living rooms, entrance halls
Beige	Most likely to go with existing furniture and carpets	Ceilings
Off-white	The ultimate neutral	
Jade/Greys	Good choice if you plan to sell your home – universally liked	

Cool

Blues	Create a fresh feeling	Bathrooms, kitchens
Lilacs	Can add formality	Period-style living rooms
Pale greens/ Lemons	Restful	Pale shades will make rooms appear larger

Warm

Terracotta	Makes a room appear warmer	Bedrooms, living rooms
Cream	A good contrast to wood	Throughout the home
Saffron/Apricot	Adds colour without dominating	Kitchens

the effect of the sun ■■■

Use a compass to find out which way the windows in your room face. The quality of light as the sun passes overhead will affect which colours work best.

North	No direct sunlight	Avoid neutral colours. Use yellows and terracotta to add warmth.
East	Sun at dawn	Cool blues for a gentle start to the day, or yellow for a bright kick-start.
South	Sun all day	No restrictions.
West	Sun late in the day	Living rooms can take both greens and pastels; use cool colours in bedrooms.

Painting

■ ■ ■As the fastest, cheapest way to redecorate a room, it's no surprise that paint is the most popular decorating choice for walls. But don't stop there: the right type of paint can cover wood, metal, and tiles ■ ■ ■

preparing to paint ■ ■ ■

Good preparation affects the finished result, so if you want what you paint to look good and last, it is essential to prepare surfaces thoroughly.

Remove as much furniture as you can from the room and cover what remains with dust cloths. Cover the carpets too. Always work in the following order:

1 Ceilings
2 Walls
3 Doors
4 Window frames
5 Skirting boards
6 Radiators

Preparing the walls

Covering existing paint with fresh paint is the simplest method of re-decoration. If there is wallpaper, you should strip it off first; however, many people do take the shortcut of painting directly onto paper. The effect is less uniform, but it may be adequate in less important rooms that you want to decorate quickly.

■ Remove nails and picture hooks.
■ Wash ceilings, walls, and woodwork with a solution of water and sugar soap (or very mild detergent). Rinse, and allow to dry.
■ Treat any mould that may have formed as a result of condensation. Scrape it off, then wash the wall with very diluted bleach, air-dry, and apply fungicide following product instructions.
■ Apply wood primer to bare wood on doors, windows, frames, and skirting.
■ Rub down metalwork with steel wool to clean off rust and flaking paint. Apply metal primer.

- Fill small wall and ceiling cracks with filler. This comes pre-mixed; simply apply it with a flat metal filling or putty knife, so that it stands slightly proud of the wall. When it's dry, smooth and level it with sandpaper.
- On the ceiling, long straight cracks will be very difficult to disguise, but it can be more effective to paper the ceiling, and then paint over it, you may need a decorating contractor to do this.
- Go over old gloss paint on wood with a sheet of rough sandpaper, to provide a surface the new paint can grip.
- Finally, check again for dirt and dust, wipe all surfaces to be painted with a damp cloth and remove fingerprints on wood with a cloth dipped in white spirit.

Choosing the right paints

To ensure there is no shade variation, try to buy enough paint before you start. The cans generally state how much area they cover, but you may need more paint than recommended on the can if:

- The walls are porous.
- You are inexperienced in painting and may overload your brush.
- You are covering a deep or contrasting colour.

Water-based paints

Many different paint finishes are now available as water-based paint. They dry quickly, need no primer or undercoat, don't smell unpleasant, and splashes can be removed if they are cleaned off quickly enough.

Vinyl silk emulsion

This water-based paint is used for walls and ceilings. It dries quickly, needs no primer or undercoat (in normal conditions), and has an acceptable smell.

Matt emulsion

A paint that gives a flat no-sheen look. It will hide uneven surfaces and small flaws, but marks easily.

Eggshell and satin

Mid-ground paint that is suitable for all around the home, it creates a tough, washable surface.

Gloss

Gives a high-sheen look and stain resistance that is great for hallways and playrooms.

One-coat paint

A thicker paint that gives excellent coverage without a second coat. However, each tin of paint covers up to one third less wall than standard emulsion. Check the label for how much you'll need before you buy.

Textured paint

Flecks in this paint give a random ripple effect that can look good on ceilings and uneven walls.

Essential tools:
a) **Protective goggles**
b) **Face mask**
c) **Latex gloves**
d) **Filler and filling knife**
e) **Dust cloth (plastic)**
f) **White spirit**
g) **Roller and paint tray**
h) **Masking tape**
i) **Sponge**
j) **Sandpaper and block**
k) **Paint brushes**

getting the job done ▪▪▪

Painting metal and wood

By tradition, this is a three-step process: primer, undercoat, and an oil-based top coat, or gloss. The result is a beautiful finish. However, oil-based paint can be more difficult to apply. The problems that can arise are:

- Streaking.
- Takes a long time to dry.
- Smells overpowering.
- Less environmentally friendly than water-based paint – it contains high levels of volatile organic compounds (VOCs).

For all of these reasons, you may decide to use special water-based paint for wood instead. The finish is almost as good (slightly less shine) and in most cases you don't need an undercoat.

Painting specialist surfaces

Most surfaces can be painted if you first use a primer to seal surfaces. Specialist paints, such as those used for ceramic tiles, metal radiators, and formica furniture, have useful extras – for example, radiator enamel contains chemicals that won't yellow on prolonged exposure to heat. Check your DIY store for the many specialist paints available and follow the instructions on the can.

Equipment checklist

- Dust cloths.
- Protective goggles or face mask.
- Overalls to protect your clothes.
- Latex gloves. These thin disposables gloves allow more control of the brush and are cheap.
- Sugar soap, to wash grease from walls.
- Ready mixed filler and filling knife.
- Sandpaper and block to wrap sandpaper around (use a wood scrap) for smoothing patches and preparing existing woodwork.
- Masking tape – to protect window frames, light switches, and so on, from paint.
- Roller frame and sleeve and paint tray, if you are using these. They can be sold as one unit and come in varying sizes. Choose a large 23cm (9 in) roller for maximum speed, plus a mini-roller 7cm (3 in) for small areas and around obstacles.
- Paintbrushes: use a 10cm (4 in) brush for walls, and a 5cm (2 in) brush for small areas. You may also want a cut-in brush with an angled edge, for greater accuracy around corners and ceiling edges.

For wood and metal
- Paint stripper, to remove an existing paint finish in bad condition.
- White spirit, to remove paint from brushes that won't soak off in water.

brushes or rollers ▪▪▪

Brushes

How to use

Sold in varying widths, and with natural or synthetic bristles. Begin painting by dipping the bottom third of the brush into the can and, taking care not to overload the brush, paint the surface with even strokes.

Suitability

Good for all surfaces, this slower, more traditional way to paint can be easier for novices. Narrow brushes are perfect for small areas and for painting around features or details.

Cleaning

Always clean brushes promptly. Brushes used with water-based paint can be run under a tap, loosening the paint in the water flow, or washed out in a bucket of water. Pour the paint water down the drain. Soak the brushes briefly in soapy water, if needed, then rinse and dry them with a paper towel. To remove oil-based paint from brushes, leave them standing in a container of solvent or turpentine that reaches the top of the bristles or wipe up-and-down on sandy soil to get rid of much of the paint. When clean, wash them with washing-up liquid and water, then dry.

Rollers

How to use

A rotating synthetic or wool roll attached to a long handle. To begin, pour paint into the well of a roller tray. Dip the roller in the paint and run it back and forth on the tray to get an even distribution of paint on the roller. Apply paint to the wall with it by using long, even strokes.

Suitability

Rollers are ideal for textured paints. In general, this is a fast way to cover large areas, although you may use more paint in the process. With a handle extension on the roller, you can quickly paint ceilings. When using a roller, it is essential to cover anything that is not being painted, as fine splatters of paint will fall on surfaces all over the room.

Cleaning

Use old newspaper and rotate the roller over it to remove excess paint. Take the roller out of its frame and wash off water-based paint in running water, or clean it in a bucket of water as with brushes.

- Leave to air-dry thoroughly before returning to frame.
- With oil-based paint, you may prefer to use a fresh roller-sleeve each day.

Paint Pads

How to use

This is a square pad of foam or mohair attached to a handle. Dip the pad into a paint tray, and then press and slide onto the wall in firm, continuous strokes.

Suitability

Good for applying thin coats when you want a smooth surface. It can produce lots of drips, which must be painted over again before they dry. But once you master the technique, you can cover large areas very fast without leaving brush marks on the surface. Pads can reach into corners and awkward areas where rollers can't, such as above window frames.

Cleaning

Wash it with soapy water, making sure that all the paint has left the pad. Clean off oil-based paint with solvent.

How much paint?

Measure the dimensions (height x width x number of walls) of the area you're to paint. A typical 3 metre (10 foot) square room has a paint area of 27 square metres (30 square yards).

	Sq. m/litre	Sq. m/gallon
Primers	6–10	5–9
Undercoat	18	15
Emulsion/Latex	18	15
Oil-based paints	20	17
Non-drip oil-based	14	12

Basic paint effects

Adding texture to a painted wall is a cheap and relatively simple process. It can take a long time to do, however, so choose a small room for your first attempt. Eggshell paints, which take longer to dry, will give you more time to work but ordinary emulsion is easier for beginners. If it goes wrong, just paint over it, allow it to dry, then start again.

Sponging

Paint the wall in a neutral shade. When it is quite dry sponge on a contrasting colour, using a natural sponge. For a softer look, add a third, related colour.

Colour washing

A fast effect for large walls. Watered down emulsion or a specialist, near-transparent glaze is painted lightly and randomly over a base shade.

Rag rolling

Crumple up a muslin or cotton cloth, dip it into paint, then roll it or press it onto a wall.

Stencilling

Use decorative cut-outs to paint intricate patterns, and motifs directly onto the wall. Ideal for borders and as pretty on furniture as on walls. Spray paint can be used if surrounding areas are well-masked.

Stamping

Pre-cut wooden blocks into shapes, dip them in paint, then stamp them straight onto the wall. To avoid drips or uneven impression, stamp onto newspaper or a cloth each time the stamp is loaded.

sponging

colour washing

rag rolling

stencilling

stamping

Wallpaper

■ ■ ■ **Pasting patterned paper or wallcovering onto your walls gives a nicer finish than paint alone. It can take a while to master the technique, but quality wallpaper will look good for years** ■ ■ ■

preparation ■ ■ ■

As with painting, you need to start from a clean, dry, and stable surface. This means you'll have to remove existing wallpaper first.

1 Thoroughly soak existing paper with warm water or wallpaper stripping fluid.
2 Peel the paper off with a stripping knife, taking care not to dig into the plaster underneath. This may take some time manually, so hire or buy an electric steam stripper for a large or difficult room.
3 Fill cracks with filler – see *Preparing the walls* page 82 – then sand them over for a smooth finish.

choosing the right paper ■ ■ ■

Let the design you prefer dictate your choice of paper; most modern papers are relatively simple to hang.

■ Paper-backed vinyl is harder-wearing than paper alone, as it can be scrubbed with a soft brush and wiped with diluted mild detergent.
■ Embossed and anaglyptic paper is designed to be painted over, in either emulsion or gloss. It is a good choice for uneven walls, as it will hide surface irregularities and is easily washed with mild detergent.
■ Choose damp-resistant wallpaper for the bathroom and kitchen.
■ If you are concerned about using the right amount of paste, choose ready-pasted papers. Simply wet the paper, by drawing it through water in the small trough supplied, and paste it to the wall.
■ Avoid very thin paper; they may tear when you put them up and will probably not last as long.

Checklist
- Dust cloths – buy plastic sheeting from the DIY store or use old curtains or sheeting.
- Overalls or old clothing.
- Large synthetic sponge and bucket – for washing walls to remove old paper.
- Wallpaper stripping fluid – to remove wallpaper (or hire an electric steam stripper).
- Stripping knife – wide, flat blade for scraping off paper without digging into plaster.

For all wallpaper jobs
- Filler – see painting section for details.
- Plumb line or spirit level – to check that each piece of paper is hung straight.
- Retractable tape measure – use on paper and walls.
- Paste table – these are cheap and lightweight folding tables for cutting and pasting wallpaper.
- Paste and paste brush – paste is mixed with water just before use, but it doesn't keep well, so just buy what you need.
- Stirring stick – a length of wood or an old wooden spoon will do the job just as well.
- Paperhanging brush – these have long, very soft bristles to smooth the paper in place.
- Stepladder – for reaching up to the ceiling. See *Ladder safety tips* on page 21.
- Paperhanging scissors – for a long cutting action.
- Retractable knife/Stanley knife – use to cut paper accurately around corners and awkward places.
- Seam roller – this mini-roller gives a professional finish to the wallpaper joins.
- Dry cloth – for wiping over the wallpaper to smooth and remove any excess paste.

DÉCOR

(a) Dropcloth
(b) Paper cutting scissors
(c) Craft knife
(d) Stripping knife
(e) Seam roller
(f) Paste
(g) Plumb line
(h) Retractable tape measure
(i) Paste brush
(j) Paperhanging brush

TYPE	EFFECT	CHECKPOINTS
Dark colours and large patterns	Rooms seem smaller	You'll need more paper if it has a long pattern repeat
Vertical stripes	Low rooms seem taller	Will highlight doors and walls that are badly aligned
Light colours and small patterns	Small rooms seem larger	Can make a big room look too fussy, will show grease and dirt more quickly
Plains	Keeps focus on furnishings, rather than walls	Easiest to hang, as no print-matching is required

hanging wallpaper ▪ ▪ ▪

You'll need a full day to paper an average-sized room.

▪ Read the hanging instructions printed on the back of the wallpaper roll label.

▪ Cut each strip with a safety margin for trimming and matching prints.

▪ To carry the wallpaper to the wall, fold the paper into a concertina-style, so that the pasted sides are facing, and then the unpasted, outside section is facing. See the picture below.

▪ Position paper up to the ceiling, leaving a couple of inches at the top for trimming, making sure any pattern is aligned. Line up the edges with a plumb line on the wall, and use a paper hanging brush to apply the top of the paper to the wall.

▪ When the top is straight, brush the bottom half of the paper into position, making sure it lines up with the plumb lines. Then go over the whole strip with the brush to remove any bubbles or wrinkles.

▪ If you find that you have bubbles or folds in your paper, do not be afraid to peel off the wallpaper and lay it again, in order to get it straight.

▪ Wipe excess paste off with a wet sponge (check in the instructions that this will not harm the paper).

▪ Repeat with adjoining strip, sliding it into place to match the pattern, if there is one.

▪ Trim the top and bottom once you have a few strips on the wall.

▪ On seams, don't leave any gaps or overlap. Use a seam roller (as shown below) to firmly apply the paper to the walls, rolling over the seam once or twice at the most.

Folding up lengths of wallpaper correctly will help you hang the paper.

A seam roller will firmly attach an overhang, or wallpaper seems, to the wall.

Newly hung wallpaper should be creased at the join of the wall and ceiling.

Laying wallpaper around a window frame. The excess will need to be trimmed.

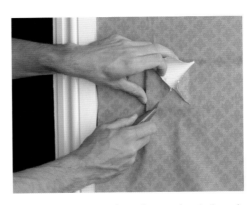

Laying paper around an electrical switch and cutting to fit.

A paper-hanging brush being used to ease wallpaper around an external corner.

how much to buy ■ ■ ■

■ A standard wallpaper roll measures 10m (11 yds) by 53cm (21 in). In most rooms, that is four lengths of wallpaper from each roll. This chart assumes a plain or small pattern design. If you have a large pattern repeat, you might achieve only three strips per roll and a lot of wastage. This also requires 25% more paper. Always buy an extra roll to allow for any problems; many shops will refund unopened ones.

Number of rolls of paper required for the average room

Height of room (includes skirting)	Perimeter (add up the width of all four walls)				
	9m (30ft)	12m (38ft)	16m (54ft	21m (70ft)	28m (94ft)
2m (6ft 6ins)	4	5	7	9	13
2.45m (8ft)	5	6	9	11	15
3m (10ft)	6	8	10	13	18

solving common problems ■ ■ ■

Problem You have hung a length upside down.

Solution
■ Carefully peel off the paper, starting at the bottom, and loop it into two or three loose folds.
■ Turn around the folded paper and re-apply it, starting at the top.
■ The paper will be unwieldy and liable to stretch. You'll have up to 30 minutes before the paste dries.

Problem Difficulty taking paper around corners.

Solution Don't try – cut the paper instead!
■ Cut the paper so that it reaches the corner, plus an extra half inch for turning.
■ Use a plumb line to position the next piece truly vertical as it is unlikely that the corner will be.
■ Hang this piece so that it overlaps the turned strip.
■ For vinyl papers use vinyl overlap adhesive, as vinyl won't stick to itself with ordinary wallpaper paste.

Problem The paper tears as you hang it.

Solution If the tear is small, it can be smoothed and repaired; if not and you have enough paper, discard it and start again.

If you're not sure whether you'll have enough paper, cut all the remaining strips.

When there is no extra paper, smooth paper back into place. Keep the white side of the tear on the underside and it should be scarcely visible. Go over it with seam roller.

If this fails to work, make a patch over the tear and:
■ Hold a spare piece of paper against the damaged area, matching any pattern.
■ Tear, rather than cut it to size. The feathered edges will blend better with the wallpaper underneath.
■ Stick on with wallpaper paste, or overlap adhesive.
■ Press it into place with a seam roller.

Problem Raised blisters appear on the surface of the paper; this is because there is insufficient paste, excess paste, or an air bubble is underneath it.

Solution Use a retractable knife with a new blade to make two short cuts, at right angles to each other, and use these to peel back two small flaps of paper.
■ Put a spot of paste on the wall.
■ Wipe away excess paste.
■ Ease out any air bubbles with a dry cloth.
■ Smooth back the cut flaps and even-out the join with a seam roller.

Lighting

■ ■ ■ **Lighting is an important factor in the design and function of any space. Much more than just a bulb under a shade, the way a room is lit can transform its mood and dictate how you use and enjoy it** ■ ■ ■

types of lighting ■ ■ ■

The best lighting should mimic as many elements of daylight as possible. By day, we take it for granted that we can do detailed work, relax with the TV, or simply look around the room and admire the ornaments! To do the same after dark, you'll need three types of lighting.

General or ambient lighting – the fixed bulb or group of bulbs is suspended from the ceiling or on a wall. In a room where you simply want to be able to see everything, this may be all that is needed.

Task lighting – focuses light only where you need it for a specific task, such as reading. It does not light up a room.

Display or accent lighting – lights that are used to highlight features within a room.

Natural light and halogen spot lights combine to give this living room a restful yet contemporary ambience.

all around the home ■ ■ ■

Living room
■ Ceiling lights: choose open shades to disperse light across the room. If fitted with dimmer controls, these will also create a relaxed mood for entertaining.
■ Table-top lamps can be placed on side tables to provide softer illumination.
■ Uplighters are bulbs shielded by a shade underneath so that a room is lit by light that reflects off the ceiling. Position the shade between 30 to 60cm (12 to 24in) from the ceiling for soft light. This technique is used to take light into the corners of long, narrow rooms and make a room appear taller.
■ Candles increase their reflection if you arrange them in groups and stand them in front of a mirror.
■ Use spotlights within glass cupboards to highlight displays inside them.
■ Fit concealed single bulbs above special paintings.
■ Feature lights, such as lava lamps, are display items themselves.

■ Full-height standard lamps can be positioned behind chairs to provide a reading light.

Dining Rooms

■ Two table lamps on side tables give a softer effect than a single ceiling light.

■ A low-hanging pendant lamp above a dining room table keeps the focus on the diners. This also appears to lower the ceiling and creates an intimate atmosphere.

■ Avoid straight shades because you'll cast shadows around the table. Instead, use open shapes or chandeliers.

Kitchens

■ If you have a dining area, choose a pendant fitting to distinguish it from the rest of the kitchen.

■ Recessed spotlights fitted inside glass cabinets highlight the cabinet and its contents.

■ Recessed lights – strong, spotlights that throw all their light downwards – fitted into the ceiling are effective and unobtrusive.

■ Under-cupboard lights illuminate worktops, so that the chef can work with plenty of light.

■ Track spotlights – lines of three or more spotlights – can be positioned exactly where you need extra light.

Entrance hall and stairs

■ Avoid lights that project upward. You need standard, semi-directional light to be able to see clearly and accurately. Choose 'traditional' pendant or straight-sided shades.

■ Use the most powerful bulb that your lampshade will safely allow.

■ Fit an all-weather light outside your door. Use a light-sensor if you are out during the day and want the light to come on at dusk.

Bedrooms

■ A central up-light that projects upward gives a soft feeling and shields your eyes from glare. Install a dimmer control.

■ Low wall-mounted lights or pendant fittings beside the bed can be practical for reading and provide a soft light in the room. Similarly, an extendable angled light can be swung to one side

when it is not being used for reading.

■ Fluorescent lighting works well above the dressing mirror.

■ Candle bulbs fitted around the mirror will give a total no-shadow effect.

Bathrooms

■ In a small space, keep pendant fittings close to the ceiling to eliminate shadows.

■ Use down lighters recessed into the ceiling.

■ Fit strip lighting above mirrors.

Bulb basics

■ **Tungsten or incandescent bulbs**
This is the most common type of bulb. A thin metal filament inside this bulb glows when hot, casting a yellowish light. Long life bulbs last around 2,000 hours. Choose from clear bulbs, which provide the brightest light, or pearl bulbs that radiate a more gentle glow.

■ **Fluorescent tubes**
Particles inside the tube glow or fluoresce, when switched on, creating a white light, with little shadow. Will last over 6,000 hours.

■ **Compact fluorescent or energy-saving bulbs**
These small tube bulbs work in the same way as standard tubes, but fit standard light fittings and last more than 5,000 hours.

Safety tip
Always turn the electricity off before replacing bulbs, or checking or changing fittings. You may want a professional electrical contractor to install light fittings and dimmer controls.

Tiling and mosaics

■ ■ ■ **Ceramic tiles and mosaics provide a hard-wearing, easy-to-clean finish in the kitchen and bathroom. Water-proof and stain-resistant, they are decorative and practical** ■ ■ ■

Ceramic tiles

Made from fired clay and usually glazed, these can be used in a variety of settings:

■ On both walls and floors they're extremely hard-wearing.
■ As backsplashes around sinks and above kitchen and laundry room worktops, they are waterproof and will repel water and stains.
■ As wall-to-wall tiling, in place of paint or paper, they are the ultimate low-maintenance material for bathrooms and shower rooms; if tiles are correctly fitted, they will outlast the bath and basins they surround.
■ For details on floor tiles, see page 101.

Hand-fired and cut tiles

Coloured and fired in a kiln by craftsmen, they may or may not have a protective glaze.

■ Unglazed tiles – which have a matt finish – stain easily and will be porous.
■ The surface of each tile may not be entirely uniform, but it does add to the decorative effect.
■ There is no standard size for handcrafted tiles, which can be square or rectangular, but most are between 7.5cm and 15cm (3in and 6in) wide and the cost will reflect the craftsmanship.

Factory-produced tiles

These are cut from sheets of clay and have a protective glaze on the surface.

■ Tiles come in every colour as well as printed designs to suit most colour schemes and interiors.
■ The most popular size is 15cm (6 in) square, but they are also available as 10cm (4in) and 20cm (8in) tiles, in the shape of rectangles, and tiles for mosaics.

buying tiles ■ ■ ■

■ Many people cut costs by having just three rows of tiles above the basin and bath. If your budget is restricted but you want to tile the whole wall imaginatively, try plain white factory tiles, with occasional picture tiles for interest.
■ Tiles of different depths will not work well together and present difficulties when factory tiles are interspersed with handcrafted tiles. This can be done, but you must match the tile thickness, as well as width and height.
■ It's great to be bold with colour and design, but remember that your bathroom colour scheme may change and re-tiling is expensive.
■ Always buy ten percent more tiles than you need in order to allow for breakages. Many tile shops let you return unopened boxes after you've completed a job.

This bathroom uses blue tiling and natural light to create a striking effect.

MOSAICS

Mosaics are tiny pieces of smooth clay tiles that are held perfectly spaced, by a nylon mesh (which is buried under the adhesive when fixed) or paper face (which is peeled off once the adhesive has hardened). Fixed as they are like standard tiles, their big advantage is that you can cut around individual mosaics to fit difficult areas.

HOW MANY TILES

Tile size	No. of tiles per sq. m
100 x 100 mm (4 x 4 in)	100
108 x 108 mm (4 ¼ x 4 ¼ in)	86
150 x 150 mm (6 x 6 in)	44
200 x 150 mm (8 x 6 in)	33
250 x 150 mm (10 x 6 in)	27
300 x 300 mm (12 x 12 in)	11

Tip
Choose heat-resistant tiles for areas behind cookers and boilers; the glaze on standard tiles could crack if exposed to high temperatures.

revamping tiles ■ ■ ■

Tiles are so hard-wearing that most people change them purely because their style has become dated, or because, by updating other fittings in the room, the existing tiles no longer match the furniture. If you're tired of your tiles, however, you don't have to replace them, why not:

■ Paint them a different colour. Use specialized primer, then paint.
■ Change the grouting colour with grout stain.
■ Decorate with tile-transfers; peel and stick on a colourful design every few tiles.
■ Tile over the existing tiles. Rub them down, use a primer, and then stick the new tiles over them.
■ Get creative with ceramic paints. Stick a template of your outline onto a tile and get painting.

Soft furnishings

■ ■ ■ **Soft furnishings is the collective name given to all the elements of a home that are made of fabric. It includes upholstery, curtains, cushions, quilts, and duvet covers** ■ ■ ■

choosing fabric ■ ■ ■

With such a wide variety to choose from, making a decision can be difficult. Considering these points will help:

■ How much wear will fabric need to withstand? Seats need hard-wearing fabric, but cushions do not. So you might choose heavyweight cotton for the sofa, then add a beautiful but less robust silk-based fabric for cushions.

■ Easy-care fabrics for upholstery are important if you have children and pets. See page 45, *Fabric care guide*, and page 66, *Buying furniture basics*.

■ Always view a fabric sample in your home. See how it looks by day and in artificial light.

■ Man-made fibres tend to have greater resistance to sun damage than natural ones. Silk is the least resistant among natural fabrics; those with woven patterns will be slower to fade in the sun than printed ones.

■ Large patterns and dark colours can overpower a small room.

■ Few rooms can hold two different patterns. If your sofa has a strong design, balance it with plain curtains.

■ Use stripes sparingly and balance them with plain fabric elsewhere in the room.

■ Offset pale walls with deep-coloured curtains.

■ Use the colour wheel on page 80 to find what contrasts would work with existing items in your room. Be adventurous with contrasts; the most unexpected contrasts will often work well.

■ The fabrics used in a room don't have to be the same material, but should share similar characteristics. Formal fabrics such as velvet and brocade will group well together in a living room, as will gingham and printed cottons in a kitchen.

recovering upholstery ■ ■

There are four options for a covered chair or sofa that is structurally sound, but in need of a replacement cover.

1 Disguise it with a throw. This is a blanket-sized piece of fabric that can be draped over a chair or sofa and tucked under the seat. A sofa might require two throws to cover it.

2 Stitch a new cover yourself. Making a loose cover that is held in place by a grip-fastener and ties requires careful cutting and accurate sewing skills, but no upholstery skills.

3 Buy stretch-covers. These typically consist of material with a high elastic content that stretches over the old cover. This is a budget option.

4 Call in a professional upholsterer. He will remove the existing cover and fully fit a new one, with the fabric of your choice. However, this can be as expensive as buying new furniture.

cushions ▪▪▪

▪ Choose removable covers in washable fabrics.
▪ Give a fixed cushion a removable cover by unpicking one seam and replacing it with an iron-on grip-fastener.
▪ Extra-large cushions can double as floor seats.
▪ Experiment with sizes, shapes, and fabrics, especially if your upholstery is in neutral shades. This is a good way to add new life to tired furniture and a simple way to make a room more colourful and cozy.
▪ Don't restrict cushions to the living room. They add colour, comfort, and decoration to kitchen chairs and in bedrooms.
▪ Choose firm cushions if you are using them to support your back.

bedding ▪▪▪

Easy-care fabrics and modern duvets have made bedroom linen and bed making effortless.

Blankets
Made from wool, wool blends, cotton, polyester, and non-woven acrylic. These are long lasting and many are machine washable. They need to be topped with a thin quilt or bedcover.

Duvets
The quick and easy way to make the bed: a daily shake and airing is all that is needed. Duvet covers are a useful way to add a large block of colour and pattern to the bedroom.

▪ Use them to draw the eye from tired décor.
▪ Reversible duvet covers give two styles in one.
▪ Create effect by choosing a neutral cover and adding a strong coloured throw and cushions.

Duvet fillings include:
▪ Goose-down gives lightweight comfort and warmth.
▪ Down and feather is not as lightweight and is less expensive than 100% down.
▪ Polyester is more compact than natural material.

Suitable for those who like the feeling of being cosy.
▪ Cotton is lightweight, but flat.

Tip: A two-in-one duvet consisting of two separate duvets, one lightweight, one middleweight, can be fastened together to give heavyweight warmth.

choosing pillows ▪▪▪

Synthetic pillows are a better choice for asthmastics, or people who are sensitive to allergens. These can be regularly washed to remove dust and mites. To improve your sleeping position, choose a:

▪ Soft pillow if you sleep on your stomach.
▪ Medium pillow if you sleep on your back.
▪ Firm pillow if you sleep on your side.

Bulk or physical weight is not a reliable indicator of firmness. Always be guided by the pillow's label.

a total look ▪▪▪

See page 76, *Designing a room* for ideas on creating your special interior.

▪ Buy a good book that gives fabric style guidelines, such as whether cotton goes with wool or whether stripes and patterns will ever work well together.
▪ Choose loose covered sofas, chairs, and cushions and change the colours and fabrics as you like.
▪ If buying permanent covers, look for sofas or chairs where you choose the fabric and it's made up and fitted for you before you receive it. You can match your fabric to your interior much better this way.
▪ Recover existing chair seats or footstools to match.
▪ Because curtains are very expensive, buy them with longevity in mind. The plainer they are, the more adaptable to a change in style they will be.
▪ Cushions can highlight the colours in the room.

Curtains and blinds

■ ■ ■Curtains are more than just a way of shutting out the darkness. Window dressing is an important aspect of the overall look and atmosphere of a room ■ ■ ■

choosing curtains ■ ■ ■

Curtains can be made from just about any fabric that has draping ability. Although they use a surprisingly large amount of material – which can mean a bulky sewing job or a big expense – they do offer the following advantages:

■ Add blocks of colour and design to a room.
■ Provide privacy, including during the day, when sheer curtains remain drawn yet let in light.
■ Keep rooms warm in winter; especially if lined.
■ Provide protection from draughts.
■ Shield rooms from the sun by day.
■ Act as dividers to partition off sections of a room – for example, the bed area in a studio flat.
■ Create a formal or casual mood for rooms.

Bedrooms
■ Provide protection from morning or evening sun.
■ Offer total privacy, if your windows are overlooked.

Suitable fabrics
■ Avoid sheer materials and unlined cotton unless you like the sun in the morning or need privacy.
■ Choose lined curtains in heavyweight cotton, linen, and mixed fibres.
■ Fit black-out lining in children's rooms.

Living rooms
■ To create impact in this room think about length, fabric quality, and style.
■ If there's a busy road outside, you might want to muffle sound with a heavy curtain.
■ Net or sheer curtains provide privacy.
■ Choose heavier curtains to keep in the warmth.
■ Think about patio door treatments.

Handy hints
■ Avoid small-detail patterns if windows are large.
■ Enlarge small windows with plain curtains.
■ Make the most of narrow windows by combining two types of window dressing – for example, heavy curtains tied apart with tie-backs, plus an inset roller blind.
■ Vertical stripes will make a room appear taller.
■ Use muslin and net materials for daytime privacy.

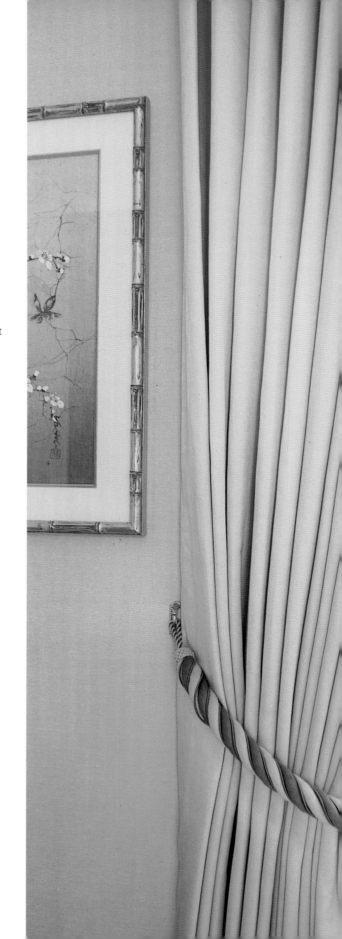

Suitable fabrics
- A wide range of fabrics are suitable.
- Choose fabrics to reflect the style of the upholstery in the room, from lush velvet to muslin, and match or contrast colours. See page 80, *Using colour.*

Kitchens
- Fabric used here needs to be easily washed, as it will attract grease, and must also be hard-wearing.
- Must be non-flammable material.
- Should shield food from the heat of the sun.

Suitable fabrics
- Choose washable 100 per cent cotton.

- Avoid nylon and mixed fibres that are flammable.
- Consider café-style curtains that run on rails across the lower half of the window. This keeps the sun away from the preparation area, while allowing the cook to see outdoors.

Bathrooms
- Use washable fabric that is resistant to mould.
- Ensure full privacy if windows have standard glass.

Suitable fabrics
- Choose machine-washable cottons, linen and mixed fibres.
- Consider vinyl blinds for narrow windows.

measuring up ▪ ▪ ▪

Curtains are sold ready-made, in varying widths and lengths, or made-to-measure, to accurately fit your window. This is expensive, but the choice of fabrics and designs is enormous. Whichever type of curtain you choose, you will need to take accurate measurements first.

- Always measure the width of the curtain track or pole – not the window. Include track overlap.
- For the length, measure from the top of the track or the underside of the pole rings to where you want your curtain to end. For full-length curtains, or ones

that you want to sit on the sill, subtract one-half inch to allow for the fabric to stretch a little.
- Pre-made curtains are sold ungathered, and the label states the width of window they are intended to fit. However, this depends on the type of treatment you choose. For ones that need more than average fabric, buy wider curtains.
- You may also want a valance. This can be either a fixed strip of fabric or a wooden surround, which will fit the wall directly above the curtain pole or track. Fabric valances may be gathered or straight, and should be purchased at the same time as the curtains.

CURTAIN HEADING TREATMENTS

Tab Tops
Informal treatment
Best with unlined fabrics

Curtain stays relatively flat, draped through fabric loops

Minimum one width of pole

Pencil Pleats
Standard heading

Curtain gathered evenly along its length

Two widths of track (with overlap) or pole

Double Pleats or Goblets
Formal effect
Good on heavy fabrics

Curtains are gathered to form evenly spaced pleats, which are then stitched into place

Two widths of track

---

hanging curtains ▪▪▪

DÉCOR

Tips and hints
Curtain clips turn any hemmed fabric into a curtain, with no need for heading tape. Simply fold over the top, clip, and hang.

Curtain Track

Made from plastic or metal and designed to be invisible, these curtains are attached via runners and hooks in front of the track. They may be closed by hand or, with a pulley system, kept neatly at one side.

Tracks

■ Keep the focus on the curtains.
■ May be teamed with a fixed valance.
■ Allow for a variety of curtain headings.
■ Work with all styles of fabric and design.
■ Are very effective at reducing draught.

Curtain Poles

These suit most fabrics. Curtains hang either below a wooden, metal – or occasionally plastic – pole, via pole rings and hooks, or are threaded directly through it. Poles have decorative ends called finials.

Poles

■ Look best with less formal curtains.
■ May use less material than a track.
■ May need to be changed to match different curtains.
■ Hold the curtain further from the window than a track does.

buying blinds ▪▪▪

Advantages

■ Simple blinds are a low-cost option.
■ Ideal where space is limited with insufficient room to draw back curtains.
■ Give privacy by day.
■ Effectively keep out the sun.
■ Can fit difficult sloping attic windows.
■ Ideal for kitchens and bathrooms, they are easy to clean and waterproof, but suitable everywhere.
■ Can be teamed with curtains at the same window.

Disadvantages

■ Don't retain heat, so not a very good choice for north-facing rooms.
■ Won't muffle traffic sounds.
■ Allow in some light, so are not ideal for bedrooms.

There are three main types of blinds

Venetian
Horizontal slats, made of PVC, metal, or wood, that open to give full light, or angle to give privacy and some light; they are raised by pulling a cord.

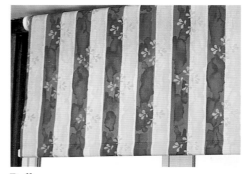

Roller
A piece of straight fabric that rolls up round a tube at the top of the window. You can vary the length of roll-up during the day to keep out sunlight as necessary.

Roman
A piece of fabric that pleats into neat folds as it is drawn upwards rather than rolling up, and, when drawn, shows a neat valance. It is usually sold made-to-measure.

Framing

■ ■ ■ **Displaying photographs and pictures is a fast way to add personality to your home. Pictures give substance and texture to plain walls** ■ ■ ■

Unless you have a fabulous work of art, pictures and photographs work best in groups. These don't have to be uniform: a variety of styles, hung in groups, rather than in straight lines, create a good wall display. You can also go for impact by using one very large poster or two medium ones on a plain, colour-washed wall. As well as the obvious family portraits, you could also frame:

■ Art postcards
■ Colour plates from old books
■ Close-up photographs of flower heads, or black-and-white landscapes
■ Memorabilia from films, magazine covers, or even your childhood
■ Children's handprints or early drawings

choosing the right frame ■ ■ ■

The purpose of the frame is to protect what's inside, by surrounding it with dry, rigid materials. However, it should also enhance the photo or picture it holds.

■ Aim to reflect the style of the picture. A portrait may look better with a formal brass frame, a modern print with a contemporary steel one, and a child's drawing surrounded by colourful painted wood.
■ Harmonize with the style of the room by choosing a frame that fits both subject and location.
■ Some frames already include a mount, or you can buy it separately. Typically a contrasting colour card, a mount adds impact and can be used to screen off the outside edges of your picture.
■ For larger prints and photos, consider using non-reflective glass that will allow you to enjoy your picture even when the sun is shining on it.

hanging ■ ■ ■

■ If you don't have a picture rail, always use picture hooks to hang frames. A single picture hook – which you nail into the wall – should support a typical frame of up to 60cm by 90cm (2ft by 3ft).
■ For bigger pictures, use a double hook or two singles, for a stronger, steady hold.
■ To hang a standard frame, turn the picture face down, and pass brass picture-hanging wire (or strong string) through the two eyelets on the back that are horizontal. Bring both wire ends back to the centre, twist secure with pliers, and then cut.
■ Clip-frames are the easiest frames to manage; slide off all four clips and position the picture between the glass and rigid backing. Replace the clips, turn the picture upright, and thread picture wire or string through the two eyelet holes that are now horizontal, continuing as for standard frames.

Carpets and hard flooring

carpet ■ ■ ■

Easily the most popular option, this is now seen as a choice to be used for some, but not all rooms.

Advantages:
■ Warm and soft underfoot.
■ Quiet, and generally absorbs sounds.
■ Can enhance colours used on walls and furnishings.

Disadvantages:
■ Generally expensive.
■ Fitted carpet requires professional fitting.
■ May become stained.
■ Limited life.

Use: Throughout the home.

hard floors ■ ■ ■

Wood
These may simply be the original floorboards, sanded and varnished, or a new floor of tongue-and-groove boards which can be overlaid onto the existing floor. Both of these options are relatively simple, but very labour-intensive projects. You can also have a contractor fit wood parquet blocks.

Advantages:
■ Wooden floors have a special beauty.
■ Choice of woods, such as oak, beech, and maple.
■ Hard-wearing and long-lasting.
■ Can add rugs for comfort.
■ Can use wood stain for different colours.

Disadvantages:
■ Expensive to buy, if not using existing boards.

- Noisy to walk on; does not absorb sound.
- May feel drafty if using existing boards only.

Use: Anywhere in the home, but care must be taken in bathrooms where water may penetrate.

Laminate

Not wood, but a photographic copy of the wood grain, stuck onto an inexpensive base, typically fibreboard or a wood composite base, the surface of each board is covered with hard-wearing, laminate plastic.

Advantages:
- Looks like real wood at a fraction of the cost.
- Relatively simple job.

Disadvantages:
- Will dent if heavy objects fall on it.
- Can't be sanded or re-sealed.
- Limited life: may need replacing after ten years.

Use: In the same way as wood.

Vinyl

A manufactured flooring made from flexible plastic that often has a printed design. Sold as sheets or tiles.

Advantages:
- Washable and waterproof.
- Warm underfoot, especially cushioned vinyl.
- Also sold as tiles, which are easy to install.

Disadvantages:
- May dent easily.
- Must be laid on a completely smooth floor.
- Will show signs of wear after a few years.

Use: Ideal for bathrooms, kitchens, or utility areas.

Linoleum

A natural alternative to vinyl, this is made from cork, wood-flour and linseed oil.

Advantages:
- Easy to clean and hard-wearing.
- Scuff-resistant.
- Soft and warm underfoot.

- Slip-resistant.
- Can buy with inset tiles to create striking designs.

Disadvantages:
- Expensive in comparison to vinyl.
- Needs a revitalizing treatment every ten years.
- Water-resistant, not waterproof.
- Requires professional fitting.

Use: Kitchens and utility areas.

Cork

A natural material, cork is manufactured into blocks and cut into thin tiles. These can be factory-laminated or sealed once they are laid.

Advantages:
- Soft and warm underfoot.
- Easy and inexpensive to install.
- Ideal for bathrooms and children's playrooms.

Disadvantages:
- Can be slippery when wet.
- Limited colours available.
- May get marked and dented easily.
- Very limited life.

Use: Bathrooms, kitchens, and playrooms.

Clay, stone, and slate

Stone and slate may be cut to size and stone can also be processed into polished, composite tiles. Clay is processed into ceramic tiles.

Advantages:
- Easy to clean.
- Cool in high temperatures.
- Water and stain-resistant.
- Rugs can be added for comfort.

Disadvantages:
- Noisy underfoot; does not absorb sound.
- Expensive to buy and difficult to install.
- Anything fragile will break on impact.

Use: Around the home, but most suitable for entrance hall, dining room, kitchen, and bathroom.

carpet

laminate

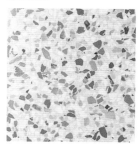

linoleum

cork

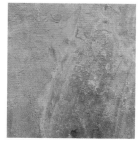

slate

semi-soft floors ▪ ▪ ▪

Rubber

Either a natural material, derived from plants, or a synthetic imitation.

Advantages:
- Warm underfoot.
- Hard-wearing.
- Improves with age.
- Choose studded or ribbed rubber for non-slip safety.

Disadvantages:
- Limited availability and colour choices for domestic use (widely available for industrial floors).
- Needs installation by a professional.

Use: In the kitchen.

Natural woven flooring

The natural fibres from sea grass, sisal, and jute are woven and then a backing, usually rubber or latex, is applied. These floors are semi-soft to make a textured surface that is mostly hard-wearing. An exception is jute, which is made from bark, and is only suitable for bedrooms.

Advantages:
- Adds warm tones and texture to floors.
- Looks particularly good in conservatories and halls and is suitable in houses that have other natural flooring, such as wooden floors.
- Sisal, made from a cactus-like plant, is hard-wearing enough for entrance halls and living rooms.
- Can buy mixed with wool, for softness.

Disadvantages:
- Not suitable for hay fever sufferers.
- Isn't soft underfoot.
- Gets dirty quickly, and attracts grit and grease particularly.
- Sea grass can be slightly slippery, and is unsuited to stairs.

Use: Around the home. Not suitable where mentioned above, or for floors that will get wet.

wall-to-wall carpet ▪ ▪ ▪

Carpet offers a vast range of choice in colour, texture, and quality of materials. To meet the needs of each particular room, you must consider not only the colour and pattern, but also the materials and manufacture.

Once you have decided on your colour scheme and style of carpet, it is important to look at the following points:

- How was the carpet made?
- What materials were used?
- What is the manufacturer's wear grade? Most give a five-point scale, with five points indicating that the carpet is suitable for heavy traffic areas.

sisal

sea grass

Type of carpet

Most new carpets are tufted (made by pulling individual lengths of yarn through a pre-woven backing). While the feeling of the carpet underfoot will depend on the fibre used, how the carpet looks from above depends on how the yarns have been treated.

■ Texture/twist pile is the most popular; this carpet has a short, cut pile with a twist set into the yarn with heat for resistance to crushing.
■ Velour carpets are twisted, then heat-set straight for a soft texture that, unfortunately, shows every footprint.
■ Berber carpets are made from low loops. They give a neat, no-footprint look but can be snagged easily.
■ Basic cut pile carpets are either shaggy (long pile) or velvet-finish (short) and made from looped fibres that have been cut to length. They may crush easily.
■ Velvet piles may show animal fur and dust.

Around the house

Choose the carpet to withstand a particular room's level of wear.

Dining rooms: Stain-treated nylon blend, with Berber, short-loop pile, so that marks from chair legs are less noticeable.
Bedrooms: Light to medium-wear: soft acrylic, plush velour or short velvet pile.
Bathrooms: Bathroom carpet with water-resistant backing – polyester velour, for a luxury feel.
Stairs: Heavy-duty synthetic mix with short, dense pile.
Entrance halls: Heavy-duty, stain-treated nylon or polypropylene (the entrance hall is the busiest place in the house).
Living rooms: Heavy-duty, but also needs to be soft: avoid Berbers and choose mid-length twist pile in wool, wool blend, or synthetic blend.
Kitchen: Stain-resistant carpet tiles in synthetic blend. These are easier to clean – simply lift a tile to treat a stain.
Playrooms: Choose light to medium-wear carpet tiles or budget 'children's design' carpeting in stain-treated synthetic.

Carpet fibres

More than 97 percent of carpets include synthetic materials. Synthetics are often blended together to get the best properties of several materials.

Nylon: Hard-wearing for every room in the home, with some resistance to crushing; cheaper nylons can feel harsh underfoot, may fade in sunlight, and give occasional static, but offer some stain resistance.
Olefin: Hard-wearing, but not soft enough for living rooms, it resists static and tends to be found in short, low-looped carpets, so crushing is not a factor. Offers good fade and stain resistance.
Acrylic: Offers moderate wear for bedrooms and bathrooms, with some crush resistance, looks and feels like a soft wool carpet so often called "art wool". Unlikely to fade, with good stain resistance.
Polyester: Moderate wear and soft, luxury feel for bedrooms, at a budget price. Once flattened, the pile is difficult to restore. Some stain resistance.
Wool: Hard-wearing, crush resistant, soft, and warm underfoot; use throughout the home, except in bathrooms, as wool fibres retain too much moisture. Offers some stain resistance.

Carpet buying checkpoints

■ Before you buy, bend back a piece of carpet. If you can easily see the backing, don't buy it, because the fibres are too loosely woven.
■ Think carefully before buying a very bright colour; you may have to live with it for twenty years.
■ Patterned carpet can restrict what you choose for soft furnishings. Plain, but textured carpet is more versatile. Remember that you can add pattern and colour with rugs on top of a carpet.
■ Cushion underlay should be placed between the carpet and the floor. Without it, the life of a carpet will be greatly reduced. Sold in rolls, it may cost up to half the price of a cheap carpet.
■ Professional installation is recommended, and essential for difficult areas like stairs.
■ Axminster and Wilton carpets, generally made of wool or wool blends, have a backing that is woven at the same time as the pile. This makes the pile particularly resistant to flattening.
■ Stain treatments, like Scotch Guard and Teflon will prevent man-made fibres from absorbing stains.

Feng shui your home

■ ■ ■ Followers of this ancient Chinese art of placement believe that the arrangement of your home can foster good fortune ■ ■ ■

what is feng shui ■ ■ ■

The theory behind Feng Shui is that if you arrange your home in such a way that the rooms and objects inside them are in harmony with nature, then the earth's powerful lines of energy, called chi, will run smoothly and bring good fortune to the occupants. This is considered to be auspicious.

By contrast, if you position things in the wrong, or inauspicious, place, you risk blocking those energy lines or, worse, sending all the positive energy straight out again.

Feng Shui – it translates literally as wind and water – is a huge subject. But to enhance the energy lines in your home, you could consider the following:

feng shui around the house ■ ■ ■

Entrance hall

■ Keep it clear. A cluttered home reflects a muddled mind.

■ Use a bright light to attract good energy into your home.

■ 'The frog that brings silver or gold' is a popular Feng Shui symbol. Put a small frog ornament discreetly by the main door to invite wealth into the home.

■ Hang cut crystals by an east window to catch the morning sunlight and create family harmony.

■ Take care that a mirror doesn't reflect the door – all your good energy could bounce right out of the house.

Living room

■ Encourage good Feng Shui by arranging chairs within a regular hexagonal shape around a coffee table. Bad positioning would be an L shape, with seats in front of tall furniture. If you must have tall furniture, stand plants in front of it.

■ No sofas or chairs should have their backs to a door.

■ Open doors onto an empty space, not in front of furniture, otherwise the flow of energy into the room will be blocked.

Kitchen

■ Remove any clutter. In fact, all you should do in this room is cook; using it for homework or reading the newspaper is distracting.

■ It should only have one door, in order to help the cook be more peaceful and relaxed. An ideal kitchen faces southeast.

■ The most harmonious place for the cooker is on an island, with limited space behind, to prevent people walking behind the chef.

■ Knives send out negative energy, so keep them out of sight to defuse arguments.

Dining room

■ Watch where you sit; a dining chair with bars on the back creates the outline of a poison arrow and means bad luck.

■ An ideal room needs to be a regular shape, preferably square. If your dining room has protruding corners – for example, a chimney that's been blocked up – disguise the corners with large plants.

■ Hang a large wall mirror. The doubling of food on the table (as shown by the mirror reflection) promises that there will be plenty for everyone in reality, too.

Bedroom

■ Point your head south, but don't let the foot of the bed face the door. The bed should be as far from the door as possible, to permit the free flow of energy into the room.

■ Everything in Feng Shui must balance. Bedrooms should have matching bedside tables and lamps, even if you are single.

■ Never have computer or exercising equipment in

Feng Shui practice makes use of wind chimes to guide the flow of chi energy.

your bedroom. This is a place for regeneration.

■ Take the TV and radio out – the energy in the room should be focused on sleep, not connected to activity.

■ Curtains are more auspicious than blinds.

■ In a child's room, keep beside the bed a photograph of the child held in the arms of the parents. This will promote a feeling of security.

Workroom

■ Choose a northeast-facing room or one towards the front of the house.

■ Use a wooden desk – it should be round if your job is creative, or square with rounded corners if you deal with figures. Square corners mean money could slip off the desk

■ Keep fresh red flowers to absorb negativity.

■ Hang up pictures of your goals, not family photos.

Lavatories

■ These are generally not good in Feng Shui, because you can inadvertently flush the good things from your life. In ancient China, toilets were kept outside the house. However, the best you can do today is keep the door shut and close the toilet lid, to stop wealth from draining away.

COLOURS

Paint walls or add ornaments to create the right atmosphere.

Red: the most auspicious colour. It's linked to happiness, passion and growth (too much may make you hyperactive).
Yellow: patience and wisdom.
Orange: creativity, teamwork, and healing.
Pink: love and romance.
Black: money and power (use sparingly).
Brown: use sparingly, it may cause you to move more slowly.
Purple: high ideals and loyalty. A good colour.
Blue: kindness and, for business, the colour of reliability.
White: a difficult colour. Symbolizes light, which is good, but in China white it is also considered the colour of death.

Selecting and arranging flowers

■ ■ ■ **Whether you're picking flowers from the garden or selecting them at a florist's store, choose what catches your eye. Displaying flowers is about having fun, not following formal rules. Here is a simple guide to the key types of flowers that are best for arranging, and when to choose them** ■ ■ ■

flower spikes ■ ■ ■

These buds grow from a centre stalk. They give height and balance to a mixed arrangement, but can be used just by themselves. They particularly suit tall, narrow vases and open, shallow dishes, especially when fixed with foam and wire. Good choices include:

Bloom	When to pick or buy
■ Gladioli	A few flowers open; buds showing colour
■ Snapdragons	Flowers open; no pollen
■ Delphiniums	Most of spike in flower
■ Stocks	Few flowers open
■ Lupins	Bottom half of spike in flower

single flowers ■ ■ ■

Round and full faced, with one flower per stem, these blooms are easy to arrange. They suit informal vases and jugs, and can also be used singly in one-stem displays. Good choices include:

Bloom	When to pick or buy
■ Narcissi	*Single* buds showing colour; *double* flowers fully open
■ Tulips	Buds showing colour; leaves taut
■ Irises	Few flowers open
■ Lilies	Few flowers open, no pollen
■ Roses	Buds open or flowers tight-centred, with some leaves on stems; avoid tight buds – they may not open
■ Standard carnations	Flowers open, but no white threads
■ Sunflowers	Flowers open; stems firm
■ Dahlias	Most flowers open
■ Gerbera	Flowers open

filler flowers ▪▪▪

Attractive stems with lots of little flowers give arrangements a soft, full look. Generally, they don't have sufficient impact to be used on their own. Pick or buy filler flowers when the leaves look fresh and the buds are just opening. Good choices include:

Bloom	When to pick or buy
▪ Baby's breath	Buds just open; leaves look fresh
▪ Eucalyptus	Leaves look fresh
▪ Ferns	Look fresh
▪ Spray carnations	Buds just open
▪ Statice	Buds just open; leaves look fresh

Ferns provide an attractive backdrop to these gerberas, using complementing colours. The large flower heads are not dwarfed by the ferns.

choosing vases ▪▪▪

Be as inventive with vases as you can. While traditional crystal, glass, and bright ceramics are good choices in some settings, you can also opt for a more unusual look, whether your décor is modern urban or country. Try some of the following stylish alternatives:

- ▪ Earthenware pots
- ▪ Enamelled household jugs
- ▪ Galvanized steel buckets
- ▪ Coloured glass bottles
- ▪ Test tubes, for single flowers
- ▪ Rectangular clear glass tanks, with a layer of pebbles at the base
- ▪ Mismatched pretty glass jars, especially striking with foliage or single blooms
- ▪ Baskets, lined with polythene

A classic mistake is to use vases that are too big and bright – the flowers should be the star of the display, not the container. By tradition, the tallest flowers should be two-and-a-half times the height of an upright vase – so a 20cm (8in) high vase would need filler flowers or foliage of around 50cm (20in) high.

Be creative – take a couple of flowers from a bunch and display them in an altogether different way in another room.

The main flowers could be shorter than this. For a more modern look, cut the stems of roses or other heavy-bloomed flowers, such as camellias or peonies, 5cm (2in) below the head. Mass them together, floating, in a low tank or wide vase.

simple arrangements ▪ ▪ ▪

These ideas can be adapted to create simple but effective everyday flower displays. Choose seasonal blooms to create special arrangements for centrepieces and table top decorations to suit holidays and special occasions.

(a) Tying flowers in a vase keeps the display looking neat and prevents flowers falling away from each other.

(b) Loose arrangements can use both leaves or flowers, adding class and fun at the same time.

(c) A low display floral arrangement – ideal as a table decoration.

Tied bunch in a vase

You will need about 20 long-stemmed mass flowers (see page 106) for this display. Don't be afraid to mix different varieties: lilies combine successfully with carnations and roses. Experiment with colour, too – this display works well in three colours. You will also need a tall vase (clear glass is ideal for this classically simple look), secateurs, and raffia or string to tie the stems.

1 Remove all foliage from the bottom half of the flower stems.
2 Using your thumb and forefinger, hold the longest stem halfway down. Still holding on, add further flowers in descending height order, each one at a slight angle and on both sides of the initial pivot stem.
3 Loosely tie the bunch with raffia or string. Trim the stems level.
4 Place in the vase, then fill with water to within 5cm (2in) of the top.

Loose arrangement

Choose about 20 stems – a mixture of spikes, single, and filler flowers (see pages 106–7). Select them from the same colour family, such as yellows and oranges, or use the colour wheel (see page 80) and pick contrasting colours. The following combination is very successful: three lilies, three delphiniums, six roses, six chrysanthemums and two baby's breath. Mass them in a medium-height vase or jug.

1 Half-fill the vase with water.
2 Criss cross the stems of the filler flowers as you put them into the vase. This creates a grid to hold the other flowers in place.

a   b   c

108

3 Starting at the outside rim with the shortest or smallest flowers, work toward the centre, adding flowers in ascending height to create a very loose triangle. For a modern, natural look, try to group flowers of the same type together.

4 Stand back and look at the arrangement as you go along. It needs to look good when viewed from a distance.

Low display

Using florists' foam or wire as a rigid support allows you to hold flowers in place when working on a shallow dish. It can also be used within a vase or a low, wide bowl.

Bold, full-headed flowers work well in compact, low arrangements – with dahlias, peonies, hydrangea, for example – and you will need about 20 stems. Cut flower heads short with secateurs to create a mass of intense colour.

1 Place the wet, cut foam block on the dish or in a low bowl.

2 Cut the stems 5cm (2in) below the flower head.

3 Press each stem into the foam until it is entirely covered. Check the display from all sides and from overhead.

Cut-flower checkpoints

■ Cut flowers in the garden to avoid drips on the carpet. Place the stems in a bucket of water to prevent wilting.

■ If even simple arranging seems too time-consuming, buy bunches of the same flower – like tulips, gladioli, and irises – choose a narrow vase approximately half their height, and simply drop the bunches in to it. Turn the flower faces to point outwards.

How to stop flowers from wilting

■ **Condition vulnerable stems that have been sitting for some time in a dry bouquet by placing them in a bucket of lukewarm water for at least two hours. Tulips and other flowers grown from bulbs should stand in shallow water only.**

■ **Flowers may fail to stand up straight if they are kept too warm, in direct sunlight, or without sufficient water.**

■ **Wrap a group of wilted stems in damp newspaper, and stand them upright in a bucket of lukewarm water overnight.**

■ **If flowers remain wilted, use a taller vase, or cut the stems and push them into florist's foam.**

caring for bouquets ■ ■ ■

Conventional bouquet

■ Choose a vase (see page 107), making sure it is wide and tall enough for the flowers.

■ Half-fill the vase with lukewarm water, and add a sachet of cut-flower food.

■ Remove all the stem leaves on flowers and foliage that would be submerged in water.

■ Cut flower stems diagonally at the base, taking off the bottom 2.5cm (1in) if damaged.

■ If the bouquet is pre-arranged, everything should fall into attractive heights once placed in a vase. If it is not arranged, see the ideas opposite.

■ Display in a cool, draft-free place.

■ Check daily, removing blooms past their best.

■ Top up the water daily and change the water after several days, adding fresh cut-flower food.

■ Every few days, spray mist the flowers.

■ When only a few blooms remain, transfer the arrangement to a smaller vase.

Cellophane-wrapped, hand-tied flowers in water

■ Do nothing. The cellophane is watertight and designed to act as a vase. Simply stand on a mat on the table.

■ If you want to untie the flowers and arrange in a bouquet in a vase (see opposite), do so over a sink (to catch the water).

■ Snip the first blooms that fade just below the flower, keeping the stem in place.

■ When many flowers fade, undo the arrangement, and rearrange the remaining flowers in a vase.

Hanging baskets and window boxes

■ ■ ■ Even if your flat or house does not have a garden, you can use window boxes and hanging baskets to add colour and interest to the outside of your home with year-round displays of flowers and foliage ■ ■ ■

creating a hanging basket ■ ■ ■

■ In small spaces, take advantage of hanging baskets to vertically extend your growing space and create trailing spheres of colour. Screw purpose-made brackets to the wall, from which to suspend the baskets, and bear in mind the advice on position when considering planting.

■ The most effective and stunningly beautiful baskets are crammed full of plants. For summer, choose a selection of long-flowering bedding plants, such as petunias, fuchsias and geraniums, plus trailing foliage, such as ivy. For winter, evergreen

foliage, heathers, and ferns retain the good looks of a healthy basket.

■ Don't stop at flowering plants and herbs: a number of vegetables do well in hanging baskets, such as tumbling cherry tomatoes and chilli peppers.

■ Baskets need to be lined – select from foam, felt, and recycled wool liners to retain moisture and, in winter baskets, to conserve warmth.

■ You don't have to make your basket from scratch if you don't want to. Baskets come already made-up from nurseries, or you can buy easy-to-make packs.

Planting a hanging basket

1 Choose a large hanging basket with a matching-sized liner. Fit the liner inside the basket, then add water-retaining granules, mixed with a small amount of compost, according to product instructions.

2 Cut small slits at regular intervals along the basket lining. From the inside, push through the top of each plant, so the root and bottom stems remain inside the basket. Cover with a thin layer of compost.

3 Plant the top of the basket, leaving enough room for the plants to spread. Include flowering bulbs in the basket to maintain the lifespan. Give the basket a really good watering when you've finished.

DÉCOR

Simple maintenance

Drying out is the main problem with window boxes and hanging baskets. In summer, they need to be watered at least once a day.

■ Ideally, water when the container is not in direct sunlight – at early morning and dusk.
■ To rescue a dried-up basket, remove it from the bracket and stand it in the shade in a bowl of lukewarm water.
■ Keep containers in flower for longer by regularly removing dead blooms.
■ Regularly add new flowers and foliage to window boxes and baskets.
■ To hide a basket's hanging chains, train trailing leaves to grow up around them.

setting up a window box ■■■

■ Choose window boxes to make a statement, and reflect the style and décor of your home: organic terracotta for a Mediterranean feel, perhaps; simple wood in the Shaker style; or galvanized metal for a modern, urban setting. But remember that the planting is the main attraction.

■ Window boxes, especially those made from terracotta, may simply stand on the windowsill. The safest way to secure a wooden, plastic, or metal box is to screw galvanized metal brackets through the box into the wall. You'll need a power drill to do this.

■ In a flat with a balcony, you may choose to attach the box to the balustrade or let it stand directly on the floor. Balustrade boxes require lightweight compost and polystyrene chips rather than heavy stones at the bottom of the box for drainage. Floor boxes can accommodate heavier plants and soil.

Choosing the planting

Select plants to reflect the look of your container – bold urban-style boxes benefit from the architectural shapes of cacti or yuccas, clipped box or bay tree. More traditional country containers suit soft, tumbling, pastel-toned flowers and herbs. Consider also the micro-climate and location: the higher a

window box, the hardier and more low-lying plants need to be, as they will be subject to strong direct sunlight in summer, and cold winds and frost in winter. Heathers are a good choice for exposed north-facing boxes. Sheltered window boxes can handle bulbs, most bedding plants, and all-year herbs, such as thyme, sage, and mint.

Aim to provide year-long interest. This may mean making your box a temporary home to narcissi in spring, then summer bedding plants or geraniums, then autumn bulbs. To make the best use of minimal space, remove plants as soon as they have peaked, and repot to finish off in a cool room.

Planting a window box

1 Scatter the bottom of the window box with a drainage layer of broken terracotta pots, or stones. Cover with a layer of water-retaining granules mixed with a small amount of compost, according to product instructions. Add a layer of compost. Press down gently.
2 Set the well-watered plants in the compost. Fill the area around each plant with compost, and firm the compost down.
3 Water thoroughly, and add a thick layer of mulch, such as composted bark chips, to retain moisture.

Caring for houseplants

■ ■ ■ For best results, concentrate on foliage and flowering plants that are renowned for being easy to care for and hard to kill. Save delicates and exotics for the experts ■ ■ ■

keeping houseplants happy ■ ■ ■

REPOTTING

Repot when you can see roots coming through the bottom of the pot. Choose a slightly larger pot; one that is much larger may cause leaf-drop through shock.

1 Put bark chippings into the base of the new pot to help drainage. Cover with 2.5cm (1in) of new compost.

2 Tip the plant carefully out of its old pot and place it in the new compost. Fill the spaces around the sides of the plant with new compost.

3 Pat the compost down with your fingers, and water sparingly.

1 Find a good position for the plant.

■ Plants like an even temperature and bright, indirect sunlight.

■ Keep plants away from cold draughts, central heating vents, and from behind drawn curtains.

2 Get the amount of water right.

■ Plants like some water, but not too much. Water plants in a sink (ideally using boiled, cooled water). Let the excess drain away, before replacing a plant on its saucer. Standing in a saucer-reservoir all day kills more plants than over-dry soil. Place a water-indicator strip in the soil to tell you when to water.

3 Feed the soil.

■ Plants flourish when fed nutrients designed to promote stem and leaf growth. Feed according to the care instructions with standard plant food, or choose long-life food spikes that release nutrients into the soil for up to 60 days.

4 Keep the leaves clean.

■ Plants should be dusted with kitchen roll dipped in tepid water. Others, such as African Violet, have leaves that must be dry-dusted. Blocked leaf pores cannot take in carbon dioxide efficiently.

5 Deal with insects promptly.

■ Keep plant leaves and buds free from pests. Wash off small numbers of aphids and spider mites. If you are not organically minded, reach for spray guns of houseplant insecticide for serious attacks.

TROUBLESHOOTING

Leaves

■ Curl, then fall off	■ Too cold or over-watered
■ Most fall off	■ Shock, caused by sudden change in temperature or light, usually when moved
■ White or straw patches	■ Water too cold
■ Wilt during day	■ Too much light
■ Brown tips	■ Plant bruised by pets or people brushing past
■ Holes	■ Insect damage
■ Fail to grow	■ In winter, few plants grow fresh leaves or stems; in summer, indicates underfeeding, over-watering, or dark location

Flowers

■ No flowers	■ Too little light; overfeeding; pot too small
■ Flowers die quickly	■ Too little water and too much heat

food matters

A well planned kitchen

FOOD MATTERS

■ ■ ■ **This most important of rooms can be the hardest to plan, because it needs to combine a variety of functions – storage, cooking, and eating – and cram in a range of appliances, too. It's wonderful, of course, to stock a completely new kitchen, but simple changes to an existing layout can make a big difference to its smooth running** ■ ■ ■

what makes a great kitchen ■ ■ ■

A kitchen has four key functions and they need to be planned carefully so you can work in your kitchen safely and efficiently: storage, food preparation, cooking, and living space. Even if you aren't considering re-decorating it, how you want to use your kitchen is probably the most important factor in planning. A keen pastry cook will want plenty of worktops and storage space for equipment. If you just use your kitchen for heating frozen foods and eating breakfast, then you may want to create space that is comfortable enough to welcome friends for coffee. Parents with small children may care most about non-slip flooring and ample refrigerator space.

tips for re-organizing ■ ■ ■

Storage
■ Make the best use of your cupboard space. Use cupboards between knee height and eye-level for items that you use most often. Store items you use infrequently, such as an ice cream maker, above and below this line. Herb and spice jars arranged at eye-level, and cleaning materials in the cupboard under the sink, both work well.

■ Try to keep items close to where they're needed. The cupboard under the sink is ideal for cleaning equipment, for instance, but make sure you install childproof locks if you have small children.

■ Store as much as you can inside cupboards. Unless you have a good deal of room, items such as coffee jars and mugs should be kept on hooks or in cupboards so that you keep your worktops clear.

■ Keep boxes of things you seldom use, such as birthday candles and cake containers on top of high kitchen cupboards.

■ Install hooks and racks on the insides of cupboard doors. On a tall larder door, you might hang aprons, pans, and brushes, and other fairly flat, unbreakable items. Shallow plastic or metal racks hold objects in place as the door opens, and so are ideal for more fragile items.

■ Choose multi purpose small appliances such as a food processor, rather than a mixer and a blender, to free cupboard space.

■ Utilize corner cupboards by adding revolving storage racks.

■ Moving the freezer to a utility room or garage is better than working in a cramped kitchen.

■ In particularly small kitchens, you may need to store some items in other rooms. For instance, wine glasses might go into a living room cupboard, ready for party drinks.

■ It's unlikely that you'll be able to move appliances, but simply re-hanging a refrigerator door from the other side can improve congestion. This is a simple job: refer to the manufacturer's care leaflet.

■ You can buy new cupboard doors from kitchen companies, at a fraction of the cost of new units. You can only do this if the rest of the cupboard is in good condition. Removing old doors and installing new ones will take a weekend.

■ Spend half a day painting shabby wooden door fronts. White or pastel shades will make the kitchen appear larger.

■ It's an easy task to replace your cupboard door handles. It will take about two hours in a small kitchen and is a simple way to update your cupboards.

Improve the efficiency and appearence of your kitchen through simple re-organization, easy DIY changes, or carefully planning a completely new kitchen.

Food preparation

Re-organization

■ Don't clutter worktops, especially those near the sink that are most useful for food preparation. Most kitchens need all available surfaces to prepare a full meal. Cluttered worktops are unhygienic because you'll be tempted to clean them less often.

■ A wooden cutting board that fits over the sink creates extra worktop space.

■ Consider making space for two rubbish bins, so that you can use one for waste and one for recycling.

Cooking

Reorganization

■ If possible, locate your cooker hob, oven, and microwave away from the main traffic in the kitchen. This will reduce the risk of colliding with someone while carrying hot pots and pans. Also make sure there is plenty of space in the cooking area for setting down hot dishes.

■ A microwave does not get hot, so it's fine to locate it next to the refrigerator.

■ Better organization of the oven and cooker hob means using your cooker more efficiently. In a small kitchen, using the oven more and the rings less will reduce steam and smells.

Updating

■ Install a good fan for ventilation over your cooker hob. This will cut down on steam, smoke and grease, keeping your kitchen fresher and cleaner.

■ See page 118 for tips on choosing new appliances.

Living Space

Reorganization

■ Plan the seating to reflect how the kitchen is used.

■ Don't cramp the kitchen with a large table, if all you do is eat breakfast there. Install a wall-mounted, fold-down table instead, and store the large one in a convenient place, ready for entertaining. If your kitchen is really tiny, you could convert a shallow drawer into a pull-out table strip. Look for kits in kitchen shops.

■ Other space-saving devices include tables with gate legs which fold down on each side, to leave a narrow rectangle on top, and extending tables, which hide an extra leaf under the main table.

■ Stools will mean you can fit in extra people around the table, and they are easy to stack and store when not in use.

■ Removing the kitchen door may make more room, for example to fit in a table, but you won't be able to shut out noise from the rest of your home or contain cooking smells.

■ Locate the second living area as far away from the cooker as you can.

■ A low-hanging light over the table, which can be worked with a dimmer switch, will create the right atmosphere for relaxing and entertaining.

Updating

■ If you use your kitchen mainly for drinking coffee with friends and re-heating leftovers, then focus on soft furnishings, such as cushions and rugs, to make the room more comfortable.

■ Steam and grease from the cooking means furniture and furnishings need to be hardwearing. Use cotton-based, washable fabrics to cover cushions.

■ It will take under a day to paint the walls of a small kitchen. Go for a deep contrast to your existing appliances (see *Using colour*, page 80).

■ Change the flooring. Wood or laminate flooring is easy to clean, and will make a nice change. It will probably take one weekend to remove existing floor covering and prepare the surface, and a second weekend to fit the new flooring.

planning a new kitchen ■ ■ ■

Many kitchens are sold on the style of cupboard door fronts. While it's important that your kitchen looks visually stunning, and is made of durable materials, the key to success lies in:

■ Analyzing your kitchen lifestyle to give the best allocation of space for storage, food preparation, cooking, and living.

■ Planning appliances in conjunction with the sink and worktops.

■ In most kitchens, the ideal is to form a 'work triangle' – that is the trail your footsteps follow as you go from the refrigerator to the sink and cooking area. Poorly located appliances mean that you continually walk the length of the kitchen, and have nowhere to set down hot or cold dishes. Ideally the main 'traffic' through the kitchen should not cross the triangle.

■ Make sure you allow for plenty of electrical outlets for appliances.

■ List what you want to do in your kitchen. Serious cooking? Entertaining? The laundry? Store ten days worth of groceries? Use this as a checklist at every stage of your planning.

■ Write down things about your current kitchen that you hate and things that work well.

FITTED VERSUS FREESTANDING

Ten years ago, practically every new kitchen consisted of rows of cupboards and appliances fastened to the wall. Now, free-standing cupboards and appliances, or a mixture of the two, have become popular.

Fitted

✓ Makes full use of small kitchen
✓ Available in all price ranges
✓ Large choice of cupboards
✓ Easier to keep clean
✗ Professional fitting is expensive
✗ DIY installation is possible, but complex
✗ You can't take it with you when you move

Freestanding

✓ Can be bought in stages, as your budget allows
✓ Freedom to mix and match
✓ Can move furniture around to change its look
✓ Can take it with you when you move
✗ Less widely available, especially as a budget option
✗ More time-consuming to clean
✗ Tend to lose out on worktop space

Small appliances

■ ■ ■ **There is a wide range of electric worktop appliances available to save you time and effort in the kitchen. In fact, there is probably a gizmo for just about every kitchen task** ■ ■ ■

tips for buying small appliances ■ ■ ■

■ Be selective! You're unlikely to have room to house everything in the kitchen. Gadgets are fun, but none is absolutely essential.

■ Choose gadgets that will give you the most pleasure in the kitchen, and add the rest to Christmas and birthday lists.

■ If storage space is limited, choose multi-function appliances, such as food processors, that do more than one job.

■ If an appliance looks difficult to clean, don't buy it, because you'll probably find you don't use it very often.

■ Look beyond fancy features to what powers the unit. A strong motor will mean it lasts longer.

■ Most small appliances don't warrant repair costs. Accept that you're buying a relatively short-term product and set your budget accordingly.

Mixers or blenders

A worktop food processor does these jobs just as well, but if you can't afford one, choose between a hand-held mixer or blender. A hand-held mixer is a wand with a mini double blade at the tip. It is useful for liquidizing small quantities in a bowl or cup (which means less washing up), and is ideal for preparing purées such as infant food and making milkshakes. A blender has a large jug that makes it ideal for soup.

Use and maintenance

■ During food preparation, clean the blade on the hand-held mixer under a running tap, but always disconnect it from the power first.

■ Follow the manufacturer's instructions to dismantle and clean it. Some parts are probably dishwasher-safe.

Breadmakers

Turn out perfect loaves every time with a machine that tells you what ingredients to add and then does the rest of the work for you. If you buy a model with a delay timer, you can set it at night and wake up in the morning to the smell of fresh bread. Bear in mind, though, that this is a bulky machine, so make sure you have somewhere to store it.

Use and maintenance

■ Crust colour control lets you choose crispy or soft-topped bread.

■ Consider adding fruits and seeds to create more exotic loaves.

■ More expensive models can also make jam!

■ Wipe out with a dry cloth after each loaf is removed. Do not submerge breadmaker in water.

Can openers

An electric can opener takes the effort out of opening cans. They are especially useful for the elderly, whose wrist grip may be poor. But if you are short of space, you'll be better off with a manual can opener you can store in a drawer.

Use and maintenance

■ Worktop models often open metal bottle tops too.

■ From time to time, lubricate metal parts with a drop of lubricating oil.

Coffee makers

Basic coffee makers simply boil water, and then filter it slowly through ground coffee. More advanced models can also grind beans and have a built-in timer, ideal for making your morning coffee.

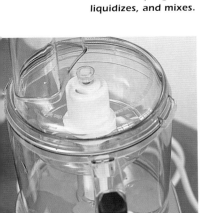

The food processor is an electronic extra-hand in the kitchen – it chops, grinds, liquidizes, and mixes.

Use and maintenance

■ A standard-sized model holds eight cups. Coffee that stands for hours can taste stale, so only buy a bigger size if you have a large household.

■ These machines need regular cleaning. Refer to manufacturer's instructions for details.

Deep fryers

The built-in thermostat that controls fat temperature makes an electric deep-fat fryer safer to use. Food also cooks far more quickly and comes out crisper. You can also cook battered prawns, Japanese vegetables, and apple fritters.

Use and maintenance

■ Models with washable or replaceable filters will absorb grease and cooking smells.

■ A cool-touch body is safer in homes with children.

■ A condenser collects steam released during cooking and stores the water in a drawer for easy disposal.

■ Lift out the basket to empty out fat completely (see *Waste disposal*, page 37). Clean the fryer with soapy water.

■ Some models have a dishwasher-safe lid and basket.

■ Change disposable filters frequently.

Espresso machines

This is a machine that pushes water through tightly packed ground coffee (caffé espresso means 'pressed coffee'). The most basic cooker hob espresso makers simply boil water and use the steam pressure to make the coffee, and the most sophisticated have a range of attachments to make coffee exactly the way you like it. Many models have powerful steam and hot water arms for frothing milk to make cappuccino and lattes.

Use and maintenance

■ More expensive machines let you adjust the strength of the coffee to taste.

■ Wipe down after each use, as coffee residue can become sticky and hard to remove.

■ Look out for models that have a removable drip tray and milk reservoir for easy clean-up.

Esspresso machine – great if you're a coffee lover.

Food processors

Their main function is to liquefy food or break it down into smaller pieces. They are the professional cook's first choice for chopping, slicing, grating, and puréeing safely, with accuracy and speed. They can also mix up cake mixtures, knead bread dough, whisk egg whites, and whip cream. Bear in mind that different models do this with varying success. If you're a basic cook, you're likely to be pleased with the results. However, an expert cook may want the superior results of specialized appliances – a mixer is better for whisking egg whites. From crushing ice to mixing a cake, the wide range of tasks this machine can tackle makes it the most important food preparation appliance you can have. Buy this before a mixer or blender as it can adequately do their jobs. Budget models, with less powerful motors, mean there are food processors to fit the smallest budget.

Use and maintenance

■ You'll need attachments for specific jobs, such as grating disks (in thin, medium, and thick sizes) for vegetables and cheese. Some will be included with

the processor, but you may want to buy extras. A juicing attachment, for instance, works like a standard juicer.

■ When processing hard-to-blend foods, stop every now and then so that the motor can cool in order to avoid overheating.

■ Place the appliance on a tea towel or a plastic mat, to prevent it from moving around the worktop.

■ Take the processor apart in order to clean it thoroughly in soapy water after each use.

■ Be very careful when handling the stainless steel, double-sided processor blade; it is razor-sharp.

■ To hand-wash the blade, hold the central plastic knob and use a handled scrubbing brush to clean the blades with hot, soapy water. Then leave to air-dry.

■ From time to time, apply vegetable oil sparingly around the rim of the lid, to ease its fit onto the bowl.

Hand-held whisk mixers

If you are a serious cook, you'll want one of these in addition to a food processor, because they incorporate air into a mixture to create lighter cakes and firmer egg whites.

Use and maintenance

■ There is hardly any cleaning involved here – just the two whisking blades which detach from the appliance – so mixers are perfect for quick jobs such as mixing icing or instant pudding.

■ To minimize splashing, start slowly and build to a higher speed. When finished, wait for the blades to stop spinning before lifting them clear of the mixture.

■ Using just one blade means you can whisk small quantities.

■ You can also whisk food in a saucepan on the cooker hob.

■ Hang beaters on a small hook to prevent them from becoming damaged in a drawer.

■ Place a drop of general-purpose oil into the holes where the beaters go to ease any stiffness.

Ice cream makers

These machines make ice cream and sorbet from natural ingredients, including fresh-picked fruits, so they can be as healthy (or as cream-laden) as you like. This fun appliance is great for summer treats.

Using a juicer, make tangy, fresh tomato juice or your favorite fruit cocktails.

Use and maintenance

■ Ensure before you buy that the bowl provided with the appliance will fit into your freezer.

■ Choose models with a special opening that allows nuts and chocolate chips to be added.

■ A see-through lid lets you check on progress.

■ The paddle and lid are generally dishwasher-safe.

Juicers

In basic models, unpeeled fruit and vegetables are grated into a strainer basket and juice is extracted from the pulp. High quality models have a separate juicing attachment that means you can also juice citrus fruits. Without this, the pith and skin on fruits such as oranges make the juice too bitter. When buying, go for the strongest motor you can afford.

Use and maintenance

■ Hard fruits like apples and pears are best, but you'll probably want to use whatever fruit and vegetables are cheap and plentiful. Juicers use a large amount of fruit and the cost of these raw ingredients may mean you won't use your juicer too often. To make two glasses of orange juice, you'll need up to ten small oranges!

■ Soft berries like raspberries and strawberries can clog the strainer unless followed up with harder fruits to push them through.

■ A juicer can be difficult to take apart to clean, but you will need to clean it thoroughly every time you use it because dried-on fruit is hard to remove.

Sandwich makers

■ Ideal for making quick, tasty snacks. Interchangeable plates on more expensive models mean you can toast a variety of breads.

Use and maintenance

■ Take care of the non-stick surface. Avoid scourers, and use a plastic spatula to lift stubborn sandwiches.

■ Don't soak a sandwich maker in water! You can detach the plates to clean on most models.

Stand mixers

The traditional choice of cake-bakers, these mixers use beaters in a revolving bowl to evenly combine ingredients. They can be bulky and heavy.

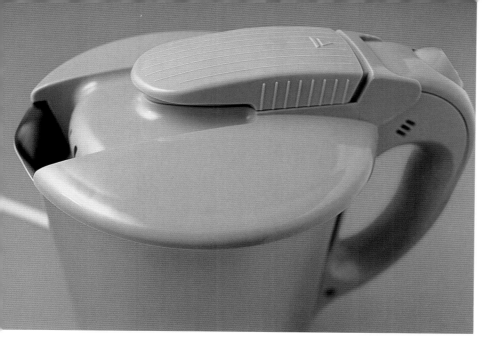

Use and maintenance

■ The right attachments can mince and shred.
■ An extra bowl can be useful for complex projects.
■ Flour that gets into the appliance via air vents can clog mixers, so wipe down the machine regularly.
■ Prolong motor life by choosing the correct speed for the job (refer to manufacturer's instructions).
■ If you have a large amount of butter to cream for a cake, divide it into small batches, then mix.

Toasters

This is probably one of the most widely used small appliances. Make this breakfast-essential more versatile by choosing a model with extra features.

Use and maintenance

■ Variable width slots let you toast muffins, rolls, and home-sliced bread.
■ A low setting means you can heat bagels.
■ A rack on top lets you warm croissants.
■ A frozen bread setting makes cooking time longer, so bread can be toasted straight from the freezer.
■ Toaster elements get hotter if they are in use for any length of time, so re-adjust the toasting controls as you prepare large batches.
■ Regularly remove the crumb tray for cleaning. Many crumb trays are now top-rack dishwasher-safe. If hand washing, dry very thoroughly. If the tray doesn't lift out, the only option is to invert the toaster over the dustbin.
■ Use a small, dry paintbrush to clean the toast carriage mechanism.
■ Never use a knife to lever out toast trapped

inside, as you could get an electric shock. Unplug the toaster. Use the high lift level, if your toaster has one. If not, wait until it is cool, then use plastic tongs or wooden skewers to remove it.

Kettles

The quickest kettles will boil in around two minutes. The choice between a traditional, rounded stainless steel kettle and a generally cheaper plastic jug depends on personal preference, although jugs are better for measuring and boiling small quantities. A 360-degree connector base means you can put the cordless kettle back on the base from any direction; this is a good idea if both left- and right-handed people use the kettle. Cordless kettles are safer, as you can lift the kettle easily from a fixed point with no electrical cord to consider. Concealed elements allow small quantities of water to be boiled and are more resistant to limescale build-up than exposed coils.

Use and maintenance

■ For hygiene and better taste, empty out old water, rather than just adding more to refill it.
■ To cut down on limescale build-up in the kettle, filter water first or add a filter tap to your sink.
■ Regularly remove build-up, especially in hard water areas. Use a brand-name product, especially for kettles. Boil a half-filled kettle. Turn it off and add build-up remover. Pour out when the fizzing stops, rinse, and boil the kettle twice before using.

Major appliances

■ ■ ■ **These are usually expensive, so it is worth taking your time to weigh the pros and cons when you are choosing major kitchen appliances** ■ ■ ■

tips for buying major appliances ■ ■ ■

Whatever the function of the appliance, certain key necessities remain the same. Bear these factors in mind when you go out to look at different models.

■ Check out power levels, plus operational features that are important to you, such as a self-cleaning oven, or auto-defrost on a refrigerator.

■ Take along measurements if the appliance has to go into a fixed space, such as a gap for a slot-in dishwasher. Also check with the sales associate on particular points, such as whether the oven will hold a large turkey.

■ Will it work the way you want to use it? Does the oven have a timer, if you are out at work all day? Look for extra features that make this particular model more suited to you.

■ Will it look good in your kitchen? Consider style, colour, and ease of cleaning.

■ Does the manufacturer have a good record on this type of product? Ask friends and look at buyers' guides in consumer magazines and on the internet.

■ Think about safety – if young children will be in your house, buy an oven with a heatproof door.

the microwave ■ ■ ■

There is no direct heat involved in microwave cooking. Waves of energy vibrate molecules, causing friction and heat. Food cooks extremely quickly and then goes on cooking for a short time after the microwave switches off. It is important to follow cooking times exactly, because microwaved food can overcook and spoil very quickly.

Tips for buying a microwave
There is a wide range of microwaves available, from the cheapest, basic microwave that is best for defrosting and heating foods, to more expensive microwaves with additional features such as grills or convection ovens.

■ The main drawback of the basic microwave is that it cannot brown or crisp-bake food. A microwave with a grill enables you to brown the surface of dishes.

■ A microwave combined with an electric convection oven is around twice the price of the cheapest microwave-only models. However, it will offer more versatility in the food items that you are able to cook.

■ The size of the turntable will limit the amount you can cook at one time, although you can stack food.

■ Microwaves make cooking simple with programmes such as auto-defrost and auto-cook, which calculate defrost and cooking times for particular foods.

Use and maintenance
■ The drawback of microwaving is that you can only cook a limited amount at a time, so it is best to keep meals simple.

■ Use microwave-safe cookware only. Never use metal dishes, or dishes with a metallic glaze – you'll destroy your microwave.

■ When heating food, microwave instructions give cooking and standing time. Never skip the standing time – the food will not be cooked.

■ Stir food halfway through cooking and before eating to eliminate any cold spots. If it is not piping hot, increase the cooking time.

ovens and cooker hobs ■ ■ ■

Ovens and cooker hobs are a vital part of any kitchen, so ask friends and family for recommendations, and research the market before you buy. One of the first decisions you must make when buying ovens and cooker hobs is what kind of fuel to use. Use our chart to compare the advantages and disadvantages of differing fuel types.

Use and maintenance

■ Keep cooker hobs very clean. Dirt will reduce the area of contact on the surface of a pot or pan and affect how efficiently foods are cooked.

■ Read the manufacturer's instructions for the correct warm-up time for ovens. Only start timing your food after this has elapsed.

FOCUS ON FUEL

Gas

Oven

✔ Moist heat stops food from drying out, especially roasts, and bakes great cakes.

✘ The oven may be hotter at the top, cooler at the bottom. If you choose a fan-assisted gas oven, this will ensure that the heat is evenly distributed.

✔ It is more energy efficient than electricity.

Grill

✔ It becomes hot in an instant.

✘ Heat may not be evenly distributed.

Cooker hob

✔ Good heat control means you can switch from hot to low-heat in an instant. You can stop milk from boiling over simply by flicking the control switch.

✘ You have to remove rings to clean.

✘ Some smell of gas is unavoidable.

Electric

Oven

✔ Even oven temperature ensures recipes cook as planned.

✔ Drier heat is good for bread and fruit cakes.

✘ It may be slow to heat up, especially older models.

✔ Fan-assisted electric ovens cook food faster than gas.

✘ It can dry out roast meats.

Grill

✘ It is slow to heat.

✔ You can use half the grill to save energy.

✘ It is less energy efficient than gas.

Cooker hob

✘ It is slow to heat, although halogen models (reflectors that glow when switched on) are available.

✘ It is very slow to cool, so you can't switch from boil to simmer quickly; if a pan is about to boil over, you have to remove it from the heat.

✔ No smell comes from an electric oven.

Cast iron cooker (Aga)

Oven

✔ Food retains moisture.

✔ No warm-up time (the oven is always on).

✔ Totally self-cleaning.

✔ You can cook a large turkey, baked potatoes, and a dessert at the same time.

✘ You can't accurately predict oven temperature.

✘ You can only change temperature by placing food at different positions.

✘ It can make a room feel very hot in summer.

Grill

✘ It does not have a grill. You can, however, make toast on the cooker hob.

Cooker hob

✔ It provides instant heat on two large, direct-contact hot plates.

✔ Its large surface area means you can cook with six saucepans at a time.

✘ It has only two options – boil or simmer.

refrigerators and freezers ▪ ▪ ▪

Essentially, these are just temperature-controlled kitchen cupboards. They work by using a refrigerant gas to cool the air as it is passed along a sealed pipe system inside the refrigerator and freezer.

Tips for buying refrigerators or freezers

▪ Side-by-side models mean that fresh and frozen foods you use most often can be kept at eye-level.

▪ Vertical freezer – refrigerator combinations make full use of a narrow space. Buy a model that reflects how you shop. If you eat mostly frozen meals, you'll want a larger freezer and a smaller refrigerator.

▪ Models in which the freezer is at the bottom cost a little more, but it is probably worth paying the price. Most people use the refrigerator more, you will have to bend down less if it is on top.

▪ Chest freezers, with a lidded top, are ideal if you buy in bulk, or want a second freezer for garden produce. They cost less to run than upright ones.

▪ Extras in the refrigerator, such as racks for eggs and drink dispensers, are available if you want them, although they may add to the price.

▪ The amount of food you can store in the refrigerator is probably the most important factor. So find out how much cubic storage it offers, not the dimensions of the cupboard.

▪ When you are checking how it will fit in your kitchen, remember to make allowance for space above the appliance for ventilation.

Use and maintenance

■ If the refrigerator is not going to be used for any length of time, switch it off, clean the inside thoroughly, and leave the door open to allow air circulation and prevent mould and smells.

■ In the event of power failure, providing that the door is kept closed, the food in your freezer should stay frozen to a safe temperature for up to twelve hours. Any items that have de-frosted during such an incident should be thrown away. If in doubt, throw it out. (See page 134 on *Storing food.*)

FREEZER TEMPERATURE

■ Refrigerator should be kept at 5°C (40°F) or less.
■ Freezer temperature should be -18°C (0°F).
■ When fast-freezing, the temperature should drop to -26°C (-12°F).

dishwashers ■ ■ ■

Dishwashers save time and effort, and clean dishes more hygienically than hand washing does. Stick to full loads as they use less water than hand washing. The arguments for dishwashers quickly stack up.

Tips for buying dishwashers

■ Full-sized models hold up to twelve place settings; smaller models hold up to eight; and compact models including those that sit on counters hold four to five place settings.

■ Check noise levels if you expect to be in the kitchen while the dishwasher is running.

■ Dishwashers break down more frequently than almost any other appliance, so it's probably worth getting a service guarantee.

■ Dishwashers need detergent in every wash, and possibly a rinse aid. These combine to make dishwashing more expensive than washing dishes by hand. However, the most energy-efficient models can wash 120 pieces of tableware in just two bowls full of water, which takes some beating!

■ To get maximum energy savings, you'll need to operate the dishwasher only when full. Choose a dishwasher small enough for your everyday needs, and do more wash cycles when entertaining.

Use and maintenance

■ Always follow manufacturer's recommendations about what is dishwasher safe.

■ Clean the filter after each wash (or thoroughly scrape plates before loading). Food debris and grease that collect in the filter and aren't removed may re-coat the next load.

■ Check indicators on the machine regularly to raise salt and rinse-aid levels. You will get less effective cleaning when these are low.

■ Always refer to manufacturers' loading instructions. Incorrectly stacked items may not be cleaned properly.

DO NOT USE IN THE DISHWASHER

■ Lead crystal
■ Antique or hand-painted china
■ Wooden spoons and bowls, or containers made of thin plastic (they may warp)
■ Uncoated, cast-iron pans
■ Silver and stainless steel cutlery at the same time

FOOD MATTERS

Tools and utensils

■ ■ ■A surprising number of tools are needed to prepare and cook everyday food. Don't be discouraged by the long list; practically all the tools a basic kitchen needs are inexpensive and widely available ■ ■ ■

must haves ■ ■ ■

Can opener
Many have a magnet to hold the lid firmly in place, which makes it safer to use. Electric can openers are safer still (see page 118).

Cutting board
Use wooden or plastic boards – both are similarly hygenic. Use separate boards for raw meats and fish and clean thoroughly after each use.

Colander
Made of metal, enamel, or rigid plastic a colander is great for washing vegetables like spinach and fruits, as well as straining cooked potatoes, rice, and vegetables after cooking.

Corkscrew and bottle opener
Everyone will recommend a different type, but look around for one that is easy to use and suits your budget. They often have a bottle opener attached.

Dry and liquid measures
See *Conversion tables*, page 186.

Grater
Grates foods such as cheese and carrots. Look for one with an edge for slicing semi-soft foods.

Kitchen scissors
Use these to open packets and cut through bone.

Knives
See page 128.

Roasting pan and rack

These are probably supplied with your oven, but you may want to upgrade to a deeper, non-stick pan if you often roast meat. A useful size is a 30cm by 20cm (12in by 8in) pan, about 5cm (2in) deep.

Spatula

A wide, wedge-shaped utensil to lift fish, slices of pizza, and pies from dish to plate.

Vegetable peeler

Various designs are available so shop around – you're sure to find one to suit you.

Salad servers

Can be used to serve just about anything at the table.

Pots and pans

See page 129.

other useful items ▪ ▪ ▪

Baking set

A starter set generally includes a flat baking sheet, a muffin tray and cake tins, that can be used for flans and pies as well. Non-stick is easier to clean.

Measuring jug

Toughened glass or plastic for measuring liquids, it is sold in a variety of sizes.

Pastry brush

This is used for greasing tins before baking, glazing pies, and for basting meat and vegetable dishes.

Mixing bowls

These are durable bowls in glass or plastic for mixing wet and dry ingredients and are often sold in sets, but if you want just one, buy a 900ml (1 pint 12fl oz) size. You can get by using other cookware.

Pestle and mortar

Useful to grind spices. You can get by with grating, crushing with a heavy spoon, or using a food processor or electric grinder or blender.

Pie dish

For this you can use a deep ovenproof dinner plate instead, or upturned casserole lid with side handles.

Potato masher

Can also be used to mash carrots, and cooked fruits, such as apples. A strong fork works almost as well. Don't be tempted to put potatoes into a food processor, as they will turn gluey.

Rolling pin

For rolling out pastry or pizza from scratch. If you're not going to be doing this often, you can use a straight glass bottle instead.

Scales

Flat, digital scales will weigh quantities as low as 5g (⅛oz); with a plastic bowl set on top, they can cope with several kilos (pounds).

Slotted spoon

This is for lifting food from its juices. Alternatively, use your colander and strain food over a pan.

Soup ladle

This can also be used to serve punch at parties.

Whisks

These incorporate air into sauces, eggs for omelettes, and fluffs up cream and packet mousses. If necessary, you can do this using a fork.

Cook's fork

Use this to hold cooked meat while carving. You can get by with a table fork instead.

Salt and pepper mill

Enhance food with freshly ground salt crystals and peppercorns.

Wooden spoons

Cheap and handy for beating, mixing, and stirring, these come in a variety of shapes and sizes.

cutting and chopping ■ ■ ■

There are more than twenty specialized kitchen knives designed for every task – from preparing a grapefruit to filleting fish. The most important thing is to find a knife, or knives, that you feel comfortable handling. Do not feel pressured into having a full knife rack. There is no need for this in a typical domestic kitchen.

Knife essentials

Large cook's knife
A rigid, triangular blade 15cm to 20cm (6in to 8in) long with a sharp point and a gently curved edge. This knife can tackle most jobs. The rounded edge means you can rock the knife to finely dice food.

Small cook's knife
This blade, around 7.5 to 10cm (3in to 4in) long, is good for chopping and paring fruit.

A bread knife
A large, serrated blade with a flat end will slice the crust, but not squash the soft bread underneath.

Vegetable knife
A long, narrow blade with a finely serrated edge, will cut through vegetables without bruising.

Carving knife and fork
This blade, at least 25cm (10in) long, is used for carving hot meats.

Boning knife
This strong knife with a razor-sharp point removes bones from raw meat and poultry.

Meat cleaver
A large, heavy rectangular blade. Steaks and other meat joints may be cut with this.

Knife safety tips
■ A sharper knife is safer than a blunt one because it is less likely to slip.
■ The simplest way to sharpen a knife is to store it in a knife block that has a self-sharpening slot.
■ Serrated knives need to be professionally sharpened every few years.
■ Never keep specialized knives in the cutlery drawer. As well as being a hazard, they'll blunt each other. Store them on a rack or in a knife block.
■ Wash knives immediately after cutting fruit because the acid could cause corrosion.

Small cook's knife   Bread knife

Large cook's knife   Cleaver

pots and pans ▪ ▪ ▪

Tips for buying pots and pans

▪ You'll need several different sizes of saucepans. The basics would be a small pan 15cm (6in) diameter, a deeper pan 20cm (8in) diameter, plus a milk pan with a pouring spout 18cm (7in) diameter.

▪ Non-stick pans are much easier to clean, and you'll use less oil for frying, but pans with no coating heat up more quickly.

▪ Strainer lids save washing time because drained food does not need to be transferred to another container (such as a colander or sieve).

▪ Most pans need sealing with oil before first use, and from time to time after that.

▪ You will need to use non-stick utensils with non-stick pans to avoid scratching the surface.

▪ A wok, which is a deep, wide pan with slanting sides, is the best for stir-frying.

The material that pots and pans are made of will affect how they cook food, and how long they will last. Four materials that most are made from are listed, with the cheapest and least hardwearing pans first.

Stainless steel

Inexpensive.
Hardwearing, but may get dented in time.
Fine on all stove tops.

✓ Doesn't scratch if scoured.

✗ These are not fast pans to heat up, but many stainless steel pans have a layer of copper or aluminum in the base to improve this.

Special care: Wash promptly after cooking salty foods to avoid surface marks.

Aluminium

Medium-priced.
Strong and hardwearing: should last at least ten years. Be aware, however that research has linked aluminium pans with Alzheimer's disease.
Can be used on all cooker hob surfaces.

✓ Ideal starter pan set, especially when covered with effective non-stick coating.

✗ Non-stick pans can be heavy.

✗ Uncoated pans can be stained by fruit.

Special care: Dry promptly to prevent watermarks.

Cast iron

Expensive.
Very hardwearing.
Can only be used on ceramic and halogen cooker hobs if the pan bottom has an enamel coating.

✓ The thick base will help prevent food from burning, so cast iron is the top choice for frying pans, because it distributes heat evenly and cools slowly.

✗ Slow to heat, so not good for quick sauces.

Special care: Follow manufacturer's instructions on preparing pans before you use them for the first time.

Copper

Expensive but looks professional and stylish.
Exceptionally hardwearing. Good copper pans will last a lifetime.
Works best on electric cooker hobs.

✓ Conducts heat perfectly. Milk heats up in a copper pan faster than in any other.

✗ Can't be used to boil sugar or make jam because pans can't withstand the high temperatures needed.

Special care: Pans are lined with stainless steel (this is the best kind) or tin for easy cleaning. Keeping the outside spotless may be hard work. To clean them, dip half a lemon in salt then rub it over the pan. Dry and polish.

Tableware

■ ■ ■ **There is a fabulous choice of beautiful china, cutlery, and glassware in stores. With such a huge range of designs available, you can choose something that is practical and yet hardwearing for everyday use, and attractive enough for formal dining ■ ■ ■**

crockery ■ ■ ■

Everyday china is often sold in complete sets. A 16-piece set will contain plates, side plates, bowls, and cups and saucers for four. To entertain formally, you'll probably want to buy more, eight is a good number to keep. Items may be sold individually, or per place setting.

WHAT YOU NEED

A basic place setting:
Dinner plate
Side plate
Bowl
Cup and saucer

For entertaining, you may also want:
Soup bowls
A large platter for fish or meat
Vegetable serving dishes with lids
Gravy boat
Cream jug

Choosing crockery
Although popularly called china, crockery is made from a variety of materials. Your budget will be a big factor in your choice, but the following information should help you weigh up the options.

Earthenware
Made from clay, which is dried, fired at a high temperature, and then glazed. It may chip and smash easily, but it is inexpensive to replace, and is dishwasher-proof.

Bone china
Made from china stone, this is china clay combined with up to 50 percent animal bone ash for added strength. It is fired at extremely high temperatures and has a beautiful translucent appearance. Hardwearing and resistant to chips and breaking, it will crack if dropped. It is expensive, so many people choose to save it for dining. Although it is dishwasher-proof, patterns on bone china will probably fade with repeated washing. Always check the manufacturer's instructions.

Stoneware
A mix of china clay, stone and silica sand, it is hardwearing and chip-resistant. Used in quality everyday plates, most fine china products are dishwasher-proof.

Porcelain
Made from china stone and clay, it is fairly hardwearing, but prone to chip. It is sometimes dishwasher-proof, but check this before buying.

cutlery ■ ■ ■

Cutlery comes in a range of fabulous designs, made from beautiful materials such as stainless steel and silver. However, choose cutlery that feels comfortable in your hands. Remember too, that you may love the design of a knife or spoon but it may not be practical for everyday use.

■ Store silver cutlery in a chest, so that sharp prongs and edges can't cause scratches.
■ Always hand-wash items with wooden handles.
■ Never leave stainless steel or silver in contact with any acidic products such as vinegar or lemon juice.

WHAT YOU NEED

A basic place setting:
Table knife
Table fork
Spoon
Teaspoon

To entertain formally, you may also want:
Fish knife and fork
Soup spoon
A butter knife
Cake fork
Carving knife and fork See page 128)
A minimum of two serving spoons

Tips for buying china

■ If you have a dishwasher, check that items are marked 'dishwasher safe'.
■ Before you buy, check that the pattern will not be discontinued. Reputable firms guarantee that a design will be produced for between two to ten years, leaving you time to add pieces.
■ China-matching companies will track down discontinued designs. China manufacturers will be able to suggest companies that are selling their old stock.
■ Ensure that dinner plates will fit inside kitchen cupboards. The largest plates may be too wide.
■ Most plates are fine in a warm oven, but you need special 'oven-to-tableware' plates for cooking.

Caring for china

■ A final rinse in a weak solution of water and vinegar will restore shine to china plates.
■ Load dishwasher-safe china so the pieces are not touching, or they could chip.
■ Never put metal-rimmed plates in the microwave.
■ The underside of many plates is quite rough, so put a paper napkin between each special plate when you put them back in the cupboard.

Glassware

■ ■ ■ **Glassware comes in many different shapes and sizes, often designed to make a particular drink taste better. But don't think that you have to have them all** ■ ■ ■

WHAT YOU NEED	
If you have the cupboard space, there is glassware designed for pretty much every drink.	
Red wine, large	Stemmed glass with plenty of room to allow the wine to breathe.
White wine, small	Stemmed glass means that the wine stays chilled longer.
Champagne flute	Narrow glasses are thought to keep the champagne bubbly for longer.
Brandy	The wide bottom and narrow top allows the brandy to be swirled around to oxygenate it.
Liqueur, small	Stemmed glass or mini-tumbler fits neatly beside your coffee cup.
Sherry or port	Smaller than wine glass because the measures are usually smaller.
Spirits	Tumbler with plenty of room to add mixers and ice.
Shots	Tiny tumbler to hold a double measure of spirits only.
Beer	Tall, straight-sided glass.
Soft drinks	Tall tumbler so you can add plenty of ice.

Three glassware essentials

If you only have limited storage space, these are the glasses you will probably find most useful.

■ Long-stemmed glasses for wine, champagne, brandy, or liqueur.
■ Tall tumblers for soft drinks with plenty of ice, beer, or fruit juice mixes.
■ Wide, short tumblers for spirits and mixer drinks.

Glassware terms

Recycled glass
Rougher, thicker glass that is often coloured.

Cut glass
Cut glass refers to the patterns set into the glass.

Crystal
Crystal is hand-blown glass that contains sand and lead that make the glass sparkle.

Lead crystal
Lead crystal is top-of-the-range glass, and contains up to 24 percent lead. Quality lead crystal can be more than ten times the cost of ordinary clear glass.

Tips for buying and caring for glassware

■ A small selection of glasses in different styles is more useful than a large set all the same.

■ Heavy, wide-based glasses are less likely to be knocked over.

■ Long-stemmed glasses can be difficult to stack safely in a dishwasher.

■ Crystal glasses should be washed by hand, because they will lose their sparkle in a dishwasher.

■ Rinse glasses very thoroughly; a trace of detergent will make champagne go flat.

■ It's safer not to store a glass standing on its rim because that is the most fragile part of it.

■ A glass decanter allows red wines and spirits to develop their bouquet.

Storing food

■ ■ ■ **Few of us have the time or dedication to shop daily for groceries. That means we need plenty of safe and hygienic storage space for food** ■ ■ ■

Canned foods

Canned foods have been treated at high temperatures to become long-lasting. Cans should be kept in a cool, dark and well-ventilated cupboard. Once opened, the contents should be transferred to a container with a lid and stored in the refrigerator for no more than 48 hours.

Bottled food

Bottled food is either heat-treated, like pasta sauces and puréed baby food, or uses preservatives (including natural ones like vinegar and sugar).

Dried food

Unopened, and kept in a cool, dry cupboard, dried foods – like uncooked rice, pasta, and cereals – have a storage life of one to two years. Once opened, they need to be kept in airtight packaging, sealed with clips. Some dried foods should be eaten within four weeks, for full freshness and flavour, such as breakfast cereals. Others, like pasta, have a very long shelf life.

Vacuum-packed

Vacuum-packed means that all the air is sucked from the packaging. This stops food inside it from deteriorating and 'locks in' flavour more effectively than standard packaging. Storage times (and where they are best stored) vary. Vacuum-packed hot dogs, for instance, need refrigeration while prunes do not. Once a package that requires refrigeration is opened, treat its contents as fresh food and store as such.

Semi-perishable fresh produce

Semi-perishable fresh produce such as bread, potatoes, and some fruit and vegetables can be stored for a limited time in cool, dry conditions. Storage requirements vary, see *Tips for storing food in the refrigerator*, page 135. It is generally easy to see when these foods have passed their best.

Perishable foods

Perishable foods, such as dairy, meat, salads, and eggs, should be stored in a refrigerator a 5°C (40°F) or less. Some fruit and vegetables can also benefit from storage in a refrigerator, see page 135.

Frozen foods

Frozen foods, or fresh foods you choose to freeze yourself, should be stored in a freezer at -18°C (0°F) or less. Over time, some frozen foods may lose taste and texture. See *Home freezing guide*, page 136.

*Always read the storage 'best before' date and storage directions on all your food products.

FOOD MATTERS

refrigerators ■ ■ ■

Stocking your refrigerator shelves

■ Store dairy produce (butter, cheese, and yoghurts), eggs, salad dressings, and sauces on top shelves. Use middle shelves for cooked meats, convenience foods, sausages, cream, and fish.

■ Store salads in the salad drawer to retain crispness.

■ Store raw meat on the bottom shelf. It is essential to separate raw and cooked meat. If you put foods like raw meats at the bottom of the refrigerator they cannot drip onto other foods and contaminate them with harmful bacteria, which may be present especially in raw minced beef and poultry. (These bacteria are killed by thorough cooking at correct temperatures.)

■ The doors are the least cool places, so use them to store things like beer, which is in the refrigerator because you prefer it cold, not because it needs to be refrigerated.

■ Air needs to circulate freely around food, in order to cool it effectively, so never overstock your refrigerator.

STORAGE TIMES IN A REFRIGERATOR

This chart gives you an idea of how long items should be stored in a refrigerator assuming food is perfectly fresh when you put it in there. Always refer to 'eat by' and 'use by' dates on packaged foods. With meat and fish, a good general rule is: if in doubt, throw it out.

Fish	24 hours
Shellfish	24 hours
Raw minced meat	24 hours
Raw chicken or turkey	2 days
Sausage	2 days
Sliced meats	2 days
Cooked meats	2 days
Chops, pork or lamb	3 days
Steaks, beef	3 to 5 days
Milk	4 to 5 days
Bacon	7 days
Hard cheese	7 to 10 days
Cream cheese	10 days

Storing food in the refrigerator

■ Apples (and oranges and pears) will stay fresh longer in the salad compartment of a refrigerator. Remove any packaging and keep a small stock of fruit in the fruit bowl, and then re-stock from the refrigerator.

■ Avocados should be left to ripen for one to two days at room temperature or a week in the refrigerator. They can then be stored for three to four days on a lower refrigerator shelf.

■ Bagels, if unopened, should be kept in a refrigerator. Once opened, store as fresh bread.

■ Bananas will discolour in temperatures below 10°C (50°F), so don't store them in the refrigerator. They also emit a gas which makes other fruits ripen very fast. To avoid this, use a banana tree to raise bananas above the rest of the bowl.

■ Bread without crisp crusts may be stored in a refrigerator. However, it goes stale just as quickly even though the tell-tale mould signs don't appear.

■ Eggs stored in the refrigerator with pointed end downward means yolks are less likely to break when egg is cracked. Store cooked eggs in sealed containers as their smell will taint other foods.

■ Green vegetables, like cabbage and spinach, should be kept in a salad crisper.

■ Fresh herbs, such as rosemary, chives, and sage, can be kept in individual plastic boxes or lidded glass jars in the refrigerator for one to two days.

■ Melon loses flavour in a refrigerator. Ideally, it should be stored at room temperature and then chilled before serving.

■ Mushrooms keep best in a paper bag at the bottom of the refrigerator.

■ Organic foods do not contain synthetic preservatives, so it is important to follow storage instructions.

■ Preserves with reduced sugar content need to be stored in the refrigerator (sugar is a preservative).

■ Raw meat and poultry should be wrapped in a plastic bag. Remove the giblets from poultry and store them separately.

■ Tomatoes do best stored at room temperature until ripe, then in a salad crisper. If they are kept too cold, their centres will spoil.

freezers ▪ ▪ ▪

Tips for freezing food

▪ Meats (raw and cooked), dishes you have prepared, and bread can all be frozen without extra preparation. Simply wrap them securely in aluminium foil or freezer bags, making sure to remove as much air from the packaging as you can, as oxygen destroys the vitamin content and colour of food.

▪ Always label and date food.

▪ To freeze berries, spread on baking trays lined with wax paper. When frozen, pack them in bags.

▪ To freeze a whole fish, either freeze it in a container of water or freeze it on a freezer-proof tray, then dip it in water to provide extra insulation from air and put it back in the freezer.

▪ Liquids expand up to 10 percent when frozen, so leave a space at the top of any containers of liquid that you put in the freezer.

▪ Never re-freeze foods that have thawed.

▪ If you don't have an auto de-frost, de-frost your freezer regularly. Ice build-up will decrease efficiency.

HOME FREEZING GUIDE

This chart gives an idea of storage times for frozen foods. Foods you freeze at home generally keep for less time than those bought already frozen. This is because the commercial freezing process is far quicker and more effective. Things that do not freeze well include cream, cottage cheese, pies with aspic inside, jelly, and potatoes.

Food	Storage time	De-frosting time in a refrigerator
Oily fish	Up to 2 months	Can be cooked frozen
Salmon	Up to 3 months	Approximately 24 hours for whole fish
White fish	Up to 3 months	Can be cooked frozen
Frozen vegetables	Approx 6 months	Can be cooked frozen
Beef steak	Up to 6 months	Approximately 2–4 hours
Minced meat	Up to 6 months	Approximately 1–2 hours
Duck	Up to 6 months	Approximately 24 hours
Chicken pieces	Up to 6 months	Approximately 4–6 hours
Pork	Up to 6 months	Approximately 6 hours per 450g (1lb)
Whole chickens	Up to 6 months	Approximately 24 hours
Whole turkey	Up to 6 months	Approximately 2–3 days
Lamb	Up to 12 months	Approximately 6 hours per 450g (1lb)
Beef	Up to 12 months	Approximately 6 hours per 450g (1lb)

It is generally safer to de-frost food either in a microwave or in the refrigerator, not at room temperature.
See Cooking terms and techniques, *page 144, for tips on how to prepare vegetables for the freezer.*

stocking your larder ▪▪▪

A well-stocked larder is the secret of a smooth-running kitchen. As well as being able to cook meals for unexpected guests, with the basic ingredients on hand, you'll be able to concentrate on creating varied, nourishing meals. Apart from larder essentials, such as breakfast cereals, biscuits, fruit juice concentrates, and instant hot drinks, there are a number of items it is very useful to have as stand-bys for pepping up recipes and adding quick flavour to dishes. The best thing to do is experiment to find out which ones you find most useful.

Tips for good larder stand-bys

■ *Dried pasta,* such as lasagna, spaghetti, and penne, will keep well even once opened, so it's worth building up a stock of different types.

■ *Rice, noodles, and couscous* are vital for both last-minute meals and bulking-out meals for the hungry.

■ *Dried beans and peas:* all kinds – from kidney beans and chickpeas beans to garden peas – are great for adding to soups and casseroles and beans are an excellent source of protein.

■ *Dried fruits* like apricots and raisins are useful for baking, can be added to breakfast cereals, and are a good alternative to sweets.

■ *Plain and self-raising flour* can go stale within three months once opened, so don't overstock this. If you only have larder space for plain flour, you can add baking powder for recipes that need self-raising flour. Cornflour is useful for sauces.

■ *Baking powder, baking soda,* and *dried yeast* are useful cooking ingredients. Bicarbonate of soda also has cleaning uses (see page 24).

■ *Dried herbs,* such as parsley, basil, and rosemary, can lift everyday meals such as casseroles and roasts. Dried herbs are stronger than fresh ones so just one or two teaspoons will be plenty.

■ *Ketchup, soy sauce, mustard,* and *pesto* can be used to add zest to barbecue marinades and cooking sauces.

■ *Dried spices,* such as cinnamon, red pepper, cloves, and peppercorns, are another easy way to add flavour to dishes.

■ *Canned tomatoes* are great for bulking-out more expensive ingredients like meat and for using in pasta dishes, soups, and casseroles. Sieve them to make a delicious base for pizza toppings.

■ *Canned tuna* is a perfect stand-by for snacks, pizza toppings, quick fish-cakes, and salads.

■ *Syrup, honey,* and *molasses* means you'll have something to add to a variety of dishes, from toppings for pancakes to marinades for barbecued food.

■ *Jam and preserves* can be used for quick cobblers and pies. Apricot jam makes a tasty glaze for oven-baked ham.

■ There is a wide range of *vinegars* and *oils* available. Red and white wine vinegar are useful for salad dressings and for mixing marinades. Extra virgin olive oil is a healthier choice than standard vegetable oil, and is ideal for frying, using on salads, and as a recipe ingredient for cakes and desserts.

■ *Stock cubes* and *vegetable paste* are ideal for adding flavour to soups, casseroles, and sauces.

■ *Nuts,* especially walnuts and almonds – ground and whole – make a great high-protein snack and can also be used in cakes and salads. For convenience, you might want to store ready-shelled nuts that are sold in vacuum packs.

Larder checkpoints

The best place for a larder is against an outside wall, because this will provide cool, dry conditions. The ideal temperature is 10°C (50°F).

■ **Never store food next to an oven.**

■ **Never use food from cans that are leaking, bulging, or badly dented.**

■ **Ensure adequate ventilation. A floor-to-ceiling larder needs a vent.**

■ **Group similar foods together so you can find them quickly.**

■ **Remember that your freezer and refrigerator are extensions of your larder. So include room for larder essentials such as ready-made pastry and homemade stocks.**

■ **Take dried foods out of their opened packages and then seal them in airtight jars and tins. See Recycling, page 39, for ideas. Transfer any food you don't use from a can to an airtight storage container, then store in the refrigerator.**

Entertaining

■ ■ ■ **Whether you are planning a formal dinner, buffet party, or barbecue, you need to plan ahead, create the right atmosphere, and provide plenty of food and drink for your guests** ■ ■ ■

tips for party planning ■ ■ ■

■ Give clear invitations. A start and finish time for parties ensures that your guests know what to expect.

■ Sending invitations by mail or e-mail gives you the chance to include directions to your home and takes up less time than talking to each person individually.

■ If you ask your guests to let you know if they can come, you then have time to invite others if some guests can't make it. Alternatively, ask for apologies only.

■ Schedule large parties for the weekend. Typically, a brunch will start by 11am, lunch by 1pm, and events without a meal, between 2 and 5pm. Cocktail parties usually run from 6 to 8pm (it is important to establish an ending time as well). Cocktails and dinner start around 7pm, and there is no need for a finish time.

■ Don't over-invite. Decide on the number of people that you can comfortably cope with, and then put names to that number. If you can't fit everyone in, consider two smaller occasions.

■ Decide on a smoking policy. If you're happy for your guests to smoke, put out ashtrays. If you would prefer guests to smoke outdoors, designate a space.

Set the table with cutlery, china, condiments, glasses, napkins, candles, and flowers in plenty of time, before your guests arrive.

formal dinner party ■ ■ ■

If you plan your dinner party carefully, you'll enjoy it much more. You want to enjoy as much time as you can sitting with your guests, and not spend the evening rushing to and from the kitchen.

■ Decide on the main course, then plan a starter and dessert to complement it.

■ Check your guests' dietary requirements and dislikes. If your guests are vegetarian or vegan, you may find you can make a modified version of the main dish. Or you can serve food everyone will eat, such as non-egg pasta, or couscous. Alternatively, you could serve completely different main dishes.

■ Avoid dishes that need hands-on attention, like a stir-fry. Casseroles let you relax with your guests, not work over a stove.

■ It is a good idea to have at least one course that can be served cold and can be prepared in advance.

Arrange the cutlery from the outside in the order that you will serve courses. This is a standard layout. Include a fish knife and fork if necessary.

When you get to the appropriate stage in the meal, just carry in serving dishes so that you serve food to your guests at the table.

■ Time the meal to be ready 30 minutes after the the guests arrive. Schedule your cooking to this, but remember that this will mean the main course needs to be ready around 50 minutes after the event starts (later still if you have a starter and soup).

■ Don't wait for late guests. It is far better for everyone else to enjoy a meal at its best, and let latecomers simply join in when they arrive.

Emergency

If a part of your cooking goes drastically wrong, stay calm.

If it is the appetiser or dessert that's gone wrong, leave out the course or substitute it with ready-made soup or ice cream. If you have some cheese or dips in the refrigerator, serve these with some freshly cut bread and tortilla chips. If it is the main course, adapt what was to have been the starter with a salad (see Good larder stand-bys, page 137), microwaved baked potatoes, or cook pasta in ten minutes, then serve it with olive oil or a tin of tomatoes from your larder, plus whatever herbs you have in the kitchen and parmesan cheese. If all else fails, call for a home-delivered pizza!

Formal dinner party tips

■ If you don't have a dining room, you could convert the living room. Remove sofas and large chairs (or move them to the side) and disguise a utility table with an attractive cloth. Make sure that you don't cram too many guests around your table. A round table with a 90cm (3ft) diameter seats six people, a 135cm (4½ft) table seats eight, and a 150cm (5ft) table seats ten. A rectangular table 180cm by 90cm (6ft by 3ft) seats six. As a general rule, each guest needs 75cm (30in) of elbow room.

■ You may find it easier to keep the main course and plates on a side table, in the room where you'll eat.

buffet parties ▪▪▪

Buffet parties are ideal for more informal occasions. You can set all the dishes out on a large table and leave guests to help themselves. You may find it easier to use several rooms to serve the food, for example main course in one, dessert in another, if space is limited. Set out a long table with the plates, knives, and forks at one end, and the dishes arranged along it to lessen lines and crowding. A running buffet, where guests take finger food directly from dishes that you offer, requires the least amount of space. You don't need a table set with food, just plenty of refrigerator and storage space in the kitchen.

Buffet party tips
▪ Assign tasks to others if possible; make one person responsible for opening the door and taking coats, while someone else serves drinks.
▪ Paper plates and disposable spoons, knives, and forks, mean less dishwashing.
▪ If you serve food that requires a knife and fork, rather than fork or finger food, you will need to provide seating or make sure your guests won't mind sitting on the floor.
▪ Warn your guests beforehand whether the buffet is a meal or just nibbles.
▪ Plan ahead where you want to serve drinks. In the kitchen, glasses can be rinsed under the tap. Drinks in the hall might ease congestion. Drinks in the living room is convenient, but takes up space.
▪ Decide whether you want to give your guests unlimited access to drinks, or put someone in charge of preparing them.

Creating a party atmosphere
▪ Your guests are much more likely to mingle and dance if you take out the chairs!
▪ Create a mood with lighting. Use candles or dim the lights.
▪ If you have a lot of guests who don't know each other, plan games like charades or play card games to break the ice.
▪ Plan what music you are going to play – perhaps soft background music to begin with and dance music for later on.
▪ Think about what your guests have in common, so that you can make personal introductions.

Barbecues
A barbecue is essentially a buffet party outdoors, so many of the same rules apply. One of the most important things to remember is to light the barbecue early. Charcoal barbecues can take more than an hour to reach cooking temperature.

Barbecue safety
▪ Never leave a barbecue unattended when children are around.
▪ Ideally, you should locate the barbecue a decent distance, and down wind, from your guests.
▪ Glass, china, and outdoors don't mix. Use paper cups, plates, and plastic cutlery.
▪ Undercooked meat is a barbecue hazard. Pierce meats with a sharp knife to check that juices run clear, and burgers must contain no pink meat. It can be easier to partially cook food on an indoor grill, immediately before bringing outside to the barbecue.
▪ The barbecue may take an hour to cool, so make sure it is positioned where no one will get burned.

Barbecue tips
▪ Barbecues range from basic charcoal disposables, costing very little, to sophisticated models that run on bottled gas and cost hundreds of pounds. Unless you know you'll use a barbecue very often, it's best to buy a basic re-usable charcoal grill, then upgrade it if you find you use it regularly.
▪ An enclosed or kettle barbecue gives protection from the wind.
▪ With a gas barbecue, you will get no charcoal smell and will have more temperature control.
▪ Always have a contingency plan in case the weather is inclement. At best, this could mean taking brief shelter in the house, at worst, using the kitchen grill and everyone staying indoors.
▪ Have a range of snacks ready, so that the chef isn't hounded by hungry guests!
▪ Have a trial-run before the day of the party to check how much food you can put on the grill. Many barbecues are surprisingly small.
▪ A barbecue doesn't have to be limited to steaks and burgers. Grill fish, make kebabs with any food that can be cut into cubes or strips, such as beef and peppers, or grill soy burgers for vegetarian guests.

PARTY COUNTDOWN CHECKLIST

The day before

❑ Supermarket shop for the bulk of the food, if it is not being delivered.

❑ Buy cut flowers.

❑ Clean and prepare rooms where the party is to be held. Set up tables and store unwanted furniture.

That morning

❑ Close the doors of the rooms you won't be using and decide where coats will go.

❑ Pay special attention to bathrooms. Put out fresh towels and soap.

❑ Buy bread.

❑ Arrange fresh flowers in key rooms, and in bedrooms if guests are staying overnight.

❑ For a buffet or barbecue set out more glasses than you will have guests, as you don't want to waste time washing them up during the party.

❑ Set tables with cutlery, plates, and napkins.

❑ Prepare food. Peel and trim vegetables.

❑ For a buffet or barbecue, prepare salads and sandwiches if you have enough refrigerator space. Cooked egg, meat, and shellfish dishes must not be left at room temperature until the party begins.

One hour to go

❑ Shower and change, and relax for 20 minutes.

❑ Make sure food that needs to be heated is ready to go in the oven.

❑ Set out snacks, sandwiches, or hors d'oeuvres.

Food and drink quantities

It is an interesting fact that, the more guests there are at a buffet party, the less everyone is likely to eat. So, catering quantities are not simply a multiple of individual portions given here. As a rough guide, 20 guests will eat the equivalent of 18 single portions. For 100, prepare 85 single portions.

Barbecue food

■ Allow for two buns and burgers per person, plus an extra dozen rolls per 20 guests.

■ Plan for two hot dog buns and hot dogs per person.

■ Have 3 chicken wings per person.

■ Allow for 2 chicken drumsticks per person.

■ A 600ml (20fl oz) bottle of ketchup will serve approximately 15 guests.

■ A 400g (14oz) jar of mayonnaise contains approximately 24 servings.

■ For green salads, allow a large handful of salad leaves per person. For pasta or rice salads, cook 55g (2oz) per person.

■ Allow for 55g (2oz) of french fries per person,

Buffet food

■ Hors d'oeuvres – allow for four to six per person. Allow for ten canapes per person at cocktail party.

■ Allow about 85g (3oz) of cold meat per person.

■ Plan for about 55g (2oz) of cheese and 55g (2oz) of biscuits per person at a buffet. At a cheese and wine party, allow for up to 115g (4oz) of cheese per

person and 115g (4oz) cheese biscuits per person.

■ A 15cm (6in) quiche or pastry will serve four to six people.

■ Allow for 55g (2oz) of potato chips per person.

■ A 18cm (7in) diameter cream cake serves 6 to 8 guests.

■ 115g (4oz) dip per person plus the equivalent of two celery sticks or bread sticks for dipping.

Drinks

Wine is one of the most popular drinks to serve at a buffet but you may know how much wine your guests are likely to drink. If not, as a general rule, allow half a bottle per head for parties over 50 guests or one bottle per head for under 25.

Don't forget that many guests will not be drinking. At a larger party, this could be up to one in three. Provide a selection of interesting soft drinks or make a non-alcoholic punch. Assume a minimum of two drinks per head of the total party number.

Make sure that you provide lots of ice – allow 225g (8oz) per person and double that if the weather is hot.

DRINKS	NO. OF GLASSES
Soft drinks/soda, 1 litre bottle	6 glasses
Fruit juice, 600ml (1 pint)	5 glasses
Punch, 1.7 litres (3 pints)	8 glasses
Spirits (average 70 cl bottle)	24 measures

Shopping

■ ■ ■ **Many of us are free to shop at any time of the day or night whether it is once a week or once a month. Despite this freedom, though, most of us still need to plan ahead and stick to a budget. It is also important to buy safe, wholesome, and properly labelled food** ■ ■ ■

a trip to the supermarket ■ ■ ■

Before you go
■ Make a short list of items in the larder, refrigerator, and freezer that need re-stocking, plus any additional items you want to get. A list is a good starting point, but it often pays to make decisions about fresh produce and special offers once you get to the supermarket.

■ Clear out your refrigerator to make space for new foods and to jog your memory about what you need to buy.

■ Check the calendar for any forthcoming special or family events that will occur before you next go shopping and write down what you'll need for these.

■ Go through any new recipes you're thinking of trying. Buy the ingredients and you might just do it!

At the supermarket
■ Take a pen with you and keep your list handy, so that you can cross off items or write down extra ideas that come into your mind.

■ Focus on foods that will make the basis of a meal such as meats, poultry, fish, vegetables, and pasta. It's easy to get distracted and pick up a shopping cart full of sauces and snacks and have nothing with which to make a meal.

■ Use 'sell by' dates to help you select the freshest produce (see *Understanding food labels* on page 143). Be flexible. If you don't feel a fresh item is up to standard, buy something else.

■ Reject any items from freezer cabinets that may have partially thawed.

■ Put heavy items such as cans, potatoes, and cat litter at the front of your shopping trolley and place perishable foods such as fresh meat, cheese, milk, and delicate packages towards the back. You'll want the checkout operator to process the heavy items first, and they can then go in the bottom of your shopping bags.

■ Pack frozen items, like ice cream and fish sticks, and perishables like milk, butter, and cream all together, so that it is easy to unload them into your refrigerator and freezer as soon as you get home.

BUYING GROCERIES ONLINE
■ Save time and stress by letting the supermarket do your shopping and deliver it to you.

■ Write a skeleton shopping list before you sit at your computer. Without the visual prompt of shelves it is easy to forget essential items.

■ Use the web site's options to describe how you like fresh items – ripe or ripening bananas, for instance.

■ Stock up on bulky items, such as potatoes and washing powder.

■ It is hard to include new products when you shop online, as you tend to search for categories you know already. It is worth going to the store every few weeks to check the latest products.

understanding food labels ▪ ▪ ▪

By law, manufacturers have to label foods so it is clear exactly what is in them and, where appropriate, to give nutritional advice. This is good news for shoppers – although labels can still seem to be a source of confusion first and information second.

Ingredients lists

Items with more than one ingredient must list everything that they contain. The ingredient at the top of this list is the one it contains most of (by weight). So if a preserve lists sugar and then strawberries, you know it's going to have less fruit than a jam that puts strawberries first.

Additives and flavourings are included on ingredient lists, or choose foods that say free of additive, preservative and artificial-flavouring, and look for 100 percent natural ingredients.

Nutrition facts

The label provides an indication of serving sizes and states how many calories the food has per serving. The percentage Daily Value shows how much of a nutrient is present in the food as a percentage of the total amount that is required each day on an average daily diet of 2,000 calories. The label also contains details on vitamin, sugar, fibre, calcium, fat, carbohydrate, protein, sodium, and cholesterol content. This information will help you decide if the food fits into your day's nutritional needs (see page 148).

'Sell by'

This date is found on the packaging of fresh foods like meats, poultry, and dairy items. It is the last date on which the store will sell this item. At the close of business, the food must be removed from the shelf. The 'sell by' date may or may not be the last date on which you can safely eat the food. Unless there is an accompanying later date, under the label 'eat by', you must assume that it is the final day and throw the food away. Alternatively, plan ahead and cook and freeze appropriate food before the 'sell by' date.

'Eat by' and 'use by'

This date is found on the packaging of fresh fish, vegetables, meat, and dairy. It is the last date on which you can safely eat the food. After this date, you should throw it away. This is especially true of food that is highly vulnerable to bacterial growths. Paté, fish, and raw meats should never be eaten after the 'eat by' date.

'Best before'

Found on practically all food that doesn't carry 'sell by' or 'eat by' instructions such as rice, jams, sauces, biscuits, bakery products, frozen foods, and canned and bottled goods. This is the date after which the manufacturer can no longer guarantee that the foods will be in top condition. It is rarely harmful to eat foods that have just passed a 'best before' date, though cakes and cookies may start to taste stale, and frozen food become rather tasteless.

Tips for using food labels

▪ A casserole with a label reading 'mushroom and chicken' (in that order) will have little meat content. Check the order of words on food labels carefully.

▪ Check meat products carefully, as some may contain just 10 percent meat.

▪ If the word 'flavoured' follows a food, such as 'strawberry-flavoured mousse', it may have no fruit content at all.

▪ Bear in mind that foods that are labelled 'sugar-free' usually contain artificial sweeteners.

▪ Look out for water on the list, as the percentage of water that a food item contains will be listed. You may decide not to buy ham that has 30 percent water added, choose one labelled 'no added water'.

▪ It is possible to freeze food on its 'sell by' date, but remember to eat the foods immediately after thawing.

Organic foods

National standards ensure that food labelled 'organic' is free from synthetic pesticides and fertilisers, genetic engineering, growth hormones, irradiation, or antibiotics, and that livestock is fed on organic foodstuffs. However, it does not automatically guarantee that the food is better than non-organic. Organic food now covers a wide range of produce and can be bought from supermarkets as well as specialist shops and farmers' markets.

Cooking terms and techniques

Al dente

Meaning, literally, 'the tooth', this is food – especially pastas and vegetables – that is cooked, but still has a firm bite to it.

All-in-one-method

Ingredients are combined together (not in stages, as in traditional baking) with a hand or electric mixer, or in a food processor – such as in cake mixes.

Baking

Food that is cooked in the main oven in a dish or pan, or directly on a rack, and doesn't have extra oil or water. Foods cooked this way are usually breads, but this technique is also used for the slow, dry cooking of fish, rice, and potatoes.

BLANCHING

Asparagus, 2 to 4 minutes
Brussels sprouts, 3 to 4 minutes
Carrots, 3 minutes
Cauliflower, 3 minutes
Courgettes, 1 minute
Peas, 1 to 2 minutes
Spinach, 2 minutes
Sweetcorn 4 to 8 minutes

Basting

Using juices from roasting food to seal in moisture and add flavour while cooking. The roast is removed briefly from the oven, every half hour or so, and juices are dribbled over it with a spoon.

Beating

Incorporating air into an ingredient or mixture by whisking it vigorously with a spoon, fork, whisk, or electric hand mixer. See also *Mixing* and *Whisking*.

Bind

Adding an egg, or a small amount of liquid, in order to bind a mixture together. This is used in cake recipes and sauces.

Blanching

A quick way to prepare foods with a high natural water content (vegetables) for the freezer. Food is dropped into boiling water, then removed from the heat after a set amount of time (see below left). This is a protective process because the blanching destroys enzymes that cause the food to spoil (lose colour, flavour, and texture) during freezing. Food will still need to be cooked after you remove it from the freezer. Before blanching:
Chop large vegetables like cauliflowers into small florets.
Trim and prepare (cut the ends off green beans and shell broad beans).

Blending

Mixing dry, generally powdered, foods with a cold liquid to form a smooth paste, for example, blending a teaspoon of cornflour with a small cup of milk to make a sauce. It also describes the action of liquefying solid foods, like vegetables, in a blender to make a thick soup.

Boiling

Cooking food like eggs and vegetables in water, at a moderate to high heat. To boil a medium-sized egg: gently lower the egg into the saucepan of already boiling water, slightly reduce the heat. Once the water reboils, cook for five minutes, 12 minutes for a hard-boiled egg. Alternatively, put a medium-sized egg into a pan of cold water. When the water boils, cook it for four minutes, or ten minutes to hard-boil.

Pasta driers such as this are great if you're making lots of fresh pasta, but try to avoid having too many gadgets that you rarely use.

Although you can make-do with a pie dish, using a specialist quiche dish will ensure that you can bake quiche to perfection.

Estimating measurements is fine if you're good at it, but otherwise measuring cups are an essential tool for the cook in any household.

Boning

Removing bones from uncooked poultry, meat, and fish, usually in preparation for stuffing or poaching. It is sometimes called filleting, especially for fish.

Braising

This is a slow method of cooking meats and vegetables either on a stove top or in an oven and is generally used for meat that is too tough to roast.

Browning

Giving a savoury dish, or occasionally a dessert, an attractive golden topping by placing it briefly under the grill or in a hot oven.

Bruise

Lightly crushing garlic or ginger to release flavour.

Casserole

Long, gentle method of cooking meat joints, small boneless pieces of meat, and vegetables with lots of liquid in a closed pot, either in the oven or on the cooker top.

Clarifying

Heating fat, typically butter, so that milk solids rise to the top. This is then either skimmed or removed using a gravy separator. Used for sautéing, as a seafood dip, a glaze topping for patés, or to pan-fry fish. Clarifying also refers to removing impurities from stock, by cooling then skimming them off the surface.

Creaming

Mixing together two or more ingredients, usually sugar and butter, until they blend into a creamy paste.

Deep-frying

Fast, high-temperature cooking in a deep pan half full of oil. The safest method is to use a deep fryer that has a basket in which food may be lifted in and out and has a lid to keep in splashes (see also *Small appliances*, page 119). The oil is ready when a cube of bread gets browned in just under a minute.

Dice

Method of cutting vegetables, cheese, or egg into small half-inch cubes.

Dry-frying

Healthier way of frying because no extra oil is added to the pan. Generally used for fattier foods, like sausages and bacon, that are put straight into a cold frying pan and cooked in their own fat.

Gratin

A breadcrumb or cheese topping that is browned in the oven or under a grill.

Grilling

Dry cooking on a rack under a high to medium heat, mostly used for bacon, steaks, kebabs, and toasting bread. Putting the rack nearer to the heat source raises the temperature, though most have temperature controls.

A rotary whisk makes light work of beating eggs, cream, and cake mixes. An inexpensive wire whisk is a popular alternative.

A copper bowl is best for whisking egg whites. The egg interacts with the metal to make the perfect meringue.

This dented chopping board and curved knife make chopping herbs and spices easy. See page 126 for more on chopping boards.

Kneading
Folding and pressing of food such as bread dough to incorporate air.

Marinating
Letting raw food stand (in a refrigerator, and usually for several hours) in a marinade of sweet or spicy liquids to absorb flavour before cooking.

Mashing
Making cooked food smooth, especially potatoes.

Melting
Heating solid foods to liquefy them, such as cheese under the grill or butter in a pan. Chocolate is best melted in a pan over another pan of hot water.

Mixing
Combining two or more ingredients.

Par-boiling
Boiling food briefly, before continuing to cook it by another method. Potatoes may be par-boiled, then roasted, to achieve a softer inside texture.

Pickling
A way of storing fresh food such as onions, gherkins, and beets, in a vinegar-based liquid.

Poaching
Gentle way of cooking foods such as fish in liquid (either using a fish kettle on the stove top or a shallow dish in a medium oven). It is also a method of cooking eggs: add two tablespoons of vinegar to a pan of water and bring it to a boil. Crack the egg into the pan, reduce the heat, and simmer for three to five minutes. Remove the egg with a slotted spoon.

Pot-roasting
Cooking meat joints with a small amount of fat and liquid in a sealed pot to increase tenderness.

Preserving
Storing fresh food, generally fruit, without losing its freshness. The food is mixed with sugar and boiled rapidly until it sets.

Puréeing
Making vegetables and fruit smooth. Essential way to prepare infant foods. Also used for drinks, sauces, and vegetable dishes. Peel vegetables, then use a food processor or blender.

Reducing
Thickening a sauce by boiling it rapidly (with no lid on the pan) so that excess liquid evaporates.

Refreshing
Plunging cooked vegetables briefly into cold water so that they stop cooking.

Roasting
Oven-cooking of meats and vegetables in their own juices, at a medium-high temperature. Also an easy way to cook vegetables, especially potatoes in a shallow roasting pan, with added oil or using juices from roasted meat.

Rubbing in
Baking term. Combine two or more ingredients (for example fat and flour) by rubbing them together between your fingertips.

Sauté
Combination of frying and braising. Fast-cooking of meat, poultry, and sometimes vegetables and fruit, in a pan that contains oil, or a mixture of oil and butter. Once the outside of the food has been browned, the heat is turned down and more liquid is added.

Searing (also called sealing)
Brief, fast-cooking of meat to create a brown crust and seal in the flavour. Can be done by putting meat into a pan and frying quickly, or turning up the oven temperature for the first ten minutes of cooking.

Separating
Dividing an egg and putting the yolk in one bowl and the white in another. Tap the egg smartly against the side of a bowl. Holding the egg over the bowl, break the shell in half while taking care to keep the egg in one half of the shell. Pass the yolk between the two halves, letting the white fall down into the bowl until only the yolk remains.

Pan frying

Fast-cooking in a pan, using a small amount of oil, butter, or fat.

Soufflé

Baked recipe dish of a sweet or savoury sauce that has had stiffly whisked egg white added to it.

Steaming

Moist-heat cooking. Food is placed directly above water, either on the cooker hob, in a colander-style pan, or in the oven, on a rack above a grill pan full of water. Food cooks slowly, without drying up.

Stewing

Slow pan-cooking of meat, or vegetables, or fruit in liquid.

Stir-frying

Cooking small, evenly cut pieces of meat, poultry, or vegetables over a medium to high heat in a wok or large, deep pan. Only a small amount of oil is used and it is essential to keep stirring with a wooden spatula or spoon to prevent sticking or burning.

Sweating

A first step in vegetable cooking, especially onions, to soften and bring out their flavour. Vegetables are added to a pan where fat (usually butter) has melted and they are cooked gently until soft.

Tenderizing

Pounding raw meat with a rolling pin, or specialized tenderizing tool, to break down muscle fibres, and make the meat more tender when cooked.

Thawing/de-frosting

Bringing frozen food up to room temperature. This should be done in a refrigerator, which is the safest way to thaw poultry or meat. See *Home freezing guide*, page 136. Some foods can be thawed rapidly in a microwave – check instructions on packaging.

Whisking

Using a hand or electric whisk to rapidly beat air into a mixture to make it light and fluffy. Especially used for cakes, some types of cream, and egg whites.

A choice of lengths of wooden spoon can be useful. Choose the one that you find the most comfortable for beating or hand mixing.

Refined versions of the original mortar and pestle are used in kitchens all over the world to prepare pastes and sauces. They are also used for grinding herbs and spices.

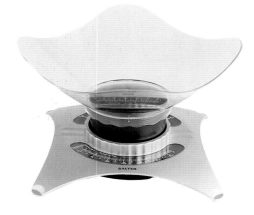

Scales are a useful tool in the kitchen – especially if you're not very good or experienced at estimating wieghts. Buy electronic scales for precise measurements.

Food nutrition and healthy eating

■ ■ ■ **You don't need to be an expert, but understanding the basics of a good diet will help your household to make balanced food choices every day** ■ ■ ■

the food pyramid ■ ■ ■

This pyramid will help you to keep a check on the amount of food you eat from each food group. Each of these food groups provide you with some, but not all, of the nutrients that you need. To remain healthy, you need to eat a mixture of foods from all these food groups every day.

Fats, oils, and sugar
Eat sparingly
Milk, yogurt, and cheeses
2–3 servings
Meat, poultry, fish, dry beans, eggs, and nuts
2–3 servings
Vegetables
3–5 servings
Fruit
2–4 servings
Bread, cereal, rice, and pasta
6–11 servings

The fats, oils, and sugars group at the top of the pyramid include salad dressings and oils, cream, butter, margarine, sugar, soft drinks, sweets, and desserts. These provide us with calories but little nutrition, so most people should eat them sparingly.

In the next level are groups of foods that mainly come from animals, such as milk, cheese, meat, fish, and eggs, as well as dry beans and nuts. These foods provide us with protein, calcium, iron, and zinc.

The third level includes foods that come from plants, such as vegetables and fruits. These foods provide us with vitamins, minerals, and fibre.

At the bottom of pyramid are breads, cereals, rice, and pasta. These foods provide us with carbohydrates (starches) which are an important source of energy. Choose wholegrains such as whole-wheat bread and whole-grain cereal.

healthy eating checkpoints ▪ ▪ ▪

■ Drink plenty of water to flush toxins from your body. Aim to drink eight glasses a day, not counting the water in cups of coffee and tea.

■ Eat less than one teaspoonful of salt per day, especially if you suffer from high blood pressure.

■ Include whole wheat among your choices from the bread and cereals group. This will provide more fibre in your diet, which is essential for the smooth working of the body's overall system. Whole-wheat foods are also more filling and will stop you wanting to snack on unhealthy sugars and fatty foods.

■ Reduce your sugar intake as sugar has no nutritional value. You can find out a processed food's sugar content by looking on the label. See *Understanding food labels*, page 143. It is difficult, but you can re-educate your taste buds to accept less sugar.

■ Balance the number of calories you eat with the amount you use each day. Multiply your weight in pounds by fifteen, or by thirteen if you're relatively inactive, to find the total number of calories you should consume. On average, women need around 2,000 calories per day, and men need around 2,500.

■ Limit your intake of fatty red meats, which contain high levels of cholesterol, and could increase your risk of heart attack. Eat grains, fish, and poultry without the skin because these are all low-cholesterol foods.

■ Vegetarians and vegans need to ensure they include protein (not found in vegetables) in at least two meals each day. See the food pyramid opposite for sources of protein.

how much? ▪ ▪ ▪

Aim for five a day

Aim to eat 5 servings of fruit and vegetables each day. These servings could be:

1 medium-sized fruit
175ml (6fl oz) of fruit juice
25g (1oz) of dried fruit
115g (4oz) of leafy vegetable
85g (3oz) of cooked beans; lentils or kidney beans.

The typical meal on your plate should be made up of a balanced diet of the food groups shown above.

■ Try snacking on raw vegetables rather than crisps.

■ Add fruit to your breakfast cereal.

■ Drink fruit juice instead of soft drinks.

fibre-rich foods ▪ ▪ ▪

Most people eat insufficient fibre, and may suffer from sluggish digestion. Eating more will improve the workings of the intestine and may afford some protection against colon cancer. To avoid gas or stomach discomfort, build your intake gradually over a fortnight so that your body has time to adapt to this new diet. Good fibre foods are:

■ Baked potatoes
■ Bananas
■ Beans and peas
■ Bran
■ Muesli
■ Leafy vegetables
■ Oat and wheat-based cereal
■ Whole-wheat breads
■ Dried apricots

Vitamin and mineral checkpoints

■ A varied diet, including a range of fresh foods, should provide all the vitamins and minerals that we need.

■ It is possible to supplement a poor diet with vitamin and mineral supplements, but adopting a healthy, balanced diet is better for you. Foods that are rich in vitamins and minerals provide other things that your body needs.

■ Many foods, like breakfast cereal, are fortified with vitamins and minerals. Check what percentage of the recommended daily allowance each serving provides.

■ Never exceed recommended doses. Excess iron is toxic.

■ In a few cases, vitamins have proven benefits. For example, taking folic acid prior to conception and in the first 12 weeks of pregnancy is known to reduce the instance of spina bifida.

■ Healthcare professionals, including nurses and pharmacists are good sources of dietary advice.

IMPORTANT VITAMINS AND MINERALS

Vitamin/mineral	Food scource	Checkpoints
Vitamin A	Liver, green leafy vegetables, orange or yellow fruits, dairy produce, fish, and eggs	Good for healthy eyes and skin; promotes bone growth; fortifies immune system
Vitamin B (includes folic acid)	Meat, fish, dairy produce, pulses, wheatgerm, yeast extract, green leafy vegetables, fruits, cereals, and breads	Needed to release energy from carbohydrates; good for healthy eyes, nails, and skin; vital before and during early pregnancy
Vitamin C	Fruit, especially citrus fruits, vegetables (particularly peppers), and berries	Helps in the healing of wounds; aids absorption of iron; and is an antioxidant
Vitamin D	Salt water fish such as cod and tuna, butter, and egg yolk	Helps to absorb calcium; good for normal growth development; helps formation of bones and teeth
Vitamin E	Fruit and vegetables (particularly asparagus), oils, and whole-wheat cereal	Good for immune system; needed for healthy cell growth; prevents oxidation of fat
Calcium	Oily fish, shellfish, molasses, milk, and dairy produce	Builds healthy teeth and bones; needed for blood clotting; regulates blood pressure
Zinc	Fish, milk, whole grains, spinach, mushrooms, red meat, shellfish, and nuts	Boosts immune system; important for cell growth and wound healing
Iron	Fish, liver, lean red meat, dried apricots, dark green vegetables, and milk	Helps in the transport of oxygen in your blood and muscle
Selenium	Lean meat, fish, shellfish, tomatoes, whole-grain cereals, eggs, garlic, and liver	Works with vitamin E as an antioxidant; protects against clogging arteries; essential for healthy immune system
Magnesium	Lean meat, fish, shellfish, rice, green vegetables, bananas, whole grains, and milk	Regulates blood pressure; aids function of nerves, bone, and muscle; vital to basic metabolic functions

chapter

4

pets

A pet for your home

■ ■ ■ **There are plenty of advantages to being a pet owner, but there are disadvantages too. So it's best to think carefully before you bring a new pet into your home. Studies show that pets chosen on impulse are more likely to be neglected or abandoned** ■ ■ ■

pet ownership ■ ■ ■

Advantages
■ Companionship
■ Teaches children about responsibility, looking after others
■ Relaxation – studies show that people with pets are more relaxed

Disadvantages
■ Extra expense
■ A big responsibility in terms of health and welfare
■ Time and work is involved in feeding, grooming and cleaning

Ask yourself the following questions
■ Can you offer a permanent home? For dogs and cats, that commitment could last over ten years.
■ Can you easily afford food, grooming, and vet's bills? The cost of keeping a pet varies from animal to animal, but caring for a medium-sized dog is a substantial amount each year.
■ Does your landlord allow you to have pets? Are pets permitted on your lease?
■ If you wish to travel abroad with your pet is it necessary to have a rabies certificate?
■ Are you able to be home at regular times to feed and exercise your pet?
■ Do you go away on trips regularly, and, if so, can you afford the kennel fees?
■ Are you sure no family member has a fur allergy? Many owners discover too late that their cat or dog makes them sick.
■ Is everyone committed to the decision? Children may be desperate for a pet, but adults often have to take on the responsibility.
■ Do you have the space available in your house for the type of pet that you want to keep?

choosing a pet ▪ ▪ ▪

Many people, when considering a pet, only choose
between a dog or a cat. However, children may want
to have rabbits, hamsters, gerbils, and guinea pigs.
Birds and fish are popular with older people.
Unusual pets – from pot-bellied pigs to snakes –
need very careful consideration. Miniature pigs, for
instance, while cute and intelligent, are always so
desperate for food that you'll need a lock on the
refrigerator and an outdoor soil area where they can
grub for goodies. Exotic pets, like snakes, aside from
the element of danger, need to be provided with
mice or rats to eat. Ferrets can also be dangerous
but are becoming increasingly popular because they
adapt well to apartment living. Go to your local
library or bookshop, or go online, to read about
different animals before you commit yourself.

finding out more ▪ ▪ ▪

Talk with family, friends, and neighbours who are
pet owners – but remember, every one has a
different story about their pets, so take what they say
as a rough guide only. Check the internet for useful
information on pets, or contact the specific pet
association for advice. If you'd like to adopt an
animal, your local animal rescue centre will be able
to give you information about a pet's personality and
habits. When selecting your pet, you will probably
want to know the following:

- Will it be good with children?
- Is it happy by itself, or do I need to keep two for
company?
- How much space will it need inside the house,
and will it also need containment space outside
the house?
- How much money and time will I have to spend
to care for it correctly?
- Is there anything about this animal, its diet,
or habitat, that makes it a challenge to care for?
- How big will it be when it is fully-grown?
- Can I buy a pet that will be fully trained or will I
have to train it myself?

Choosing your pet

■ ■ ■ There are so many factors to bear in mind when you are choosing a pet that it is hard to keep track of them all. This overview should help you ■ ■ ■

Cats

Kittens are cute and are usually easy to housetrain, but they'll climb up your curtains and race all over your furniture. Adult cats are good companions but they are also independent and, unlike most dogs, do not mind spending time alone.

Life expectancy Up to 17 years +
Special attributes Cats are generally happier as one of a pair if everyone is out at work or school all day. Long-haired cats are beautiful, but keep in mind that they require a great deal of grooming to keep them that way.

✓ Can be trained to use a litter box indoors, so are an ideal pet if you live in a city apartment. Cats are fastidious about keeping themselves clean.
✗ Cats shed fur and can cause serious claw damage to home furnishings.

Fish

Fish are very low-maintenance pets, provided you seek qualified advice on which fish to keep and how to look after your tank.

Life expectancy Variable. While some fish will probably only live for one year, a goldfish can live up to twenty years!
Special attributes Choose from freshwater (easier for beginners) or saltwater fish. Fish enjoy the company of their own species', so it's best not to keep a solitary fish.

✓ Maintaining a healthy tank is relatively straightforward and, with automated feeding, fish can be safely left when you go on vacation.
✗ Not the most entertaining pet to keep, but many people claim that they lower stress levels.

Dogs

If you want a puppy, remember that as cute as they are, puppies chew and can be very destructive. They are also very time-consuming to housetrain and socialize. All dogs should be walked a couple of times each day and should, if possible, have access to a fenced-in garden. Most dogs are not happy to be left alone for long periods and so are not ideal in households where everyone is out at school or work all day.

Life expectancy Around 12 years
Special attributes The wide range of breeds means there's a dog for almost everyone – from decorative miniature poodles to large Great Danes and mixed breeds of every size. Characteristics vary with breed, but many dogs are wonderful with children.

✓ Dogs can be kept indoors or in an outdoor kennel. They are good companions and provide home security. They also mean that you'll get more regular exercise.
✗ Dogs are messy and you'll have to be tolerant of muddy paws and fur on the furniture.

Birds

Maybe not the first pet you would think of, but birds can be very companionable, playful, and some can learn several hundred words.

Life expectancy Variable; some parrots can live longer than people.
Special attributes Birds like plenty of company and, if possible, to spend some time outside their cages. They are, therefore, ideal if you're around during the day, but don't or can't get about easily.

✓ Easy to feed and care for.
✗ Can be noisy – parrots screech loudly, and most birds are messy.

If you are abroad and your pet is bitten by a wild animal or even a domestic animal, take your pet to a vet within 24 hours. If the attacker is at high risk of rabies – for example, a fox or stray dog – handle your pet with gloves and wash any area which may have saliva from the attacker on it. Keep children away from the pet. These instructions apply whether or not your pet is vaccinated.

Rabbits

If handled from an early age, rabbits are friendly, cuddly pets. Some rabbits can be housetrained and can adapt well to apartment living.

Life expectancy 5 to 15 years
Special attributes Rabbits are sociable and they don't like to live alone. If you do decide to get two, consider two females – unless you want lots and lots of rabbits very quickly.

- ✓ A cute, easy-to-care-for pet if you're at work all day, with the bonus that it can live out-doors, so long as it has sufficient protection.
- ✗ Rabbits are good at escaping, so if they are kept outside, their run needs to be constructed with the utmost care.

Hamsters, guinea pigs, gerbils, mice

Good first pets for young children, because all they require is food, water, an appropriate climate and a clean cage.

Life expectancy 2 to 5 years
Special attributes Hamsters are nocturnal, so they wake up as everyone else goes to bed. Guinea pigs are gentle, placid creatures and have several sleep/wake cycles during the day. Gerbils are the cleanest rodents.

- ✓ Easy to feed and care for.
- ✗ Hamsters have a reputation for biting, and some gerbils can be too shy to enjoy much handling, but, as with most pets, if they have been handled from an early age, this should not be a problem.

Exotics

Exotics such as lizards, snakes, and spiders generally need to be kept in protective tanks.

Life expectancy Variable – snakes can live for over 40 years.
Special attributes Animal care charities and most veterinarians advise against keeping exotics. They may be dangerous and hard to care for properly.

- ✓ The natural dry heat preferred by many species means there is little cleaning to be done.
- ✗ They are often hard to care for properly and are sometimes dangerous, so you may lose friends!

Ferrets

If they are handled from an early age, ferrets are friendly, cuddly pets. They are very playful even as adults, and their bold, curious natures make them fun to have around.

Life expectancy 6 to 10 years
Special attributes Ferrets are related to otters, weasels, and badgers. If you have other pets, you may want to bear in mind that ferrets and birds are natural enemies.

- ✓ Small, easy to care for, and quiet. They adapt well to apartment living.
- ✗ Can be smelly (but once they are neutered and given regular baths this can be kept under control).

For most pets, it is best to go to an animal shelter or a reputable breeder. If you go to a breeder, make sure that you see the pet's mother, too. Look for:

- Bright, shiny eyes
- Healthy-looking fur/feathers/scales
- Sound teeth/beak
- No obvious deformities
- Good weight and size
- Alert, responsive nature

A visit to the vet

■ ■ ■ **It is a good idea to have a vet examine your new pet so that you can make sure that it is healthy** ■ ■ ■

how to find a good vet ■ ■ ■

■ Ask your family, friends, and neighbours for a recommendation.

■ Ask your animal's breeder or the local animal shelter to recommend a vet.

■ Look in the Yellow Pages, and arrange a visit to a clinic. Base your choice on surgery location, opening hours, and fees, plus friendliness and services offered.

visiting the vet ■ ■ ■

■ Never carry an animal into the surgery. However calm your pet might normally be, that behaviour might change when it smells the other animals.

■ Dogs should be put on a leash, cats and rabbits in specialized pet carriers. Small animals, such as hamsters and mice, can be safely transported in small, lidded shoeboxes with holes in the lid.

■ Be prepared with any questions you have about your pet, whether it's about health or behaviour.

■ Cats and dogs need vaccinations to keep them safe from harmful diseases, including rabies. You'll also need advice on treatments for fleas and worms.

■ Unless you have a very good reason to breed your animal, neutering makes sense. Dogs are much more likely to stray if they are not neutered, and cats that are not neutered are more likely to fight and increase your vet bills. Your vet will advise you on the best age at which to neuter your animal.

HANDLING SICK OR INJURED ANIMALS

■ Approach sick or injured animals slowly and cautiously. Even your own pet can become aggressive when in pain or frightened. Do not make sudden movements and be as calm as possible.

■ It is a good idea to wrap small animals in a towel or blanket. This will make it more difficult for them to bite or scratch you, and they are less likely to hurt themselves.

■ In the case of a serious emergency, call beforehand to let the vet know you are coming.

■ Disguising pills in scraps of food usually works for dogs, and sometimes for cats (try smoked salmon or cheese spread that will stick to the pill). To give a cat a worming pill, wrap the cat in a towel, so only its head is sticking out. If possible, get someone to help you. Aim to get the pill on to the back of the cat's tongue. You may find it helps to administer the pill hidden inside a small piece of butter. Once the pill is in, hold the mouth closed and blow gently into your cat's face until you see it swallow.

health care

Home medicine chest

■ ■ ■ **Every modern home needs a medicine chest. Make sure it has enough space to store medicines to treat a range of minor ailments, as well as a basic first-aid kit** ■ ■ ■

assembling a first-aid kit ■ ■ ■

Choose a strong, durable box with a tight-fitting lid. A lidded, rigid, plastic storage container, or a zipped, soft, plastic bag is ideal. Alternatively, buy a ready-made first-aid kit from a pharmacist, with room to add extras. Inside, you will need:

Antiseptic liquid and wipes	Cleaning wounds, cuts, and grazes
Antiseptic cream or ointment	Soothing cuts, grazes, bites, and stings
Bandages	
rolled, stretch-fabric	For securing dressings and supporting injured limbs
plain cotton rectangles	Supporting sprains and strains
Cotton swabs (sterile)	Cleaning cuts and grazes
Cotton wool	Padding for dressings
Dressings	
sterile pads	Covering and protecting wounds
sterile eye pad with bandage	
gauze swabs	
Gloves (latex, disposable)	Preventing infection and protecting against blood and fluids
Elastoplast	
variety of sizes	Covering and protecting cuts and grazes
waterproof	For cuts on hands
Scissors	For cutting dressings
Safety pins	Fastening bandages
Thermometer	See *Common ailments*, page 166, for types
Tweezers	Removing splinters

Storage guide

■ A cool bathroom is a convenient place to wall-mount a small, lockable medicine chest.

■ If your household uses lots of medication, you may prefer to site the chest downstairs, perhaps in a utility room. Again, ensure it is mounted high on the wall.

■ Within the chest, keep a portable first-aid kit to take out for use. See left for contents.

■ Go through your medicine chest every few months; discard out-of-date medicines safely by returning them to your pharmacist for disposal, and then replenish supplies.

■ Although accessible, make sure that the medicine chest is out of the reach of children or pets.

everyday medicines ▪ ▪ ▪

Without amassing a huge stock, it is prudent to keep remedies to treat common ailments in your home medicine chest. You might like to include:

- Analgesics for headache, fever, and pain relief (see chart, below).
- Cold/influenza-relief products, including decongestants and cough-suppressants.
- Antiseptic lozenges, sprays, and gargles for sore throats and mouth ulcers.
- Hydrocortisone cream to soothe insect bites and rashes.
- Diarrhoea remedies and rehydration medication.
- Acid indigestion tablets/liquid.
- Hangover relief.
- Ear drops to soften wax and soothe earache.
- Sunblock (PABA-B-free) with insect repellant.
- Calamine lotion for sunburn and rough skin.

Homeopathic and alternative preparations

Aconite	For shock or panic after accidents
Arnica	To minimize bruising after injury
Cantharis	To relieve pain from bites and stings
Symphytum	Relief for black-eyes
Bach flowers/ Rescue remedy	To aid recovery from emotional shock
Witch hazel	To soothe stings and broken skin
Tea tree oil	For minor cuts
Calendula	Antiseptic for cuts and abrasions

ANALGESICS CHECKPOINTS

- Never exceed the recommended dose; if you do so accidentally, seek immediate medical attention.
- Many brand-name analgesics are available as less expensive generic versions with identical active ingredients.
- For stronger pain-relief, never mix tablets, but check the packet and choose analgesics that combine ingredients, such as paracetamol teamed with codeine or caffeine.

ANALGESICS

There may seem to be a bewildering range of painkillers available, but most contain one of three main ingredients. Through experience, you will get to know which gives you the best relief, without giving you any other side effect like an upset stomach.

Item	Effects	Pain-relief	Advantages	Cautions
Paracetamol	Relieves headache, migraine, all-round pain; reduces fever	Mild to moderate	Gentle on the stomach	Many cold and influenza remedies contain paracetamol: never take more than one paracetamol-containing medicine at one time. Check labels.
Aspirin	Relieves headache, migraine, all-round pain; reduces fever; eases inflammatory pain	Mild to moderate	Can be taken at the same time as many prescription drugs but always check with your pharmacist first	Not suitable for children under 12 (can lead to a rare but serious brain and liver condition); can irritate the stomach in susceptible people.
Ibuprofen	Relieves headache, migraine, and joint and muscle pain; reduces fever	Moderate	Good for reducing inflammation caused by arthritis and sports injuries. Benefits last 2 to 3 hours longer than paracetamol and aspirin	If you are pregnant, breast-feeding or have high blood pressure discuss the implications of taking Ibuprofen with your doctor.

Basic first aid

■ ■ ■ **These are the absolute basics that should help with most minor household injuries. If in doubt, call your doctor or dial 999. For choking, breathing difficulties, poisoning, fainting and seizures, large burns, eye injuries, and resuscitation, see Emergency first aid, pages 176–84** ■ ■ ■

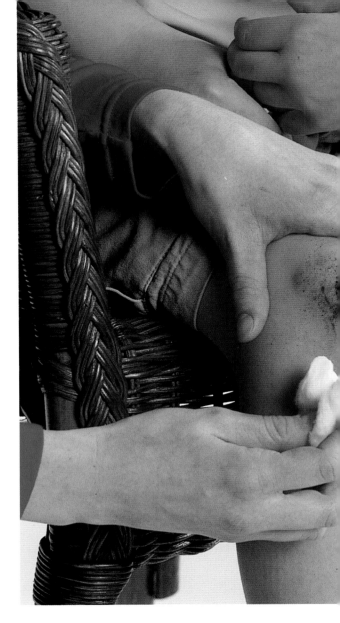

Cuts and grazes

A minor cut to the skin from a knife, piece of glass or even paper, affects only the outer layer of the skin. If it has pierced deeper, into the muscle below, or is more than 1cm (½in) long on the face or hands – 2.5cm (1in) on the body – stitches may be needed. Seek urgent medical attention. A graze is a scraping injury, and oozes a clear, sticky fluid. It bleeds less than a cut, but needs to be cleaned carefully to remove small pieces of dirt and grit. For major wounds, see *Bleeding* in *Emergency first aid*, page 180.

1 Clean the wound by running it under cold water, or wiping it with antiseptic wipes or cotton wool, moistened with diluted antiseptic solution.
2 Wash away dirt and grit, using tweezers carefully to pick out pieces embedded in the wound. Dry with gauze or a clean cotton handkerchief.
3 Tackle any bleeding; most minor wounds will have already stopped bleeding. If not, press together any gaping edges, then apply direct pressure to the wound with gauze or a clean cotton handkerchief.
4 Cover with an elastoplast or non-stick dressing. Remove when the wound is dry and healing well.

Splinters

1 Grasp the splinter with tweezers, and draw it out at the same angle at which it went in.
2 Once removed, squeeze the wound until it just begins to bleed, to flush out dirt.
3 Wash and cover as directed in cuts and grazes, above.

Insect bites and stings

For a very few people with a severe allergic reaction to insect venom, bites and stings can be life-threatening. A victim may not know that he has an allergy, so be alert for signs of anaphylactic shock: pain; swelling of the throat, lips, and tongue; an itchy rash; redness at the site of the bite; decreased consciousness; difficult, noisy breathing. Call 999 without delay, and see *Anaphylactic shock* in *Emergency first aid*, page 183. Seek medical help immediately for stings in the mouth and throat.

1 Wash the wound using soap and water. Dry with gauze or a clean cotton handkerchief.
2 Keep the stung area lower than the heart, to slow the circulation of venom in the body. Apply a cool compress to relieve any pain and swelling.

Bee stings

First remove the sting and the attached venom by scraping with a fingernail, the blade of a knife or the edge of a credit card. Do not squeeze the sting, for example with tweezers, as this will cause more venom to be injected into the skin. Once removed, make a paste of bicarbonate of soda and water, and dab it on the wound. Finally, apply antiseptic cream or ointment to guard against infection, and take analgesics, if necessary (see page 159).

For wasp stings: Dab on vinegar.

Animal bites

The priority is to thoroughly clean the area bitten to remove possible infections transmitted by the animal.

1 Wash the wound using soap and water, then hold it under cold running water for five minutes.
2 Pat dry with gauze or a clean cotton handkerchief, and cover with elastoplast or non-stick dressing.
3 Seek medical attention to rule out infection. It may be necessary to have a tetanus booster or antibiotics.

Snakebites

Most bites are from non-poisonous snakes and medical treatment is very effective. Nevertheless, it is important to get to an emergency ward as quickly as possible.

1 Wash the wound using soap and water. Dry with gauze or a clean cotton handkerchief.
2 Bandage the wound firmly, and keep the area bitten lower than the heart to slow the circulation of the venom. Do not cut the wound or try to suck out venom.
3 Seek urgent medical attention.

Swelling and bruising

The key word to remember is RICE – Rest, Ice, Compression, and Elevation. Be aware of the possibility of bone fracture; if you suspect this, seek medical attention immediately, and see *Fractures* in *Emergency first aid*, page 183.

1 Rest the affected area.
2 Ice – apply a cold compress for 15 minutes. For speed, use a bag of frozen peas, wrapped in a towel to prevent freezer burn. Repeat every three or four hours until the swelling subsides.
3 Compression – compress the area by putting on a firm support bandage.
4 Elevate the injured limb higher than the heart.
5 If the swelling does not subside, have the injury checked out by a doctor.

Minor burns and scalds

Minor burns with no blistering can be treated at home, see *Burns and scalds* in *Emergency first aid*, page 182.

Nosebleeds

Treat minor nosebleeds at home. If bleeding follows an injury to the head, neck, or back, do not attempt to control the blood flow: seek urgent medical attention.

1 Sit the casualty up, leaning forward slightly, with mouth open to clear the airway.
2 Pinch the nostrils shut for about 15 minutes. If the bleeding does not stop after 20 minutes, seek medical attention.
3 Once the bleeding has stopped, walking or even talking could make the bleeding resume. Allow the casualty to rest quietly without blowing the nose for several hours.

Minor eye injuries

The eye is a delicate organ but is otherwise generally good at recovering from injuries. Everyday injuries come from foreign objects becoming stuck in the eye. The eye will become painful, bloodshot, itchy, or begin to water when this happens.

1 Try to wash out the object with water. Use an eyebath if you have one, or an eggcup. Do not use eye-drops unless prescribed by a doctor.
2 If this fails, try to remove the object with the corner of a clean cloth (do not use a cotton bud which has loose fibres that can go into the eye). Use a mirror so that you can see where the object is, or ask a friend to help. Try to avoid pushing the object around the eye, as this can do more damage.
3 If vision is affected, seek medical help.

Preventing accidents

■ ■ ■ **More accidents happen within the home than anywhere else. Common injuries are burns and scalds caused by daily household tasks such as cooking; bruises and breakages caused by falls due to flooring or furniture hazards; and cuts caused by the use of domestic equipment, from knives to electrical appliances and power tools** ■ ■ ■

THOSE AT SPECIAL RISK

■ DIY: be especially careful when using power tools and ladders. See the safety checkpoints on *Basic repairs inside your house*, page 8, as well as those for *The tool box*, page 18.

■ Infants and children under five: to prevent accidents caused by natural curiosity to your own or visiting children, see *Childproofing your home* on page 165.

■ Elderly: be extra vigilant when you receive visits from older relatives and neighbours; falls on stairs are especially common.

safety tips for every room ■ ■ ■

Kitchens

■ Building an ergonomic kitchen will help prevent accidents (see *A well-planned kitchen*, page 114). Special dangers to be aware of when working in the kitchen include burns and cuts (see *Basic first aid*, page 160). Bear in mind the following precautions, and see the safety tips on *Knives*, page 160, and *Deep Friers*, page 119.

■ Stay in the kitchen when pans are on the hob – watch they don't get knocked off or overflow.

■ Always use oven gloves when removing pans from the oven; don't use a dish cloth.

■ Use a cordless electric kettle.

■ Take extreme care with oven cleaners, which will cause chemical burns if used incorrectly (see *Household cleaning*, page 24).

■ After cleaning a floor, leave the bucket and mop in front of the door to warn others that the surface might be slippery.

■ Buy a step-stool for reaching into high cupboards.

■ Avoid storing heavy items on the top shelf: falling cans or other heavy items can injure people. Use this space for storing light items, that are not used on a daily basis.

Living and dining room

Here, open fires and foam upholstery on chairs and sofas are special dangers.

- Fit individual thermostats on radiators to prevent them from becoming hot enough to burn.
- Check labels to make certain that all your upholstery is fire-retardant.
- Take special care to extinguish cigarettes. Keep plenty of ashtrays around if you smoke.
- Use specialist firelighters and never use lighter fluid on an indoor fire.
- Have chimneys swept regularly to remove soot and blockage that could spread flames back into a room.
- Do not dry or air clothes in front of open fires or electric heaters. They could catch fire.
- To prevent full bookcases from toppling over, fix them to the wall with a shelf bracket positioned above the top of the frame.
- Use safety glass in patio doors to prevent accidents if adults or children walk (or run) into them inadvertently.

Bathroom

Watch out for falls on slippery floors, burns from water that is too hot (see *Basic first aid*, page 160), and the rare possibility of drowning. Maintain gas appliances regularly to prevent the build-up of life-threatening carbon-monoxide fumes.

- Turn the hot-water thermostat down to 54°C (120°F) to prevent scalding. When running bath water, first run the cold and then add hot water if you have separate taps.
- Use a nonslip mat, or fix nonslip stickers on the base of the shower or bath.
- Never step out of the bath or shower onto a potentially slippery floor like wood. Have a mat ready to step onto. Use mat-grippers on the underside of bathroom mats to prevent the mat slipping.
- Never leave children alone in the bath, even just to answer a telephone; they can drown in as little as 2.5cm (1in) of water.
- Never take electrical radios, or any other electrical items, into the bathroom.

Always use oven gloves to remove food from the oven or lift pans when handles or lids become too hot. Make sure that the gloves are dry because damp gloves will conduct the heat quickly to your hands and burn them. Ensure that the gloves are not sticky as they might adhere to the oven tray, the oven itself, or to a hot pan causing your hand, and the glove, to slip.

Bedroom

Most accidents in bedrooms derive from heated blankets and night-time falls.

■ Never smoke in bed.

■ Extinguish candles, nightlights, and aromatherapy burners before you go to sleep.

■ Before getting into bed, turn off electric blankets not designed for overnight use. Once in bed, you may forget or fall asleep.

■ Electric blankets for overnight use must be spread flat on the bed, to prevent overheating. Have them serviced according to the manufacturer's recommendations.

■ Do not keep a lamp and a night time drink on the same bedside table. Install low-level wall-lights instead, or place a table on either side of the bed.

■ Keep a clear path from your bed to the door, to prevent night-time falls.

Halls and stairs

Common sense dictates that the key dangers here are falls.

■ Establish good house safety rules, such as 'don't cross another person on the stairs'.

■ Fix worn or loose carpet promptly.

■ Keep shoes, bags, and general clutter off the floor where they could become a tripping hazard: set up a central box where items can be dumped temporarily, but keep it away from the main traffic.

■ Ensure that stairs are adequately lit so that the steps can be clearly seen. If a bulb burns out, replace it immediately, during daylight. Put a light in an understairs cupboard to prevent bumps on the head.

Gardens, paths, and driveways

Again, falls are the main danger outdoors.

■ Use a non-slip outdoor mat or place non-slip stickers under a mat.

■ Clear snowy paths promptly. Once compacted, snow becomes a slipping hazard, and is harder to move. Use a shovel to scoop it off the pathway and, onto the lawn or flower beds.

■ Avoid backing into your driveway or garage if you have children or pets; you might not see them.

■ Ensure that the driveway is adequately lit at night.

CHILDPROOFING YOUR HOME

From around the time an infant is seven months old, he starts to crawl, and the home suddenly becomes very dangerous for him. It is vital to introduce safeguards to protect the inquisitive older infant from serious or fatal injuries. Start by searching every room for potential hazards. If you're having children over to visit, be aware of the danger areas and make some adjustments in your home, such as moving sharp objects or household detergents out of reach, and limiting the rooms that they are allowed to enter.

■ Place stair gates at the top and bottom of the stairs. Use stair gates to screen other areas of danger – for example, the kitchen, or before several steps down to a room.

■ Use locks on upstairs windows.

■ Tie back pull-cords on blinds – they can be a strangulation hazard.

■ Never leave plastic bags lying around – a child can suffocate if it pulls one over its head.

■ Use plug socket protectors on low-level electric sockets to stop little fingers from probing.

■ Fit corner-protectors on sharp-edged furniture – they could scar a child's face.

■ Secure fire screens protecting open fires to the wall.

■ Use the back burners on your cooker hob, and keep pan handles turned to the side.

■ Move rubbish bins and lift them off the floor.

■ Buy a choke-hazard tester – this small tube tests whether small objects would present a danger to children under three. If the item fits in or through the tube, it's too small for a toddler to handle.

■ Store household and garden chemicals up high or in locked cupboards.

■ The most common accident suffered by toddlers is scalding from adults' hot drinks. If you are concerned, remove your coffee table and serve drinks in the kitchen.

■ Make sure adults on medication don't leave medicines in handbags or pockets, where children may find them.

■ Don't rely on childproof locks – eventually most children work out how to open them.

■ If you can, design rooms with children's safety in mind, like the bathroom in this picture.

Treating common ailments

■ ■ ■ **Colds, upset stomachs, and headaches are a fact of life, although rarely cause for concern. In addition to conventional medication, it is often worth trying alternative remedies** ■ ■ ■

treating or relieving symptoms ■ ■ ■

Colds

■ Colds start gradually, and infection of the membranes of the nose, sinuses, and throat can cause a runny or stopped-up nose, sore throat, cough, sneezes, headache and slight fever. A cold lasts about a week.

Care tips

■ Rest and stay warm, but ventilate the room well.
■ Continue to eat and drink plenty of liquids, including hot drinks containing lemon or blackcurrant.
■ Medicines cannot treat colds, which are caused by over 200 viruses. But you can buy over-the-counter

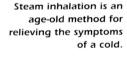

Steam inhalation is an age-old method for relieving the symptoms of a cold.

medication to relieve symptoms. Choose a decongestant for a topped-up nose; and an analgesic (see *Home medicine chest*, page 158) to relieve headaches and lower your temperature.

Alternative remedies

Aromatherapy: Inhale natural oils, including eucalyptus, peppermint, camphor and menthol, to clear a stuffy head and blocked nose. Put four to five drops on a tissue and inhale as necessary, or add four drops to a bowl of steaming hot water. Bend over the bowl with a towel over your head for ten minutes to inhale the steam. (Avoid steam inhalations if you suffer from asthma.)

Influenza

This infection of the respiratory tract is easily confused with a cold, but it starts suddenly and the symptoms are worse. They include high fever, chills, aches and pains, and listlessness, accompanied by headache, painful breathing, a dry cough and a sore throat. After two to three days, the temperature returns to normal, but it can be a week before other symptoms subside.

Care tips

■ Follow the advice, above, for colds.
■ Take analgesics (see *Home medicine chest*, page 158) to ease aches, pains, fever, and headaches.
■ Use a cough suppressant, if necessary, to aid restful sleep.

Alternative remedies

Homeopathy: The following remedies can be helpful:
Rhus tox for stiff, painful muscles;
Gelsemium for chills and fatigue;
Bryonia for headache, thirst and painful coughing.

Sore throats

The majority of sore throats are the result of viral infection. Symptoms usually clear up within three to five days. Consult your doctor if a sore throat lasts longer and you have a fever, as these are signs of tonsillitis, a bacterial infection requiring antibiotics.

Care tips
- Rest at home if you feel ill, and talk as little as possible.
- Do not smoke, and avoid smoky atmospheres.
- Drink plenty of fluids.
- Gargle with warm salt water (do not swallow).
- Over-the-counter lozenges and gargles may help.
- Strengthen your immune system by eating plenty of garlic and fruit rich in vitamin C.

Alternative remedies
Aromatherapy: Make a gargle by adding up to five drops of essential oils of geranium and tea tree to 600ml (1 pint) of warm water. (Avoid during pregnancy.)

Headaches

Most headaches are caused by stress and anxiety, but the wide range of causes also include trigger foods and poor posture. Consult your doctor if your symptoms include fever, stiff neck, drowsiness, nausea, vomiting, sensitivity to light, or if headaches occur after a head injury.

Care tips
- Take analgesics (see *Home medicine chest*, page 158, for more information).
- Try identifying the cause of the pain to find a cure for it. Have you skipped a meal? You may have a low blood sugar headache that will disappear after a snack. Are you a coffee-drinker? Try drinking a cup if you haven't for some hours. Are you dehydrated? Drink a large glass of water.
- Close your eyes and relax for a few moments.
- Get some air and exercise on a ten-minute walk.

Alternative remedies
Massage: Work around the neck, face, and scalp to help reduce tension in the neck and shoulders that may be causing the headache.

Homeopathy: The following remedies can be helpful:
Nux vom for hangover headaches;
Acid phos for eyestrain headaches;
Aconite for a sudden headache like a tight band;
Bryonia for pain that is worse with movement;
Belladonna for throbbing pain that is worse in hot sun;
Hypericum for bursting pain that is worse in damp conditions.

Nausea and vomiting

Causes can include food poisoning, early pregnancy, adverse reaction to drugs, motion sickness, inner ear problems, and shock. Consult your doctor if vomiting lasts more than 12 hours, if you cannot keep fluids down, or if you have abdominal pain, fever, drowsiness, or headache. Do not take anti-nausea medication during pregnancy.

Care tips
- For vomiting caused by food poisoning, avoid solid food for 24 hours. Avoid milk.
- For morning sickness (that can last all day), eat small amounts of bland food frequently; keep ginger biscuits by your bed for the early morning.
- Once all vomiting has stopped, replace lost fluids with over-the-counter rehydration powders.
- If someone who is ill or drunk is in danger of vomiting while asleep, put them in the recovery position (see *Emergency first aid*, page 176). Stay with them if their condition is very bad.

Tea with lemon (with or without honey) will relieve a sore throat.

Fever

Normal body temperature can range from 36.5 to 37.2°C (97.8 to 99°F). Remember that body temperature varies from person to person, and fluctuates throughout the day. Now and again, take readings on family members in good health. This helps you spot a temperature that is raised or lowered through sickness. **Call a doctor immediately if a temperature rises to 38.6°C (101.4°F).**

Diarrhoea

Frequent, loose bowel movements are the main symptom of diarrhoea. It is most often caused by food poisoning – from ingesting food or drink contaminated by bacteria, such as salmonella. Other causes may include anxiety, stress, and the side effects of drugs. Consult your doctor if diarrhoea lasts more than three days, or if stools contains blood or mucus.

Care tips

■ Stay in bed if the attack is severe.
■ Although diarrhoea will clear up by itself within a few days, you may want to take an over-the-counter anti-diarrhoea medicine.
■ It is vital to rehydrate the body; take over-the-counter rehydration powders or sports drinks with electrolytes to replace lost water and salts.
■ Do not eat solid food for 24 hours. When you start to eat again, begin with dry toast and clear soup.
■ Drink plenty of fluids, but avoid milk, coffee, and concentrated fruit juice.
■ Be vigilant with domestic hygiene. See *Storing food*, page 134, for ways to avoid food poisoning with home-prepared foods.

Alternative remedies

Homeopathy: The following remedy can be helpful: Arsen Alb for diarrhoea and vomiting.
Naturopathy: Consider allergy tests and an elimination diet recommended by a naturopath if symptoms seem to be caused by certain foods.

Indigestion

Medicines can effectively treat pain in the upper stomach and a burning feeling in the centre of the chest (also known as heartburn) that appears after eating and drinking rich foods or to excess. Consult your doctor if the symptoms last for more than a few days.

Care tips

■ Over-the-counter antacids neutralize stomach acids.
■ Acid-suppressing drugs reduce the amount of acid the stomach produces, and can be taken in advance of a potentially aggravating meal.
■ Eat smaller meals, sitting at a table, and take time to savour every mouthful.
■ Include more fibre in your diet, in the form of fresh fruit, vegetables, and whole grains.

Alternative remedies

Homeopathy: The following remedies can be helpful:
Sulphur for long-term indigestion.
Bryonia for indigestion that comes on immediately after food.
Pulsatilla for bouts that start one to two hours later.
Relaxation: Stress and indigestion are linked, so try relaxation techniques, including slow, deep breathing or yoga exercises.

Mouth ulcers

These uncomfortable spots with inflamed edges form on the tongue, inner cheeks, and gums. Stress, damage from teeth, food intolerance, nutritional deficiency, or viral infection can be the cause. Mouth ulcers generally go away within a fortnight.

Care tips

■ Use over-the-counter antiseptic lozenges or local-anesthetic spray.
■ A doctor may prescribe steroid cream.
■ Make sure you eat a balanced, varied diet with plenty of fresh fruit and vegetables, and foods rich in vitamin B, such as whole grains, potatoes, and milk.
■ Consult your doctor if you have more than ten mouth ulcers at one time.

Alternative remedies

Homeopathy: The following remedy can be helpful:
Arsen Alb if the mouth feels hot and dry.
Herbalism: Gargle nightly with warm sage tea; an herbalist may prescribe echinacea tincture to help combat an infection.

chapter

emergencies

Being prepared

■ ■ ■Coping with emergencies successfully in the home depends on your knowledge of how everything works, and on your ability to stay calm and act promptly. Familiarize yourself with the checklist below ■ ■ ■

safety essentials ■ ■ ■

Fire
■ Install a smoke alarm on the hallway of every floor of the house. If you use washing machines and dishwashers overnight, place an alarm in the kitchen or utility room as well. Never remove batteries from the alarm to use elsewhere.
■ Plan an escape route from every room (bear in mind that most fires start at night). Make sure that everyone in the house knows the evacuation drill, and also that they must never return to a burning building, even to collect pets.
■ Keep a multi-purpose, powder, fire extinguisher in a central place.

Water
■ Know where the stopcock is, and, from time to time, check that the handle has not become jammed.
■ Keep a wrench nearby for extra leverage.

Gas
■ Check the location of the main gas valve (it may be found by the gas meter) and make sure you know which way to turn it off.
■ Install carbon monoxide detectors at eye-level in rooms with gas appliances. This deadly gas given off by faulty gas appliances cannot be detected by smell. For detectors, you may choose between pads that change colour if carbon monoxide is present and a battery-operated device that emits a warning.

Electricity
■ Check the location of the electricity mains and learn how to turn it off. The switch may be on or next to the fuse box.
■ Keep a torch in an easy-to-reach spot on every floor and make sure every member of the family knows where it is.

action in the event of fire ■ ■ ■

Getting help fast
■ Give a spare key and a contact telephone number to a neighbour you trust when away from home.
■ A mobile telephone makes it easier to talk to emergency services from a place of safety.
■ Keep emergency numbers by the phone. Write down your home address and local landmarks to assist the emergency services. In a panic, it may be easier to read aloud than remember.
■ A clear house number on your front door and an outdoor light also aid the emergency services.

Smoke, as well as flames, can kill. This is particularly true of fires that start or are accelerated by contact with foam-filled furniture.

General evacuation procedure
Follow this evacuation procedure if you smell smoke or hear flames at night; if a fire is too big to tackle safely, or upholstery is burning:
1 Get everyone out of the house at once. Do not stop for possessions. Do not look for pets. Shut doors behind you.

2 If a door feels warm to the touch, do not open it. Use an alternative route.
3 Call 999 from a mobile or a neighbour's phone. Alert all neighbours.

If you are trapped in a room

1 Keep the door shut. Place a blanket or towel (preferably wet), or wedge carpet or a rug at the bottom of the door.
2 Go to the window and call for help. Do not jump out from upstairs windows unless your life is threatened.
3 If the room fills with smoke, lean out of the window, or lie on the floor, below the level of the smoke.

If you have to escape from an upstairs room

1 Throw a mattress out of the window to break your fall.
2 Lower yourself from the window, feet first, keeping hold of the sill.
3 Drop onto the mattress.

Fire prevention checkpoints

■ Never dry clothes in front of an open fire or electric heater.
■ Do not smoke in bed, and extinguish candles, nightlights, and aromatherapy burners before sleep.
■ Never store anything flammable under the stairs – it would make your exit harder.
■ At night, shut internal doors, to slow down a fire.
■ Keep keys for window locks close to windows. Ensure all rooms have at least one opening window.

Electrical fires

1 Turn off every appliance at the socket, and unplug it if you are able to do so safely.
2 Use a dry-powder fire extinguisher to put out the fire. Never use water to put out an electrical fire.
3 Alternatively, smother flames with a heavy blanket, rug, or coat (not nylon).

Electrical-fire checkpoints

■ Service appliances regularly.
■ Always use a circuit-breaker if there is a risk that the cord could be severed, for instance, when using power tools and electrical gardening equipment.

■ Ensure that the television, computer and other electrical equipment is turned off at night.
■ Do not overload electricity sockets.
■ Repair frayed electrical cords.

Fat fires

1 Do not move a burning or smoking pan or throw water on it. This will spread the fire.
2 If you are able to do so safely, disconnect the power to an electric cooker, or the burner on a gas cooker.
3 Smother the pan with a damp cloth or a large lid.
4 If the fire is out of control, shut the door and call 999. Follow the procedure for evacuation.

Fat-fire checkpoints

■ Never leave pans of heating fat unattended.
■ Do not overfill pans with fat or food.
■ A deep-fat fryer is a safer way to fry in fat (see *Small appliances*, page 119).

NATURAL DISASTERS

Emergency services should automatically arrive when flooding is imminent, or there has been a natural disaster. Follow the advice below until then.

For floods: With dry hands, turn off all gas, electricity, and water supplies at the main switches, if you can safely do so. If you have time, block off exterior doors and porous bricks with sandbags or plastic bags filled with soil. Move valuables, including vital papers, upstairs, and lift downstairs carpets. If possible, put large appliances up on wood or cement blocks or wrap them in polythene film. Stay upstairs and wait for help. Be prepared to evacuate when instructed to do so.

For thunderstorms: Go to the basement or ground floor or a room in the centre of your flat or house. Be prepared to escape in case of fire. Stay away from windows. Avoid using the telephone (unless in an emergency) or electrical appliances. After the storm, wait half an hour before leaving the house, as lightening could still appear.

For landslides and mudslides: Contact your local fire or police station. Inform neighbours and evacuate the area, if possible. If not, take cover under a desk or other piece of sturdy furniture.

Plumbing emergencies

■ ■ ■ You need to act fast to stem water flow and minimize damage to your home and its contents. Follow this guide for information on what to do, when, and how ■ ■ ■

	Problem	Cause
Burst water pipes	When water pipes burst, indoors or out, water can spurt or drip. This is usually discovered after a cold spell.	Ice needs up to 10 percent more space than water of the same volume. In winter, when the temperature drops and water in poorly insulated pipes turns to ice, the only way the ice gains this extra space is to crack the pipe. These cracks often go unnoticed, unless a pipe gets blocked (see *Frozen pipes*, below) or a thaw sets in and water starts to leak.
Frozen pipes	Water will not flow from a tap if it has frozen. A frozen external overflow pipe may in time flood the cold tank (usually in the roof).	Extreme weather. The most likely pipes to freeze are those in a roof or unheated bathroom with piping on an outside wall, or outside pipes carrying water to a drain.
Ceiling full of water	Ceiling in danger of collapse.	The weight of water from burst pipes, appliances, or bathroom floods on an upper floor may cause a ceiling to collapse.
Overflowing baths, showers, and sinks	Major overflow can seep under floorboards to affect electrical wiring or even bring down a ceiling (see above).	Leaking trim in shower tray. Failure to turn off tap. Blocked overflow.
Blocked toilet	When flushed, the toilet empties in a circulating pool that rises to the top of the bowl, then ebbs away slowly. This is a sign of blockage in the drainpipe.	Too much tissue, or bulky items like sanitary towels may have become wedged inside the toilet or pipes.

Remedy	Prevention checkpoints

1 Place a bucket under the burst pipe.
2 Turn off the water supply at the mains.
3 Put plugs in baths and sinks, to save water for boiling and emergency use. Turn on all taps to empty the system.
4 Call a plumber.
5 If the burst is small – i.e., a pinhole or small crack you can easily reach – make a temporary repair by spreading a thick layer of epoxy repair putty over it (from hardware shops; follow instructions) or wrap adhesive sealant tape around it.

■ Insulate pipes, especially those in the attic that are exposed to the most cold.
■ Cover any outdoor taps.

1 Check pipes for cracks. If there are any, treat as for burst pipes, above.
2 Turn on the relevant tap, so water can flow normally once the ice thaws.
3 Working backwards from the tap, wrap warm, damp cloths around the U-bend. Heat copper pipes with a hairdryer on a low setting, or place a hot water bottle over the pipe.

■ Install good insulation (see burst pipes, above).
■ Install a heater that is set to come on at a temperature just above freezing in rooms that are susceptible to cold weather.
■ Turn off and drain your water system before you leave for winter holidays.

1 Quickly identify the cause and, as appropriate, turn off the tap or water at the mains, or alert anybody upstairs. Ideally, one person should do this, while another immediately does the following:
2 Arrange buckets or large bowls under the centre of the ceiling.
3 Turn off the lighting at the mains. Move or cover furniture.
4 Make a small hole in the ceiling with a screwdriver to direct the water to one point for draining. Reposition the buckets beneath the hole, if necessary.

■ See burst and frozen pipes, above, and overflowing baths, showers, and sinks, below.

1 Switch off the electricity at the fuse box, and mop up as much water as possible.
2 Remove wet carpets and rugs so they can dry, preferably outdoors.
3 Look under any floorboards. If a lot of water is present, lift several floorboards to allow air to circulate. Open any windows.

■ Check the seal around showers, and repair them if necessary.
■ Never block overflow holes in baths or sinks.

1 Wearing rubber gloves, push a long-handled wire around the U-bend to try to shift any visible waste. Wait for the water level to drop.
2 When the water level has dropped, stand on a chair and flush the toilet by pouring a bucket of water into the bowl from a height.
3 If this fails, use a large plunger (see box). Flush the toilet.
4 If it is still blocked, use flexible drain rods to probe the pipe and trap in order to dislodge blockages. If it is still blocked, call a plumber.

■ Avoid blockages by keeping a rubbish bin by the toilet for the disposal of bulky materials like nappies and sanitary towels.

Gas and electrical emergencies

■ ■ ■ **Always turn off the power or gas at the mains supply before investigating electrical or gas problems. Only turn it back on when you are confident everything has been made safe. If in doubt, call an electrician or your gas supplier** ■ ■ ■

what to do if you smell gas ■ ■ ■

If there is a strong smell of gas
1 Turn off the gas next to the meter, if possible.
2 Call the gas company (the number will be on the meter or in the phone book).
3 Get everyone out of the house.
4 Open doors and windows.
5 Extinguish cigarettes and candles.
6 Turn off all gas appliances, such as cookers or heaters.
7 Do not touch electric switches: a spark could ignite escaped gas.
8 Warn all neighbours: a gas explosion may affect their safety.

If there is a slight smell of gas
1 Check that the pilot lights on stoves and boilers have not blown out.

2 Check that controls on cookers have not been left on without the burners being ignited.
3 Once you have traced the source, switch off the cooker, and open doors and windows, or wait until the smell has gone, then relight the pilot light.
4 If you cannot find the source, open doors and windows, and call your gas supplier.

If you experience headaches, nausea, lethargy, and muscle weakness in a room with a gas appliance
1 This may be a sign of carbon monoxide poisoning from a faulty gas appliance. Turn off all gas appliances, and open doors and windows.
2 Check around the appliance for yellow or brown stains; look for yellow or orange flames – gas flames should burn blue.
3 Call your gas supplier.

what to do if electricity fails ■ ■ ■

No power, no lights
1 Look outside to see if other homes are affected: if so, this is a local power failure.
2 Turn off all lights and appliances, except one bulb (so you know when power is restored), the refrigerator, and freezer.
3 When power returns, do not open the freezer for six hours.

If only your home is affected
1 Go to the main fuse box and check the switch on the Residual Current Device (RCD). If it has tripped to the 'off' position, turn the switch back on again.

COPING WITHOUT LIGHT AND FUEL

■ Keep an emergency supply of torches, candles, matches, and a portable gas burner (camping stove).
■ Be vigilant about safety. Candle fires are extremely easy to start. It is safer to walk with a torch, only lighting candles when stationary.
■ Keeping warm can be a problem. Wear woollen hats and gloves as well as thick clothes.
■ Eat frequently. Cold food will fuel your body as effectively as hot.

2 Run through the light and power checks detailed below.

3 If there is still no power, call an electrician.

No lights in one circuit (internal problem)

1 A surge of current may have caused the circuit to go into safety mode and switch itself off. This is probably the result of a blown light bulb. To locate the bulb, check all those on the same circuit for signs of damage (black around the base).

2 Replace the damaged bulb.

3 Turn the circuit switch back on.

4 If there is still no power, there may be a loose connection in the light fitting. You may want to call an electrician.

No power at a socket (internal problem)

1 Plug another appliance into the socket to rule out appliance failure.

2 Turn off the power at the mains.

3 If your system has fuses, check the main fuse box to see if a circuit fuse has blown. If so, replace it with an identical fuse with the power still off, as follows: *For rewirable fuses*, loosen the terminal screws to remove burned-out fuse wire, then feed new wire of the same thickness through the tube, so that it

connects with the terminals. Cut away excess wire. *For cartridge fuses*, simply lift out the damaged fuse and insert a new one.

4 If you have a modern system with switches on miniature circuit breakers, switch the relevant circuit back on.

5 If the system immediately fails again, call an electrician.

6 If the system stays on, try to find out which appliance caused the problem and, if appropriate, take it to a service engineer for repair.

Electric shocks

- **Turn off the source of current immediately.**
- **If you cannot cut the power, do not touch the casualty, or you will get a shock too.**
- **Stand on an insulating material (a wooden chair or pile of newspapers) and use a wooden broom to push the current-source away. Alternatively, wrap a dry towel around the casualty's feet to drag him away. As a last resort, pull on the victim's dry, loose clothes.**
- **Follow the ABC of resuscitation, if necessary, and take action for burns, see Emergency first aid, pages 176–84.**

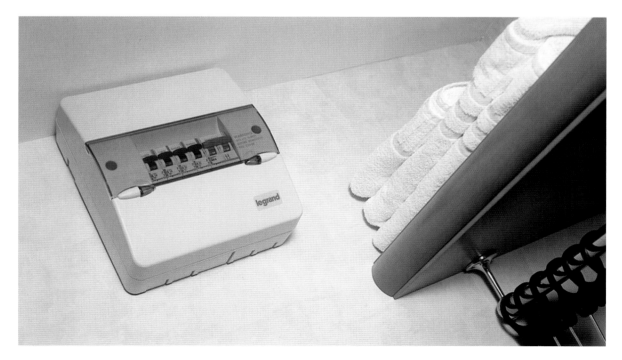

Do you know where your fuse box is, and could you find it in the dark?

Emergency first aid

■ ■ ■ **Do not wait for a life-threatening emergency before reading these pages. Familiarize yourself with the details now or take first-aid instruction** ■ ■ ■

order of priority in an emergency ■ ■ ■

1 Assess the situation – is it safe for you to help? Are you at risk of becoming a casualty yourself?

2 Is the casualty conscious? Kneel and ask: "Hello, can you hear me?"

3 If there is no response, call 999 before doing anything else. Studies show that victims who are not breathing or do not have a pulse have a substantially greater chance of survival with prompt advanced medical care.

4 Attempt first aid.

moving casualties ■ ■ ■

To avoid risk of causing further injury, do not move anyone who has been seriously injured unless they are in danger, breathing is obstructed, or you need to give CPR (see page 178).

1 Place victim's arm (closest to you) above the head.

2 Turn him onto his back by placing one of your hands on the victim's hip, and the other at his shoulder. Turn in a smooth, even line to prevent further injury.

resuscitation ■ ■ ■

The ABC of resuscitation is the single most important first-aid procedure you can learn. Once the casualty has a pulse and is breathing, deal with injuries in the following order: bleeding (see page 180), shock (see page 183), burns (see page 182), fractures (see page 183), and other injuries.

A Check the victim's **Airway** is clear. If not, unblock it. Place the heel of one hand on the victim's forehead, the fingertips of the other hand under the bony part of the jaw. Push down on the forehead, while lifting up the chin, until the jaw points straight up.

B Check that the victim is **Breathing**: look, listen, and feel. *Look* at chest and abdomen for movement; *listen* for breathing; then put your face next to the victim's head to *feel* breath.

C Finally, check the **Circulation** (that the heart is beating), by feeling for a pulse. Use two fingers to feel the large arteries on either side of the larynx (Adam's apple). In infants, feel with two fingers on the inside of the upper arm.

If there is breathing:

Put the casualty in the recovery position and begin checking for injuries.

If there is no breathing:

With the casualty on his back, look for obvious obstructions to the airway. Keeping the chin up and head tilted back, place two hooked fingers into the victim's mouth. Sweep around to find any foreign objects. Do this as quickly as possible.

If there is still no breathing:

Check again for a pulse.

If there is a pulse but no breathing:

Perform artificial respiration (see opposite).

If there is no pulse or breathing:

Perform cardiopulmonary resuscitation (CPR) (see pages 178–79).

artificial respiration ...

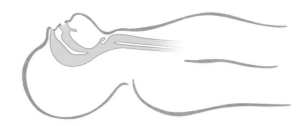

Tilting the patients head back will ensure that the airway is clear.

1 Make sure that the airway is still open and unblocked: place one hand on the forehead and tilt it back, lifting the chin with the other hand. Look, listen, and feel for breathing. Pinch the victim's nose closed, and keep it closed throughout.

2 Take a deep breath, open your mouth, seal your lips around the victim's open mouth, and blow into it, waiting for the chest to rise. Remove your mouth and watch the chest fall.

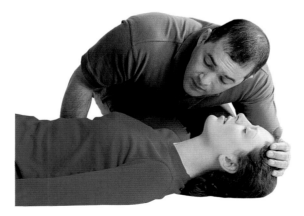

3 Repeat the breath ten times, one every six seconds. Check the pulse after every ten breaths. If you are alone, give ten breaths, and then call 999. Return at once to continue the breaths, checking for a pulse after every ten breaths until breathing starts or medical help arrives.

4 *For infants and small children:* Allow your mouth to cover both the nose and mouth. Blow gently, just enough to make the chest rise. Follow step three above but aim for 15 to 20 breaths per minute (one every three seconds) when applying breaths. Check for pulse after every 20 breaths.

cardiopulmonary resuscitation (CPR) ▪▪▪

Learning to do this effectively requires intensive classroom instruction and practice. Without these skills, CPR should only be performed if there is no breathing or pulse, and medical assistance is not immediately available. Never practice on healthy people.

1 Make sure the airway is still open and unblocked: place one hand on the forehead and tilt it back, lifting the chin with the other hand. Look, listen, and feel for breathing. Give two breaths of artificial respiration (see page 177; five for infants and small children). Check the arteries at the side of the Adam's apple (inside the upper arm for infants) for five seconds.

2 If there is a pulse but the victim is not breathing, give artificial respiration. If there is no pulse, place the victim on a firm surface and kneel beside him. (For infants and children, see opposite.)

Remember artificial respiration

A is for Airway (check airways)
B is for Breathing (look, listen and feel)
C is for Circulation (check pulse)

---

3 At the bottom of the chest, feel for the angle of the ribs. In the middle, where the ribs meet, is the breastbone. Place your middle finger on this point, with your forefinger resting on the breastbone above.

4 Place your other hand over the first, interlocking the fingers. Keeping your arms straight, press down on the chest. It should compress around 5cm (2in). Keeping your hands in place, let the chest rise, then repeat.

5 Give 15 compressions at a rate just faster than one per second – count one, two, three as you would regularly. When you reach 15, stop and give two breaths of artificial ventilation. Repeat the cycle of 15 compressions and two breaths. After 100 compressions, check for a pulse.

6 Call 999, then repeat the cycle until the pulse and breathing return or medical help arrives. If two people are present, one should give chest compressions, the other artificial ventilation. When the victim starts to breathe, place him in the recovery position as shown on page 181.

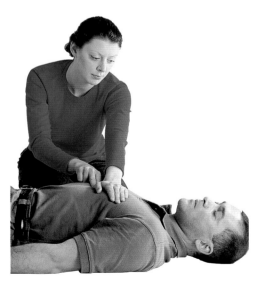

Feeling for the breastbone.

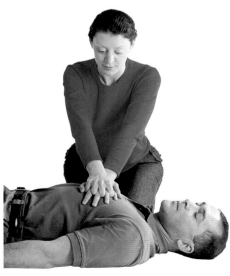

Compressing the chest.

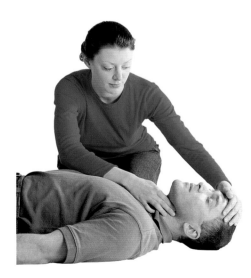

Checking for the pulse.

CPR for infants and children ▪▪▪

1 For infants, place the tips of the fore- and middle fingers of one hand on the breastbone, just below a line connecting the nipples. For children, place your middle finger where the ribs meet, and your forefinger just above, on the breastbone. Place the heel of your other hand on the breastbone, next to your fingers.

2 Press five times in three seconds, to a depth of 2cm (¾ in) for babies, 4.5cm (1¾ in) for children, ensuring the chest rises between each compression.

3 Give one breath after every five compressions, and repeat for one minute (10 cycles). Call 999, then repeat the cycle, until the pulse and breathing return or medical help arrives. When the child starts to breathe, place him in the recovery position.

choking ▪▪▪

If the casualty can still speak or cough forcibly, encourage her to continue coughing. If she cannot speak or cough, immediately treat for airway obstruction by using back slaps and abdominal thrusts.

Back slaps
Stand behind the casualty (adult or child), and bend her over. Smack smartly between her shoulder blades up to five times with the heel of your hand. If this fails, perform abdominal thrusts (right).

Abdominal thrusts
Wrap your arms around the victim's waist. Make a fist with one hand and place the thumb side against the abdomen, just above the navel. Grasp the fist with your other hand, and, with elbows out, press your fist into the casualty's abdomen with a quick, upward thrust. Repeat, up to five times, treating each thrust as an attempt to dislodge the obstruction. Return to five back slaps. Then repeat five abdominal thrusts. Continue the cycle until breathing returns or medical help arrives.

Back slaps for infants.

Abdominal thrusts for infants.

Back slaps and abdominal thrusts for infants

Turn the infant upside down, supported by your forearm, with their head lower than the body, and the chin supported between your fingers. Slap up to five times on the middle of the back with the heel of your hand. Remove any visible obstruction from the mouth carefully with your finger.

If you can't do this, turn the infant face up. Place the tips of the fore- and middle fingers of one hand on the breastbone, just below a line connecting the nipples. Thrust sharply, five times. Repeat the cycle of back slaps and abdominal thrusts until breathing returns or medical help arrives.

Abdominal thrusts for children over one year old

Place the child on his back. Set the heel of your hand on his breastbone. Make five smart downward thrusts. If there is still no breathing, place the heel of your hand just below the ribs and thrust upward five times. Roll the child toward you to repeat five back slaps. Continue the cycle of abdominal thrusts and back slaps until breathing returns or medical help arrives.

bleeding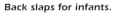

Bleeding

If an object is embedded in a wound, do not attempt to remove it; seek medical assistance as soon as bleeding has stopped.

With head wounds, be especially careful because of the possibility of skull fractures. When using pressure, do not press too hard. Keep the neck and head still.

1 If you do not suspect a fracture, elevate the wound above the level of the casualty's heart.

2 Apply direct pressure to the wound, using dressing, towel, or bare hands. When faced with major bleeding, it is not important that dressings are sterile.

3 Keep pressure in place for 15 minutes. If dressings become soaked with blood, apply more on top. Do not remove saturated dressings. Never apply a tourniquet or constricting band.

4 When bleeding has stopped, cover with clean gauze to prevent infection, and bandage firmly.

recovery position ▪ ▪ ▪

This position keeps the airway open and stops the casualty from choking on vomit, or from rolling backward or forward, even if unconscious. Keep checking for breathing and a pulse using the ABC (see page 176) and, if necessary, give artificial respiration or CPR (see pages 177 and 178). Turn casualties with spinal injuries only if breathing is obstructed, always keeping the head, neck, and back aligned.

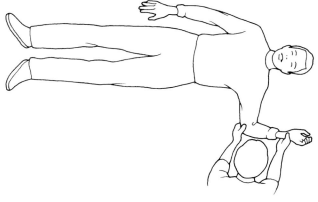

1 Lay the casualty on his back. Place the arm nearest to you at right angles to the body, with the palm facing upwards.

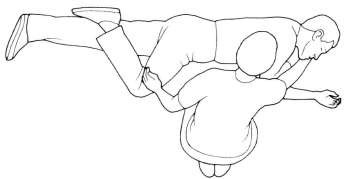

2 Bring the far arm across the chest and hold the back of the hand against the nearest cheek. Hold the far leg just above the knee with your other hand, and pull the knee up. Roll the casualty towards you until he is lying on his side.

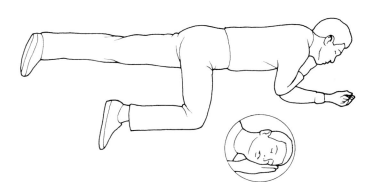

3 Adjust the upper leg so that the hip and the leg are bent at right angles. Ensure that the casualty is not lying on the lower arm and adjust if necessary. Keep the casualty's airway clear by tilting back the head.

EMERGENCIES

heat stroke ■ ■ ■

Symptoms include red-hot skin that usually feels dry, small pupils, and a very high body temperature – up to 40°C (105°F).

1 Cool the casualty as quickly as possible in any way that you can. Put him into a bath of cool water, or wrap him in wet sheets. Give him cool water to drink, but no more than 125ml (4fl oz) every 15 minutes.

2 Call 999, monitor his breathing and pulse, and perform artificial respiration and CPR, as required (see page 177–78).

dealing with flames ■ ■ ■

1 When trying to extinguish flames on a person, take care that your own clothing does not catch fire. Wrap the victim in heavy material, such as a coat, curtain, or blanket (not nylon). Lay him down and roll him over to prevent flames spreading to his face.

2 Call 999. Cut away any clothing that is not stuck to the victim.

3 Gently pour jugs or buckets of cold water over the victim to reduce the temperature. Continue for at least ten minutes. Do not do this if more than 10% of the body is burned or if the burns are very deep.

4 If loss of consciousness occurs, monitor the person's breathing and pulse, and perform artificial respiration and CPR, as necessary (see pages 177–78).

burns and scalds ■ ■ ■

Burns are caused by dry heat, such as direct contact with cooker hobs and ovens, or open flames. Scalds from steam and hot liquids, and chemical burns from household cleaners, paint stripper, and caustic soda, require the same treatment as listed below. Do not attempt to treat third-degree burns, or second-degree burns covering more than 10 percent of the body (5 percent for a child). Call 999 immediately. The information in the chart should help you decide the best course of immediate action to take.

1 Remove the victim from the source of heat. Take off rings or bracelets immediately, before swelling starts. Do not remove any clothing that is sticking to the area of the burn.

2 Hold the burned area under cold running water for at least 10 minutes, and for 20 to 30 minutes for chemical burns. Never use ice on a burn.

3 Remove clothing around the area if it comes away freely. Do not remove clothing sticking to the skin.

4 Apply a loose, sterile, non-fluffy dressing. For burns to hands and feet, place them in a clean plastic bag, secured with elastoplast on the bag. Treat for shock, if necessary (see above), and call 999 for chemical burns.

TYPE OF BURN	SYMPTOM	ACTION
First degree, including sunburn	Skin red and swollen	See above
Second degree with some blistering	Skin red and mottled with some blistering Extreme pain	If more than 10% (5% for child) of body affected, call 999
Third degree	Skin white or charred Severe pain, or none at all (if nerve endings destroyed)	Call 999. Do not cover burn; do not use water

anaphylactic shock ...

This severe allergic reaction to certain foods (including peanuts, shellfish, eggs, and cow's milk) can be life-threatening without immediate medical attention. Reactions start a few minutes after exposure and include an itchy rash; swollen lips, tongue, and throat; breathing difficulties; fainting; drowsiness and loss of consciousness; and abdominal pain.

1 Call 999. Place the casualty in a sitting position to ease breathing. Do not give food or drink. Look around for signs of what caused the shock.

2 If the victim vomits, place him in the recovery position (see page 181). If loss of consciousness occurs, monitor breathing and pulse, perform artificial respiration and CPR, as necessary (see pages 177–78).

fractures ...

Sprains, strains, and dislocations should be treated as if they are fractures. Do not move anyone following a car accident or fall: you could make head, neck, and back injuries worse (see page 176).

1 Control any bleeding (see page 180). If a bone has pierced the skin, bandage the area, building it up to the same height as the protruding bone. Steady and support the injured part without moving the victim.

2 Do not attempt to straighten an injured leg; support the limb in its current position with plenty of padding above and below the fracture to prevent movement. Call 999.

3 Do not give the victim food or drink – the casualty may need an anesthetic to set the fracture when he reaches a hospital. Use cold packs to help reduce pain and swelling.

shock ...

This can appear during the first hour after an injury, and may be caused by blood loss, dehydration or severe burns. It is a result of the body's failure to keep enough blood, and therefore oxygen, pumping to the vital organs. Symptoms include cool, moist, pale skin; thirst; confused behaviour; breathing and pulse rate very fast or very slow; weakness in arms or legs; enlarged pupils; and yawning or gasping for air.

1 Place the casualty on his back, elevate the legs to improve circulation if no head, neck, or leg injuries are suspected. Turn the head to one side.

2 Do not give water. Call 999 and stay with the casualty. If she loses consciousness, monitor her breathing and pulse, and perform artificial respiration and CPR, as necessary (see pages 177–78).

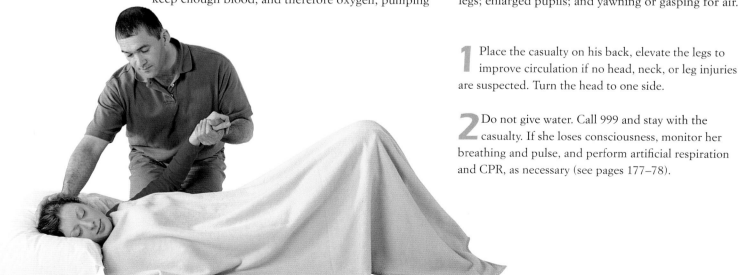

seizure emergencies ▪ ▪ ▪

These may be caused by a head injury, but are generally the result of conditions such as high fever, viral infection of the brain, epilepsy, or reaction to drugs.

1 Move furniture and equipment so the victim cannot cause injury to themselves by knocking into it.

2 Do not restrain the victim or put anything in his mouth. Loosen tight clothing at the neck, and place a pillow under his head.

3 Call 999 if a seizure lasts more than five minutes, another seizure follows immediately, or if consciousness is not regained after a few minutes.

eye injuries ▪ ▪ ▪

Treat objects that cannot be flushed out with water, or objects embedded in the eye, in the following way:

1 Carefully cover the eye with a clean pad or inverted paper cup.

2 Bandage the pad or cup in place firmly, but not too tightly.

3 Cover the other eye to prevent the injured eye from moving, and take the casualty to hospital.

diabetic emergencies ▪ ▪ ▪

Hypoglycemia – an abnormally low level of glucose in the blood – in those with diabetes mellitus can occur because the victim has taken too much medication, failed to eat, or has exercised heavily. Symptoms include fast breathing and pulse, dizziness, visual difficulties, sweating, numb hands and feet, and hunger, and may be mistaken for drunkenness.

1 Give sugar quickly in the form of cubes, glucose tablets, sweets, and fruit juice or soft drinks.

2 If the victim becomes unconscious, call 999. Place him in the recovery position (see page 181), monitor his breathing and pulse, and perform artificial respiration and CPR as necessary (see pages 177–78).

poisoning ▪ ▪ ▪

If you suspect someone has swallowed a toxic substance, do not wait for symptoms to occur. Try to identify the substance and the dose taken.

1 Call 999 and your doctor for specific instructions. Do not make the victim vomit or give him drinks.

2 Place an unconscious victim in the recovery position (see page 181), and monitor his breathing and pulse, performing artificial respiration and CPR as necessary (see pages 177–8).

ALCOHOL POISONING

The amount of alcohol that will cause poisoning varies from person to person. If someone is severely drunk and unconscious, the main risk is of airway obstruction and choking on vomit. Check the casualty's level of response by shouting and shaking the shoulders. If the casualty is unresponsive, check breathing and pulse, and be prepared to resuscitate him if necessary. Place the casualty in the recovery position (see page 181) and protect the person from cold. If you become concerned, call 999.

Glossary of terms

Analgesic

A medication that reduces or eliminates pain.

Antioxidant

A substance, such as vitamin E and vitamin C, that is thought to protect body cells from the damaging effects of oxidation (the action of oxygen).

Art Deco

Art Deco comes from the 'Exposition des Arts Decoratifs' (Exhibition of Decorative Arts), which took place in Paris in 1925. It is a decorative style seen in interiors, architecture, and jewellery, which features bold colours, geometric shapes, stylized natural forms, and the use of plastic and glass.

Caulking tool

A flat square of metal on a wooden handle used for smoothing cement or filler into joints or cracks.

Chisel

A sharp metal hand tool, usually with a wooden or plastic handle, used for carving or forming wood.

Dowel and dovetail joints

A dowel joint is a simple joint that uses wood or metal pegs slotted into holes to join two adjacent parts. A dovetail joint is a more complex joint, which is formed by wedge-shaped interlocking pieces. The wedge-shaped projections (tenons) of one piece of wood are fitted into the corresponding slots (mortises) in another piece of wood to form the joint.

Ergonomics

The study of the relationship between workers and their environment.

Flashing

Material, usually thin metal, used to weatherproof roofing joints.

Floor brads

A small, tapered nail with a small head that is symmetrical or formed on one side only.

Allen key

Long handled, L-shaped tool with a bevelled shaft, designed to slot into a screw head to turn it.

Joists

Beams made of timber, steel, or concrete, which are used to support floors or ceilings.

Lath

Wire mesh used as a backing for plaster or render.

Mallet

A large, usually wooden, hammer, often used with a chisel.

Plasterboard

Thin, stiff board made from plaster compressed between two layers of fibreboard, used to form or cover walls.

Drain rods

Long, flexible rods thast connect together and can be pushed into a pipe or drain to clear a blockage.

Shaker style

Furniture that is very plain, simply constructed, and functional.

Washer

A flat ring of rubber or metal used to provide a seal in a tap.

Conversion tables

Never mix imperial and metric values in the same project.

■ The conversions used here, which are the ones most commonly found, are rounded off to make it easy to read for general measuring needs.

■ If you need to make a precise calculation – for instance, to buy goods made overseas to fit a precise space in your home, such as Italian terracotta tiles, use exact mathematics to make the conversion, as detailed at the bottom of each list.

LIQUID MEASURES

Metric	Imperial	US
5 ml	⅛ fl oz	1 teaspoon
15 ml	½ fl oz	1 tablespoon
25 ml	1 fl oz	⅛ cup
50 ml	2 fl oz	¼ cup
65 ml	2½ fl oz	⅓ cup
100 ml	4 fl oz	½ cup
150 ml	5 fl oz	⅔ cup
175 ml	6 fl oz	¾ cup
225 ml	8 fl oz	1 cup (½ pint)
300 ml	10 fl oz (½ UK pt)	1¼ cups
350 ml	12 fl oz	1½ cups
475 ml	16 fl oz	2 cups (1 pint)
600 ml	20 fl oz (1 UK pt)	2½ cups
750 ml	24 fl oz	3 cups
900 ml	32 fl oz	4 cups (2 pints)
1 litre	35 fl oz	4¼ cups
1.14 litres	40 fl oz (2 UK pints)	5 cups

■ To convert USA pints to litres, multiply number of pints by 0.47.
■ To convert UK pints to litres, multiply number of pints by 0.568.
■ To convert litres to US pints, divide number of litres by 0.473.
■ To convert litres to UK pints, divide number of litres by 0.568.

WEATHER RANGE TEMPERATURES

Centigrade Degrees °C	Fahrenheit Degrees °F
-18	0
-7	20
+4	40
16	60
27	80
38	100

■ To convert Fahrenheit to centigrade, subtract 32, then multiply by 0.55.
■ To convert centigrade to Fahrenheit, multiply by 1.8, then add 32.

LENGTH

Metric	Imperial
5 millimetres	¼ inch
1 centimetre	½ inch
2.5 centimetres	1 inch
5 centimetres	2 inches
7 centimetres	3 inches
10 centimetres	4 inches
15 centimetres	6 inches
20 centimetres	8 inches
23 centimetres	9 inches
25 centimetres	10 inches
30 centimetres	12 inches (1 foot)
91 centimetres	36 inches (1 yard)
1 metre	39 inches
3.05 metres	10 feet
9.1 metres	10 yards

■ To convert feet to centimetres, multiply number of feet by 30.48.
■ To convert centimetres to feet, divide number of centimetres by 30.48.
■ To convert yards to metres, multiply number of yards by 0.9144.
■ To convert metres to yards, divide number of metres by 0.9144.

LONG DISTANCES

Miles	Kilometres
1 miles	1.61 kilometres
2 miles	3.22 kilometres
3 miles	4.83 kilometres
4 miles	6.44 kilometres
5 miles	8.05 kilometres
8 miles	12.88 kilometres
10 miles	16.09 kilometres
100 miles	160.93 kilometres

■ To convert miles to kilometres, multiply number of miles by 1.609.
■ To convert kilometres to miles, divide number of kilometres by 1.609.

SOLIDS

Warning! If a recipe gives both metric and imperial, it is essential to use one system of measurements throughout. (It doesn't matter which you use.)

Metric	Imperial
5g	¼ oz (1 teaspoon)
15g	½ oz (1 tablespoon)
25g	1 oz
50g	2 oz
85g	3 oz
110g	4 oz
140g	5 oz
180g	6 oz
200g	7 oz
225g	8 oz
250g	9 oz
280g	10 oz
340g	12 oz
400g	14 oz
450g	16 oz (1lb)
1 kg	2.2lbs

■ To convert pounds to kilograms, multiply number of pounds by 0.4536.
■ To convert kilograms to pounds, divide number of kilograms by 0.4536.
■ To convert ounces to grams, multiply number of ounces by 28.3495.
■ To convert grams to ounces, divide number of grams by 28.3495.

MEN'S SUITS

US and UK	Continental
36	46
37	48
40	50/52
42	54
44	56
46	58/60
48	62
50	64

ADULT BODY WEIGHTS

Metric	Imperial	US
45kg	7st 2lbs	100lb
55kg	8st 8lbs	120lb
64kg	10st	140lb
73kg	11st 6lb	160lb
82kg	12st 12lb	180lb
91kg	14st 4lb	200lb
100kg	15st 10lb	220lb

■ To convert pounds to kilograms, multiply number of pounds by 0.4536.
■ To convert kilograms to pounds, divide number of kilograms by 0.4536.

WOMEN'S CLOTHING

UK	Continental	US
8	38	6
10	40	8
12	42	10
14	44	12
16	46	14
18	48	16
20	50	18

SHOE SIZES

UK	Continental	US
3	35	4½
3½	36	5
4	36½	5⅓
4½	37	6
5	38	6½
5½	38½	7
6	39	7½
6½	39½	8
7	40	8½
7½	41	9
8	41½	9½
8½	42	10
9	43	10½
9½	43½	11
11	45½	12½

Index

picture credits ▪ ▪ ▪

Pictures reproduced with the permission of:

Dorling Kindersley Images: pp. 33, 34, 53, 74, 85 (hand sponging and rag rolling), 88, 124, 134, 136, 148, 165, copyright Dorling Kindersley.

Cephas Picture Library: p148

DIY photo library: pp. 62, 63, 64 (stand alone safe and safe in floor).

Arcaid: pp. 16–17 by Alan Weintraub; 17 by Martine Hamilton Knight (brick); 68–9 by Max Dupain; 90–91 by Earl Carter/Belle; 118 by Richard Powers; 121 by Gary Hamill Photography.

Elizabeth Whiting and Associates: pp. 6, 40 ; 41 by Spike Powell; 47, 86, 125 by Tim Imrie; 54 by DI Lewis; 66–7, 98 (Roman blind) by Mark Luscomb-Whyte; 82 by Clive Helm; 91, 98 (venitian blind); 92 by Bruce Hemming; 94 by Michael Dunn; 100, 114 by Rodney Hyett; 92–3; 98 (roller blind) by Mark Thomas; 99, 102 by Andreas von Einsiedel; 129; 130–1 by Debie Treloar152–3 Neil Davis; front cover by Clive Helm.

Anthony Blake Photo Library: pp. 119 by Milk Marque; 120 by Tony Robins; 121 by Robert Lawson; 165 by Graham Kirk.

Food Features: p. 162, copyright Food Features.

Dennis Gillson and Son: p.17.

IPC library: pp. 8, Dominic Blackmore/Ideal Home/IPC; 54, Simon Upton/Country Homes and Interiors/IPC Syndication; 70–1, Ed Reeve/Living Etc/IPC Syndication; 72, Adrian Briscoe/Homes and Ideas/IPC Syndication; 76, Paul Massey/Living Etc/IPC Syndication; 85, (colourwashing) Pia Tryde/IPC Syndication; 85, (stencilling) Andrew Cameron/Homes and Ideas/IPC Syndication; 85, (stamping) David Giles/Homes and Ideas/PIC Syndication; 104–5, Adrian Briscoe/Essentials/IPC Syndication; 107, Paul Raeside/Living Etc/IPC Syndication.

Houses and Interiors: pp. 5 by Verne; 93 by Theresa Ward and Steve Hawkins; 116, 131 by Jake Fitzjones; 133 by Verne; front flap by Verne.

Le Grand fuse boxes: p174.

British Clothing Institute: p53.

All other images copyright MQP publications.

acknowledgements ▪ ▪ ▪

With kind thanks to those who helped with props and photography shoots:
Amy's (Cook and Dine), 30 Golders Green Road, London NW11 8LL; Amy's (Tool-Ware-House), 41 Golders Green Road, London NW11 8EE; Amy's (Home and Garden), 29–31 Golders Green Road, London NW11 8EE; St John Supplies, PO Box 707B, Friend Street, London EC1V 7NE; Courts (UK) Ltd, The Grange, 1 Central Road, Morden, Surrey SM4 5PQ; The Pier Ltd, Tottenham Court Road, London W1P OAD; Dennis Gillson and Son, Naylor Hill Quaryy, Blackmoor Road, Hawarth BD22 9SU, UK.